MW01027820

MOVING TO HAWAII!

ISBN: 9781520303901
Imprint: Independently published

TABLE OF CONTENTS

Intro

1. Welcome to Hawaii

2. High Cost of Living

3. How Much Money is Enough?

4. Minimalist Living

5. Before You Go

6. After You Arrive

7. Geography of Hawaii

8. Population and Demographic Info

9. Weather

10. Which Island Is Right for You?

11. Employment

12. Starting a Business

13. State Taxes

14. Schools

15. Veterans Services and Benefits

16. Senior Citizen Agencies

17. Social Environment

18. Homes

19. Things to Do

20. What Do People Who Live in Hawaii Do?

21. Religion

22. Food!

23. Golf - (Top courses on all islands)

24. Shopping - (All islands)

25. Social Problems

26. Marijuana

27. Bugs and Other Land Critters

28. Marine Critters

29. Sharks!

30. Other Cautions

31. Plan B

32. Making the Decision to Go!

Appendix

Some Interesting Facts About Hawaii

Hawaii Frequently Asked Questions

Email and Answers

About the Author

INTRO

Aloha! This is my newest book on moving to Hawaii which doubles the number of pages in my last book, the bestselling "Moving to Hawaii – 2014" guide. This guide is fully updated for 2015, and every year it will be updated to keep it current.

My name is Vern Lovic. I have lived in the Hawaiian Islands for six years since 1984 and I am planning a move back with my family in early 2016.

Hawaii is the ultimate place to live on the face of the earth. I haven't seen it all, but I've seen Hawaii. Some say that is enough. I have had amazing times while living in Hawaii, and also some rough times. Through it all I have to say, the Hawaiian Islands are a great place to visit, to retire, or to live and work for the rest of your life.

As you know, Hawaii is part of the United States of America, yet you might question that as your plane touches down and you step out into the airport. Caucasians are a minority in Hawaii. Asians are in greater number – especially Japanese and Filipinos. I've met people from the mainland USA, Canada, Sweden, England, Germany, Australia, Tonga, Fiji, Samoa, Tahiti, Guam, Philippines, Japan, Korea, Thailand, China, and Indonesia living in the Hawaiian Islands. Hawaii is truly a wonderful melting pot of race and culture.

At present, I know a number of people living in the islands that are all from different backgrounds and socio-economic strata. One friend lives on the island of Kauai working on a farm for a few hours each day. He rents half of a small house. He makes just over $1,000 USD per month. He has been living like this for about five years now with no signs of leaving. I know a married couple living on Oahu making tens of thousands of dollars each month doing time-share sales. They own a beautiful house in Kailua, and another home on Maui. They are also not leaving anytime soon.

Though everyone knows the cost of living is high in Hawaii, it is tied to how you choose to live. Probably you could live in Hawaii too if you made it your goal to do so. There is a lot to know, but I'll do my best to give you what you need here in the pages of this book.

My goal is to help you come to a decision – can you, or can't you - move to Hawaii and make it?

Anybody can jump on a plane, stay a month, and admit failure. I want to give you as much as I know about all that is involved in moving to Hawaii, so you can decide yourself - go for it - or, not.

Wouldn't it be great if you could live Hawaii for at least a year?

In this book, I cover both the positive and negative aspects of living in this amazing place. I tried hard to balance the good and bad of living in this amazing place. I was cautious not to overemphasize either the good or bad – but I wanted to present many examples of both sides so you could have a more realistic picture of what it is really like living in what I consider to be America's most beautiful state.

So, be careful not to focus entirely on the positive aspects of moving to the islands, and definitely do not focus on the negative either. If you do end up moving to Hawaii – go with open eyes, and an open mind – ready to experience the best and worst the islands have to offer. For me, and most people who move here, the positives outweigh the negatives. By a large factor! You'll never know this until you give it a try yourself.

If you have any comments you want to give me, please write me at the email address in the back of this book. I love to receive email from people looking to move to the islands, or from those that that have already moved and are in the middle of giving it their best shot.

Aloha,

Vern Lovic

1 – WELCOME TO HAWAII!

Passengers seated all around me on the plane cheered as the wheels of our United Airlines 747 touched down, and I thought – *what is this? Why were people cheering so loudly for a plane landing?*

I guess I had mixed feelings about arriving on Oahu. I was nearly five thousand miles from the place I grew up in Western Pennsylvania. I was coming to Oahu as my first duty station in the U.S. Air Force. According to everyone's reaction around me in tech school where I received my orders, I'd hit the jackpot for my first permanent duty station at Hickam Air Force Base, Honolulu, Hawaii. Many of my teachers at my technical training school in Biloxi, Mississippi told me that Hickam was the best assignment the Air Force had available.

I wasn't at all sure about that. I had never even once thought about moving to Hawaii before the orders came. The only thing I ever heard or saw about Hawaii was the Brady Bunch television episode where they went on vacation and had a tarantula in one of their hotel room beds.

Flying from Pittsburgh to Honolulu took about nine hours. I didn't sleep at all, my mind spun with possibilities. I wondered if it was possible after I arrived and didn't like it if maybe it wasn't too late to trade my orders to go somewhere else. I knew I was stuck in Hawaii, but I didn't want to admit it to myself. I'd probably be there four years. It felt a bit like a prison sentence at the time.

After the cheers and claps, my arms tingled and I got what Hawaiians call "chicken skeenz." Then the pilot said warmly over the speakers, "Aloha, and welcome to the lovely island of Oahu, Hawaii!" Once again, applause and cheers erupted from everyone on the plane – except me. I smiled nervously, but it was all I could manage.

Looking back on it, I couldn't have been more clueless about what Hawaii was all about. Many of those around me on the plane already knew. They had been to the Hawaiian Islands before and they were obviously excited about returning. I remember people talking excitedly about arriving in Honolulu and all that they would do. I remember the flight attendants were gorgeous, and extra delightful. After we landed, everyone smiled, joked and laughed as if they were old friends.

Looking out the small windows of our plane as we taxied, I saw the most picture-perfect sunny day. As I walked down the corridor and stepped into the airport, I remember seeing more Asian people than I'd ever seen before in my life. We had one adopted Chinese girl in our town, and later we had a family from Vietnam that was sponsored by a family friend. Sadly, that was the extent of my seeing people from other cultures!

Everyone appeared to be so happy inside the Honolulu International Airport. It was surreal. Somewhere ukulele music played softly. The space was bright and airy. The scent of Plumeria (Frangipani), Tuberose, and Arabian Jasmine flowers hung in the air from the many leis being handed out by tour guides.

I was already completely overwhelmed with the beauty of Hawaii, *and I was still in the airport!*

I remember clearly, my body was tingling when I walked out of the airport on that very warm day of March 8, 1985. I was wrapped in a dreamy state that I can only describe as *magical.*

That first day I still remember vividly. At 11:30 am. after I had collected my bags, I met with Staff Sergeant Gallagher. "Bob" was my new supervisor at my job as one of the mail delivery persons at Hickam Air Force Base. We drove to the base where I checked into the dorm. There, I was also stunned by the beauty of Hickam AFB. It was like a resort! It was nice enough to be on Robin Leech's Lifestyles of the Rich and Famous. Hickam was stunningly beautiful.

Imagine me, later that week almost slipping into a pleasure-coma when I finally got to see the beaches and ocean in Waikiki, Makapu'u, Kahana, Kailua, and the views at the Pali Lookout and the North Shore.

I walked around with my head in the clouds for weeks, not fully understanding why I was there, and not sure it wasn't all going to just disappear when I woke up from the dream.

Fast forward to the present. I've seen Thailand, Laos, Malaysia, some of Cambodia, Korea, Canada, Key West, New York City, and Miami.

I've seen some beautiful places, but I have never experienced the same magical feeling I have in Hawaii. Hawaii is a place that defies logic and explanation. It's too nice. It's too perfect. It's mystical and magical… and so many other things words cannot adequately describe.

Besides the aesthetic beauty of Hawaii, there is something else to it that really defies words. I feel like I still haven't expressed it to you as clearly as I want to.

The natural beauty of the islands is unsurpassed. Everywhere I looked was a postcard view. Every plant was bright green and flowering. The smells in the air, the fragrance of the flowers combined with the salty air near the beaches, were all mind-numbing… and *soothing*.

The weather in Hawaii is nothing short of miraculous. Where else in the world is there such perfect weather? I don't think it can be beat. The weather is always bearable, and usually what I'd call *perfect*. The trade winds cool things off so it doesn't get too warm, and overall, the weather experience is part of the magic of Hawaii because there is near constant beautiful weather. Growing up with the horrible winters in Pittsburgh for the first eighteen years of my life, I felt like Hawaii was another planet.

The pure air in Hawaii outside of certain spots during rush hour is just astounding. The gentle sting in the nose of salty fresh air as one gets close to the beach where waves are breaking and on-shore wind is blowing, is one of my favorite smells and experiences ever. Inhaling this salty wet air and breathing deeply of it, gives me a peace of mind that I've never had before. It reinforces the idea that the islands are a magical place.

Exercising in Hawaii is great because the air is so clean and the terrain so varied. On Oahu, you can run in the sand at the beach, on the sidewalk along the Ala Wai canal, or up winding dirt trails on Tantalus Mountain. *Up to you!* There is no shortage of physical activities you can take up in Hawaii – even snorkeling can give you a workout if you cover some ground. For me, surfing and bodyboarding were the ultimate ways to spend time in the ocean. I spent hundreds of hours in the Pacific Ocean doing those activities, along with swimming, and bodysurfing.

The waters of Hawaii where I typically swam were clean, and often times filled with fish and the occasional large sea turtle. Swimming in such an amazing place, with the possibility of seeing dolphin jumping, spinning, and flipping above the water's surface was a lovely way to spend my free time. Seeing the occasional shark, fish, crabs, octopus, and sea turtles really gives a magical, and mysterious feeling to the islands of Hawaii.

There is always activity going on, especially on Oahu. The island is packed with fun things to do. For me, it was impossible to not have fun there. I can't remember a bad day in Hawaii, truthfully – *I cannot!*

Every day is a great day. Every day is a day you can go to the beach or do something new, like climb a mountain, swim in a new spot, explore some hidden terrain, shop in a new place, or whatever your passion is. Not only these things, but you can choose from the other islands as well – Kauai, Hawaii, Maui, Molokai, and Lanai. They are all just a short flight or overnight boat ride to a completely new island paradise. So, part of Hawaii's magic is that it doesn't end with the island you're on. There is so much more to explore, and you'll never see and do it *all*.

Hawaii's locals are real gems. You might not have the same experience I did… but, working with them and spending time after work with people who grew up on the islands was a real treat. They have an awesome outlook on life, and they are a significant part of the island magic I experienced. It was really refreshing to see their attitude about life as much more relaxed than my own. On the mainland, in the northeast, we are indoctrinated with ideas of work being everything – the main focus. Having fun happens only after we've worked hard and accomplished *enough*.

In Hawaii, I learned how to relax at work and during my free time. I spent hours laying on the beach in the morning sun. Sometimes I'd find myself sleeping on a towel at the beach for six or more hours each day on the weekend. I met people from all over the world in Hawaii. I dated women from Tahiti, Venezuela, Canada, Colorado, Philippines, and Japan. I had never even known people from these places before I arrived in Hawaii.

I learned how to camp and barbeque at the beach – *Hawaiian Style*. We'd spend the weekends camping out in tents in Waimanalo or spending it in the beach cabins at Bellows Air Force Station – and having more fun than we thought we had a right to. I think that's part of the magic. I think that's the one of the hidden ingredients that many visitors to Hawaii, and those living in Hawaii, can't quite put a finger on.

It's the magical feeling that, "I'm having a better time than I deserve to."

It's the awesome realization that, "This is the most beautiful and awesome place on the planet to experience – and I'm HERE NOW!"

It is the incredible feeling that – "I am not worthy of this amazing, dreamy, mystical place, the people, the experiences, the MAGICAL FEELING that pervades the Hawaiian Islands…"

It's too much – too perfect… I'm not worthy of it.

And I don't know what else to say to help you come to know the feeling of magic pervading life in the Hawaiian Islands. You need to go and experience it for yourself. Words can only give you a hint. The experience must be had for yourself. You have to make it happen if it is ever going to be!

I have a website dedicated to living in Hawaii - AimforAwesome.com. After you finish with this book you should go have a look because there are many more articles about living in the islands. After reading this book and a couple dozen more articles on the website, you should have a really good idea whether Hawaii is right for you. It's a big decision, but not an impossible decision.

I like to poll readers on my site to see what their views are. As much as I like to think my views are the "norm" – I've been shown many times to be way off. Polling visitors of my site helps me to keep in touch with what the rest of the world is thinking.

Below is a reader's poll I had on my website for a few days. I wanted to see if my idea of the best things about living in Hawaii were echoed by others living here.

Choose the 3 Best Things About Living in Hawaii:

- The ocean (73%)

- The weather (71%)

- The laid-back atmosphere (40%)

- The multi-cultural experience (35%)

- The food! (23%)

- Isolated from the mainland USA (18%)

- Best place to raise a family (11%)

- The hiking (10%)

- The shopping (5%)

- Great place for business (2%)

Total Voters: 128

There are good and bad reasons or motivations that people use when moving to Hawaii. Let's take a look at some of both kinds.

Some Good Reasons to Move to Hawaii:

1. You have family living in the islands already and you want to be close to them. This is a great reason, and it presupposes that you have already been to Hawaii and know what it is like. Maybe you even grew up there and you'll likely stay there as long as you want without any problem. Most Hawaii residents born and raised in the islands that move away, I think eventually return.

2. You are retired and have a check coming in that more than covers all necessities, needs, and wants. And, you are sure that check will keep on coming. Keep in mind that as you age your needs for medical care may grow enormously and quickly.

3. You have another income source whether it is royalties from a book or music, or something else, and that income is not likely to change at least for the next few years. Moving to Hawaii can be the ultimate long-term vacation. If you can make it for a couple of years, or even a year, in my mind it makes sense to make the move and experience the beauty of Hawaii for as long as you can make it last.

4. Somehow, you lucked-out and landed a good job in Hawaii either without having been here, or while you were just visiting the islands! I almost, *almost* landed a job by phone from Florida. This was for an online startup that needed someone to do all the online marketing for the company. They needed someone that could hit the floor running. I was 80% sure they would call me back to hire me. Nope. Close, but no cigar. It is very difficult to get an offer from Hawaii if you are not established there already.

Companies in Hawaii are very cautious about the people they offer jobs because many have made offers only to see the applicants disappear afterward.

5. You can sell everything and move - either living off investments or getting a job in a field where workers are in demand. I think for those over fifty years of age, this is the scenario that most often happens. You suffered your way through thirty years of work, bought a house, the kids are either in college or done, and you want more than anything else in the world to go live in Hawaii. Some people make it, and some don't. If you have the money, I always say, give it a try and see if it's for you. If you are lucky enough to get a once in a lifetime chance to live in Hawaii - *why not go for it?*

The Negative Side of Living in Hawaii

Out of every ten visitors to the Hawaiian Islands, at least five are wondering, "Is living in Hawaii possible for *me*?"

And for every five that do wonder such a thing, realistically maybe one can choose to live in Hawaii for any length of time. Maybe less than that.

Why is it so difficult for the average person to move and stay in the islands?

Hawaii is a very different place from wherever you grew up in Kansas, Okinawa, or wherever you call home.

Let's look at some of the differences that are readily apparent.

Living on a Hawaiian Island is Constrained by Space

Living on an island is a little different than living in downtown Boulder, Colorado. The Hawaiian Islands are not large. Oahu is about forty-four miles on the long side and thirty on the short side. Can you imagine living in 597 square miles? The only way you go further than forty-four miles in any one direction, is on a plane or in a boat – which sounds interesting, but there's another set of issues there I'll talk about in a minute.

Island Fever

Defined as the feeling that one is stuck on an island, and doesn't have the freedom to just go somewhere and drive for a few hours to 'get away.' Island fever usually hits first timers that move to the islands after six months or a year. The sudden realization occurs that, *this is all there is*. Sure Hawaii is beautiful... it has awesome natural beauty, views, and landmarks, and plenty to do, but this is it. This is home, and it's not a big home, it's a relatively small island to live for the rest of your life.

There are parts of the island you wouldn't want to go see. There is a lot of private property on Oahu and the other islands, and you will never see a good portion of the island you live on. So in reality, you're stuck living and exploring the public places – whatever the government has declared as such. Island fever is one of the big sources of discontent among new Hawaii residents. It shouldn't be overlooked because if you move to Hawaii, it will likely hit you at some future point in time, and maybe it will be the entire reason you decide to leave later.

Year-Round Heat

It's warm year-round. Some would even call Hawaii "hot" - but I never would, having lived in Miami, Tampa, and Thailand for nearly two decades. Those places are hot. Hawaii has the perfect weather for me, but you may find it hot all the time. I know people who sweat continually in Hawaii. They need not do anything physically, but they just sweat constantly. If you're one of those people, Hawaii may not be the right place for you to live. Some people adjust; maybe you are one of them?

No Seasons

There are no changing weather seasons in Hawaii. Only warm, balmy weather with a period during the winter where it is a bit rainier than during other parts of the year, and that is about it. Sure, once per year you might get to breathe fog on a cold December or January day, but it doesn't happen often. Not even every year.

Frequent Rain

It rains often on all the islands, in different areas. If you're planning on living on Kauai you should carry a poncho all the time because Kauai gets a lot of rain. One of the mountain peaks on Kauai is the wettest place on earth. It receives over 450 inches of rain per year. That's over an inch each day! No matter which Hawaiian Island you choose to be living on – it rains often – but usually in short bursts. Some find that annoying. If you ride a motorcycle or bicycle often, you will probably be caught in showers. That's Hawaii.

Groceries are All $5 or More

It is a bit of a shock during your first few trips to the grocery store. It seems like there isn't anything cheaper than five dollars. Most everything consumable is imported, and arrives by sea. One time I remember shopping at the grocery close to my home in Waikiki. This was the cheapest grocery around so it was always packed with locals who knew where to get the good stuff at a reasonable price. But, every single thing in my cart – and I had over thirty things – was over $5. A gallon of milk, a pound of butter I remember in particular. Unbelievably expensive - right? You'll need to get accustomed to it if you want to live here. Food on all the islands is expensive. There are secret resources locals use for food that are out of the way, but usually worth the trip. Of course, everyone is a member of Costco and Sam's Club.

Employment is Tough to Find

Jobs exist in certain career fields. If you're a waiter-waitress, nurse or other healthcare worker, or you have worked in the travel industry, you can probably find a job in Hawaii. If not, outside of a few other career areas it may be a struggle to find employment. The entire island is built on tourism. If your specialty doesn't have something to do with that, or isn't related to that in some way like sales, customer service, waiting tables, or selling retail, you might want to reconsider living in Hawaii. At the very least you should do a lot of research before you arrive to prepare yourself.

I know a guy with a lot of different skills that arrived on Oahu and tried for a year to get a job he really wanted. Finally he accepted a telephone sales job just to get some income. It's a very tough job market, and don't let the unemployment figures lull you into a false sense of security about the place. The jobs most often open are in those areas I mentioned above. Bring a whole lot of savings to live off if you don't have skills in one of those fields.

Driving Nightmare

I used my mountain bike a lot while living in Hawaii. Was it dangerous? Sure it was, most tourists are looking around and not prepared for bicycles on the streets. Still, it was more stressful to drive my Honda around Waikiki. Rush hours and weekends where there is an event of some kind going on are pure nightmare material, and you'll not want to live far from where you work unless you live in downtown and work in Kapolei or somewhere else there is no traffic. Traffic goes toward the downtown and Waikiki areas in the morning and away during 5 – 7 pm. rush hour.

Add to the driving nightmare the fact that the Honolulu police seem to be everywhere you look. There is a higher police presence on Oahu than I have experienced anywhere else in the nation. If you are late putting your seatbelt on, they are standing in the middle of the street by your condominium and writing you a ticket. If you coast through a stop sign, even slightly, they are on you. If you speed, they got you! If you ride in the wrong lane on the highway, you're had. You cannot win driving a vehicle in the islands. This in particular was no fun for me at all. Maybe because I'm such a bad driver! As I said, I used the bike or even walked when my destination wasn't too far away.

Hawaii's High Cost of Living

To some it seems ridiculously high. To others, it's manageable. There is a whole chapter on this coming up soon.

Attitudes

This one is hard to get away from. If your own attitude is poor, you'll meet some of the nastiest people you never wanted to know in Hawaii.

That's just the way it is everywhere, right?

However, if you've got a cool attitude and are open to learning how things work before and during your time there and you are friendly, outgoing, and a decent person all around, you'll be likely to meet the coolest bunch of people you ever knew.

Give first, and you'll get more in return. Such has been my experience while meeting new people in Hawaii. The Hawaiian spirit of Aloha is really a wonderful philosophy of life and I hope you get to experience it during your stay. If you're not the type of person that deals well with cultural diversity or have a lack of common sense, you may not do well in Hawaii and it can be a very cold place for the selfish, ignorant, prejudiced, clueless, and heartless.

Bringing Your Kids

Bringing your school-aged kids (keiki) to Hawaii to live might seem like a great idea… 'Let them breathe the clean air and soak up the sunshine… swim with the dolphins!' Sure. They can do all that. But, they'll still have to endure the school system. For mainland kids arriving in Hawaii for school it's sometimes (usually?) traumatic. I wouldn't recommend anyone bring their kids to Hawaii to live if they have to attend the public school system. I just wouldn't. That's me. I've considered at length whether I would want my daughter to grow up in Hawaii and attend Hawaiian public schools. I've decided – definitely not. We won't move back to Hawaii until we can afford the home-school experience, or a good private school. In either of those two scenarios I think Hawaii would be a great place for a child to grow up. Otherwise? No. That's just my bias.

If after reading all these negatives you decide that you still want to live in Hawaii because it's your destiny or something - try this…

Look at living in Hawaii as a temporary move and tell yourself you'll try living on one of the islands for a year. See if you can make it that long. By then you'll have a good idea what the island you're living on is like. You'll probably have visited some of the others and know a little bit about them too. You might choose to move to another island or you might continue on living where you are. Or, you might move back to the mainland US after a year. No harm done, right? You just spent a year in Hawaii while many people dream of having that option.

If they see you doing it, you may have many people ask how you did it because they too are starting to get that question in the back of their mind.

"Could I do it too?"

Another reader poll:

Choose the 3 Worst Things About Living in Hawaii

- High cost of living (75%)

- Illegal drugs epidemic (39%)

- Traffic (31%)

- Low pay (26%)

- High unemployment (17%)

- Isolation from other places (18%)

- Too many tourists (15%)

- Tough for businesses to make it (14%)

- Schools (11%)

- The people (10%)

- Not enough cultural things going on (9%)

- Military presence (7%)

- The constant police presence (4%)

- Bad place to raise family (4%)

Total Voters: 113

Just like there are good reasons or motivations for moving to the islands, there are some not-so-good reasons.

Some Bad Reasons to Move to Hawaii:

1. **You love smoking pot** – and what better place to get Maui Wowie, than right here in West Maui? I don't know that too many people move to Hawaii just for the pot experience, but I'll bet there are more than I think there are! Driving out west past Kahana and over by the cliffs… and then on Kauai – the same, anywhere it looks like pure Hawaii jungle – you're likely to see a guy or two just hanging out along the road. *What are they doing?* If they think you're safe enough, they will hold up a big bunch of Hawaiian grown marijuana to let you see it and purchase it if you want. They are bold, and they have lookouts for police further up the road, and there are only two ways in to get to them so they disappear when police are cruising down the road. Contrary to popular belief, the Honolulu Police Department will throw you in jail for possession and for growing or distributing pot. It isn't legal in Hawaii (yet). See Chapter 26 for more information on marijuana and likelihood of legalization in the islands in the coming years.

2. **You don't feel like you fit in on the mainland because you don't like working.** You don't like the whole environment. You want to get back to a slower place, the islands. Well, Hawaii is not Jamaica mon, and you're probably going to get a big surprise as you land at Honolulu International Airport and smell the bus and car fumes from Nimitz Highway. Mexico might be a better place to move. Florida near the beaches… or even Jamaica might be better for you.

Hawaii is unforgiving... meaning, you must have cash or you're going to be spending a lot of time with poor locals camping in the parks and along the beaches. It is very hard to adjust to that lifestyle, and very hard to make friends of the locals in that situation. You'd really be better off being homeless or destitute somewhere else. The homeless population is getting quite large in the islands. The State of Hawaii government is actually considering buying them plane tickets to go back to their state of residence! Yes, it's *that bad*.

3. **You just got an unexpected payday.** Meaning, you just got an insurance settlement, sold a business, sold a house or something else and you're looking for a way to spend it. I have said many times that if you have $10K USD saved, you could possibly make it in Hawaii. Just find a rented apartment and start the job search. What I mean is, if you start saving now and planning, in a few months when you have the money, you'll have likely learned everything you have to in preparation to move to Hawaii. If you just get a payday and you're looking to spend it in an amazing way moving to the islands, you haven't done all the necessary preparation. Don't neglect to research a lot about moving, and how life will be once you arrive. If you haven't ever been to Hawaii I wouldn't suggest you move here. It's too different from every other place you've probably ever been. I've seen more than a couple people blow their savings and move back home within just months.

4. **You have an incurable illness and you want to die in paradise.** Hawaii can be a very lonely place. I have seen and spoken with many lonely people here. Most Caucasians don't realize they'll be a minority in the islands, but more importantly – they don't know what that feels like. It's a weird feeling at first, for most of us. Though I was surrounded by military, when I went off on my own, or in a small group I realized – wow, I'm a minority. It was a bit of a shock, but I got over it quickly. Some don't. If you cannot, it will be quite difficult to make friends.

If you have an incurable illness and you think it's best to pass in Hawaii – I'm not sure it is. You'll have to make friends, and friends that really care. If you are bed-ridden, you might die alone watching Hawaii 5-0 on the television set. How sad is that? I think better to stay where you are in the mainland, or wherever your family and friends are.

5. **You want to start a business.** You have a great idea, it's amazing, and you know Hawaii is the right place for you to make it work.

Starting a business in Hawaii has got to be one of the riskiest things you could possibly do with your money. Hawaii is a different world when it comes to what people like. Do Filipinos like your product or service? Local Japanese? Hawaiians? Military? Visitors from across the globe? You'll have to really spend some time researching the marketplace in-depth in Hawaii for your business. I have seen all sorts of businesses start and fail very quickly in Hawaii. If it takes longer to fail, that's even worse because more money, time and effort go out the window. If you're going to start a business in Hawaii, make sure you spend months doing the hard research you'll need to ensure success. You probably need to live in the islands for a year or so before you have any idea at all what might work or not.

2 – HIGH COST OF LIVING

In general things cost a lot more in Hawaii than they do on the mainland. Shipping food over the ocean in boats (or planes) is one reason for this, but another is that grocers have to maintain huge stocks of food in warehouses to keep food on the shelves all the time.

This requires a lot more money to pay the rent and people for running the warehouses.

Another reason is Hawaii's 4% excise tax. Which is added to just about everything business related.

Housing Costs

Of course, the main issue factoring into the high cost of living in Hawaii is the cost of housing – owning and renting homes.

The reason land and homes are so expensive is because land is not a renewable resource. What is here on the islands is all you have to work with. With the rugged terrain there is a lot of land it isn't possible to build on.

Want to know the major reason prices are so high?

Demand. There are people WILLING to pay $600K – 900K for a regular sized home on Oahu or Maui. In most cases they are moving from Japan or California and have sold their home there and received about the same amount. It's a rather affordable move for them.

The number of people who would answer 'yes' if you asked them, 'if you could, would you live in Hawaii?' is probably very high.

I don't know many that would answer 'no' – do you?

Why is the demand so high for housing and rental units in Hawaii?

Well, there is a whole lot to like about the islands! Personally, I rate it as one of the two top places to live in the world. Krabi, Thailand is one, and somewhere on Maui is another one. It's a tough call to label one as better than the other – there are vast differences between them. Hawaii is, without a doubt, the best place to live in the USA. Hands down the winner!

Hawaii has everything I like - clean air; clean water; what I'd call perfect weather; a wide range of environments – forest, desert, beaches; a great group of people; delicious restaurants; and decent nightlife.

If you've already lived in Tokyo, Japan; Seoul, Korea; Hollywood, California, or New York City, New York, you will think Hawaii's cost of living is reasonable. If you haven't lived in a very high cost of living area before, you will probably become very cost-conscious once you start living here.

Chapter 18 covers homes and condos.

Insurance

Car insurance, health insurance, fire insurance, every insurance, is more expensive in Hawaii. If you ride a motorcycle, be prepared to sign away a good portion of your monthly income to insurance. The whole living in Hawaii experience is outrageously expensive and it may go against your common sense to live here - but you may not be able to resist!

Many Hawaii residents have two and three jobs to keep up with expenses. It's safe to say you'll meet more people working more than one job in Hawaii than you have ever met anywhere else in your life.

Groceries

I mentioned before that most grocery items are over $5. Many are over $10 now too!

Add to that the cost of gas, renting apartments that are very small and with pay for parking issues all over Waikiki if that's where you plan to stay, and it gets expensive.

According to a survey I did of residents living in Hawaii, their average food bill per person in the family was, as a minimum, around $300. I routinely ate $800 - 1K per month just for me! It is not difficult to do; there are some great restaurants on the islands. Restraint is called for! Restraint I obviously didn't have. Maybe that's why I exercise so much.

Can you live in Hawaii making $25K per year? Yes, probably. But, be prepared to be very frugal and live in a manner you may not be accustomed to, eating food you may not be so happy with.

High Electricity Costs

At 30 cents per kilowatt-hour average across the islands, and with a range of 20 cents to 34 cents, the monthly cost is around $120 – 180 just for electricity.

Hawaii's electrical generators are run on petroleum for the most part. When the price of gas went through the roof – so did electricity in Hawaii. The islands now boast the highest cost for electricity per unit – in the USA. It's about 300% of the national average.

I think the figure mentioned above is being conservative. I typically used over $200 in electricity per month. Unless you're really conscious about your electricity use, your average bill for a home will be over $200 and probably more like $300.

Water Bills

I've had water bills as low as $45 in Hawaii a couple years back. Some people with five adults and three or four kids report having to pay $300 every two months. Keep in mind, anyone with a house is using the sprinklers on their lawn, and sometimes filling swimming pools as well.

3 – HOW MUCH MONEY IS ENOUGH?

This is the biggest unknown for most people, as they consider moving to Hawaii. It is for me too. Every time I move back to the islands, it is also the main question on my mind.

How much money is enough to cover you as you move from the mainland USA, or maybe another part of the world, to Hawaii? How much do you need each month to live, and for savings for the unknown future?

It depends on you, and how you want to live before you buy or rent a home. You'll be spending hours looking at houses or condominiums and you will need a place to sleep, that's about it. You'll be out of your room all day until nighttime. You only, realistically, need a place you can sleep that is safe and clean.

You can find a room for $100 or so per night, at many locations on the island of Oahu. Hostels have rooms for $30 per night if you're desperate.

I don't recommend bringing any valuables with you, like notebook computer, jewelry, or anything else too expensive that you can't carry around with you all day in a backpack or bag.

Though the hotels insist their room safes are secure, I have lost items there when the cleaning staff or others broke into them. People I know have also been victims of theft.

I think it's better to have a trusted friend or family member send valuables to you after you find your new home.

Most families in Hawaii have household income under $70K per annum. Before finding that statistic, I would have guessed that the average income for families in Hawaii was higher. It does make sense why everyone is griping about how expensive everything is!

It's safe to say, at these income levels – you need A+ credit to buy a home in Hawaii – well, anywhere but Big Island, where homes are still somewhat affordable!

At $75K per year, for two unmarried people, it works out to just $37,500 each. Twelve thousand of that goes to taxes from each – which leaves $25K each, $50K total for two people. That isn't so great at all.

Fully one quarter of all Hawaii households are pulling in less than $35K per year in income. That's plain unlivable for more than one person.

I really think that any income over $50K per person is 'enough' to live in Hawaii. You can make that work on any of the islands. If you're making any less than that you're going to be too stressed that you aren't making enough. My most recent multi-year stay in Hawaii had me racking up $800 in food bills per month – minimum!

Even if you're staying in a studio or one-bedroom in Waikiki that is clean and has security, you'll be paying $1K per month. Want 1-bedroom? You'll pay around $1,400.

Every time we went to the grocery behind Ala Moana shopping center we shelled out $200+ for groceries. In Pennsylvania, where I grew up, you could fill the back of a truck for that! In Hawaii? You might get four or five bags if you're lucky. I remember going to the fresh fish shop on Maui in Honokowai and paying $50 - $70 for some tuna, swordfish, and shrimp. It's THAT bad! Who can go without fresh fish though? I certainly cannot. You just have to pay the price!

Car insurance, car payment, health insurance payment, kids' private school costs, personal taxes, emergency costs, going out costs... all of these add up to eat up your entire paycheck if you're making under $50K per year.

Life is what you make it, and life in Hawaii can be done at less than $50K per year in personal income, but I wouldn't really recommend it unless you are ready to live very frugally. There are people who can do it on even $30K income per year. I've seen them. They don't eat well, and they don't do anything at night. Some are happy that way, and others tolerate it for a while before they move back to the mainland and raise their standard of living back up to what they are comfortable with.

Your standard of living is kind of built into you. You were raised in a certain standard – and that usually becomes your minimum you are willing to go down to. If you made $70K back in the mainland – in a town like Gibson City, Illinois – you could have whatever you wanted. Move to Hawaii and it's like you're making $40K. You have about the same amount of spending power.

Think very hard about moving to Hawaii if money is going to be a severely limiting factor. *Can you live on less so you actually have some savings at the end of the month? Should you spend the next year before you move to learn skills that will help you get a better job? Should you start an Internet business that provides residual income in addition to what you make at a regular job working eight hours per day? Should you sell your car and get a bike in Hawaii?*

There are so many questions… and so many ways to make it work if you really want to. Don't take your move to the Hawaiian Islands lightly. Consider money very carefully, especially if you have a family relying on you.

4 – MINIMALIST LIVING

What is the bare minimum one needs to survive in Hawaii?

As I've alluded to earlier, every question dealing with money is basically up to *you*. There are many homeless people in Hawaii – so, you could go that route if you were dying to get here and spend your life in one of the most beautiful places in the world. As of yet, they cannot kick you out and make you move back to your state of residence. Maybe make Hawaii your state of residence before you become homeless – then you're set, right? Perhaps.

Being homeless in Hawaii is not as easy as it might appear on the surface, but it's probably a whole lot easier than living in a cold place without a home. I do know that the agencies providing homeless services are overworked and have little funds. Realistically they have to come up with them to help people who have lost it all and that are living in the streets.

"The cost of living in Hawaii is what you make it."

It's amazing what you can easily spend living in downtown Honolulu – Waikiki area or anywhere on Oahu. You can easily spend $1K for a studio apartment in downtown Honolulu if you want to be close enough to walk or bike to anything you need to get to. For food you can easily spend $600 per month for one person. I think to spend less you really have to budget and watch what you're eating. I don't particularly enjoy watching what I'm eating, unless it's going into my mouth. *Can you keep yourself from eating expensive food?* It's a question you'll have to ask yourself if you're planning on going the minimalistic route. Food is probably the area you can save most on if you're thrifty.

If you want to live in a room, you can probably find on Craigslist.org a room in someone's home for around $400 per month. Students at University of Hawaii typically stay in this type of housing situation because it's the cheapest option. You could share a room in a house. Then you might pay only $250 per month. You could share a room in a house with four people if the landlord would let you! *Can you live that way?* Ask yourself before you go. I sure couldn't enjoy life like that unless I got to choose the four people I lived with. Unfortunately, that wouldn't happen.

Let's say you find a room for $400. You could eat on $350 to $400 per month in Hawaii if you were smart over the first few weeks and months. Then you'd find out where the real cost savers are – the markets, the house that sells mangos or pineapples in front on a table for $1 each. The outdoor markets in the morning on the weekend have a great supply of fruits and vegetables for reasonable prices. As reasonable as you're going to find anyway.

For extras, you'll spend another couple hundred. So, you could live in Hawaii for as little as $1,000 per month without a car. Honolulu is a densely packed area that is great for walking around in. You could have a room in Honolulu and walk to work and everywhere else you needed to get to most of the time – supermarket and beach.

If you drink a lot or have some other addiction like partaking of the nightlife often, you're going to add a lot of money to your monthly expenses. If you want to move to Hawaii and remain here, you probably will have to suffer for a little while until you build up your income and make enough connections to help you weather the first few months or years.

I have a friend that moved to Oahu with virtually nothing – I mentioned him earlier. He took a job cold calling to sell insurance. He did OK, but then he found another friend that appraised property. He trained under this friend for two years, making very little income. Now he's an appraiser – certified, and doing fine for himself. He has more work than he can handle. He owns a condo and is married to a lovely Japanese woman and they have a daughter.

If you're willing to sacrifice for a while – you can move to Oahu, Maui, Kauai, or Big Island Hawaii. *You can.*

It's just a matter of *how badly* you want to do it.

5 – BEFORE YOU GO

The first time I went to live in Hawaii, as I said, I was sent to Oahu in the US Air Force. They arranged everything, and it couldn't have been easier. I brought clothes in a suitcase, and my uniforms and other gear. That was about it besides some photos of friends, and a lot of papers.

Over the years I've shipped a lot of furniture, and a handful of vehicles to Hawaii. It becomes quite an involved process when you want to move some, or all of your possessions from the mainland (or anywhere) to Hawaii.

There are things you can do to minimize what might amount to "culture shock" when you move to Hawaii. One of them, you've already done. Buying this book will help a lot as a resource. Another is using my free website. Another is watching my YouTube videos under "Moving to Hawaii" – there are four videos to watch. I review one of my earlier books about moving to Hawaii, and invariably I add some new information to the video than I have put in the book.

There is a list of helpful resources at the end of this book you can use too. Some are friends; some are places I've gone frequently. Others are resources that get great reviews from friends – but that I haven't tried yet.

What else can you do to get a good picture of what it will be like living the 50th State?

Talk to other people and get different points of view about moving here. There are over a million people on the islands, and while most of them like it – or love it, a great deal – there are those that do not. Some of them will be moving away as soon as they can afford to. You should try to find people from both sides and see what they like and don't like about life in Hawaii.

Talk to as many people as you can find that will chat with you about it.

How?

I recommend you join and get familiar with using Twitter.com.

Twitter.com is a chat service; I'll not go through all the details of how to set up an account. It isn't too difficult.

Using Twitter's "Search" function you can search the messages of hundreds of millions of members to see who is talking about "living in Hawaii" or "moving to Hawaii." Once you find some people you can send them a message and ask them if they might share some of their opinions or knowledge on the subject.

This is a very cheap, very efficient, and very common thing to do recently. Twitter has become a major resource online for finding information about anything people are talking about. I strongly recommend you join the service, spend some time figuring it out, and use the search function. I am sure you'll be able to find helpful people who will let you know their true feelings about living in Hawaii.

Be aware that some Hawaii residents aren't looking forward to anyone else coming to the islands. Hawaii is getting crowded (some say it has always been) and more people are coming everyday to see what it's like to live in paradise. People you meet online are not always the type to portray an accurate picture of what it's really like to live in Hawaii full-time. They might try to dissuade you from giving it a shot.

What is the best way to figure out if you could make it in Hawaii?

I strongly recommend you visit the islands first. When you do, talk to as many locals as you can to help you figure out what the reality of the situation is. I'm writing this book to show you the reality of living in the islands as I see it. I'm very pro-Hawaii, as you might have guessed. Everyone sees things differently. The best thing to do is find many people to talk with – all with a variety of opinions, likes, dislikes, needs, agendas, etc.

Do your homework and talk to people, or you won't have a real good idea what living in Hawaii is like.

Also, when contacting others that reside in Hawaii, remember it has its own Time Zone – Hawaiian Standard Time Zone.

Sometimes the state is six hours behind the mainland's East coast. Sometimes just five hours – depending on Daylight Savings Time – which Hawaii does not follow. Be considerate of making contact with people in Hawaii according to their time.

Airport Codes

Here is a list of the airports on the main Hawaiian Islands, along with their airport codes you can use when you're planning airline flights to Hawaii.

Typically it takes nine hours from Chicago to Oahu's Honolulu International Airport, and five to six hours from California.

Oahu Airports

• Honolulu International Airport (**HNL**) – Oahu's largest and most used airport.

• Dillingham Airfield (**HDH**) – this is a small airport used for light aircraft and is located on the northwestern side of Oahu.

• Kalaeloa Airport (**JRF**) – another less-used airport located in Kapolei, on the west side of Pearl Harbor on Oahu, Hawaii.

Maui Airports

- Hana Airport (**HNM**) – Hana airport is located on the extreme eastern side of Maui, and is for light aircraft.

- Kahului Airport (**OGG**) – the main airport for Maui.

- Kapalua Airport (**JHM**) – this is a small airport on the side of a hill near Kahana on the west side of Maui.

Hawaii Airports

- Hilo International Airport (**ITO**) – one of the main Big Island airports.

- Kona International Airport at Keahole (**KOA**) – the other main Big Island airport.

- Upolu Airport (**UPP**)

- Waimea-Kohala Airport (**MUE**)

Kauai Airports

- Lihue Airport (**LIH**) – the main arrival airport, but it is so small and quaint that you might think you landed in the wrong place. Nope, this is Kauai!

- Port Allen Airport (**PAK**)

Molokai Airports

- Kalaupapa Airport (**LUP**)

- Molokai Airport (**MKK**)

Lanai Airports

- Lanai Airport (**LNY**)

Bringing Your Pet to Hawaii

Hawaii has the rare distinction of being a rabies-free state. It just doesn't exist in the islands. Apparently, this is something they want to continue, so they strictly restrict pets coming in.

I remember back in 1985 when I first arrived in Hawaii, there were people I knew that were waiting to have their dogs and cats out of the quarantine station in Hawaii – for an entire year!

Today that has changed a bit, but your pet will still stay one hundred twenty days unless you jump through some more hoops. If you're a good hoop jumper, you just might be able to get your pet into Hawaii and joining you at your home in just thirty days. That's a big improvement over one year, right? Guess what? There is also a five-day quarantine option that you might be lucky enough to qualify for.

Fees for bringing your pet over to Hawaii range from $175 to $1,100 – not including airfare to send your pet from wherever you live currently.

Nor does that include costs to visit your pet, from the other islands. The pet quarantine facility is located on the island of Oahu, in Aiea. If you live on Kauai, you'll have additional costs that someone on Oahu, won't have.

Hawaii Animal Quarantine Facility

99-951 Halawa Valley Street
Aiea, HI 96701-5602
Web: HawaiiAG.org/hdoa
Phone: 808-483-7151, Fax 808-483-7161
Email: hdoa_info@exec.state.hi.us or aqs.rabies@gte.net

In addition to restricting the import of cats and dogs to Hawaii –
there are requirements for bringing other animals, and plants too.

For information about bringing plants to Hawaii, contact:

Hawaii Department of Agriculture - Plant Quarantine

1849 Auiki Street
Honolulu, HI 96819
Web: HawaiiAg.org/hdoa
Phone: 808-832-0566, Fax: 808-832-0584

Moving Personal Belongings to Hawaii

You might think it's impossible for someone to move all your
stuff from your current house on the east coast of the USA – to
Hawaii, including your car, truck, and riding lawnmower. But, it
is possible! It's not even that difficult. Sure, there are things
you'll have to manage yourself but, all in all it isn't that big of a
deal.

Typical costs for moving the furniture and other belongings of a
5-person family in a 3-bedroom, 2,000 square foot home with
two cars will be in the neighborhood of $15K – 20K from
Florida.

When you can, ask some people living in Hawaii that have
moved from the mainland about their shipping experiences. If
they lived in the same region as you, maybe you can use the
same local moving company to handle your furniture.

Schedule the movers to arrive a day or two before your flight
leaves for Hawaii. The good movers will come to your house in
the morning by 9 am. or 10 am., with a giant truck or two, and
begin the slow process of wrapping each piece of furniture and
box you have with blankets and very strong wrapping plastic –

so your belongings will survive the trip over the ocean without getting banged up and broken.

Pack all your small things, well padded, into boxes. Then, either put them in bigger boxes, or the movers will do it. Bicycle boxes can be found at the bicycle stores. Some will even wrap the bikes for you in bike boxes for a reasonable fee. I think it is well worth it to have them do it, they can take off the pedals and loosen the stem and handlebars to make the bike fit easily into the box. It's something less for you to worry about. Let them do it.

Some movers will let you wrap your items yourself. You may save about $1K doing it that way, but really – you'll have enough to worry about. Let them do it, rather than you taking the responsibility for wrapping every box and piece of furniture in your house well enough that it doesn't get scratched or broken in a boat container that may experience heavy seas.

I've only had one problem with shipping items from the mainland to Hawaii – my car was scratched up on the door a bit. Matson paid for the damage, so it wasn't so bad.

I've shipped three cars - a Honda Prelude, a Lexus RX300, a Toyota Tercel, and a truck, each for about $1K. This required driving three of the vehicles from Florida to Los Angeles at the "Matson Shipping" office in Long Beach, California. I shipped one car the other way from Hawaii to Florida when I left the Air Force too – and had no problem.

Time to arrive in Hawaii from California - once the boat departs?

About three weeks.

Not too bad, right?

What Items to Bring With You To Hawaii?

People usually do it one of two ways…

1. Bring everything they own and that they've collected over the decades.

2. Bring the bare essentials, and buy what is needed on the island.

People who are in Hawaii already also recommend the same plan of attack. Personally, I like the idea of selling everything and arriving with just the clothes on my back and in my suitcase. Oh, and I do always bring a vehicle.

If it sat around your present home gathering dust, you will never need it in Hawaii. The Hawaii experience is so different and it has the power to change the person you are. I no longer watched TV after I arrived in Hawaii. I just couldn't do it anymore. I felt like I was completely wasting my valuable time because now there were all these other things to do outside instead.

Good thing I didn't bring a TV here because it would have been pointless.

And that's what I mean, bringing things that were part of your life in the mainland USA, probably doesn't make sense.

Think hard about whether it's worth it to take things you may never use again. Shipping is expensive. Why not sell all your stuff, pocket that money AND the $10K - $20K and buy what you need when you arrive in Hawaii?

Makes sense to me – but up to you of course.

The clothing you need, will depend where you will live, but in general, shorts and loose, light shirts is all you need. You will probably buy new clothes when you arrive, so again, I recommend taking the minimum.

Bring important documents – ID, tax papers, business papers, medical records, prescriptions and scripts, diplomas and whatever else is essential.

United Parcel Service serves Hawaii and it only takes five to ten days to receive your items when sent through the mail from the mainland.

Shipping for Autos and Household Goods

Matson Navigation Company
Web: Matson.com
Phone: 800-462-8766 (toll-free)

Horizon Lines (CSX Lines)
Web: Horizon-Lines.com
Phone: 842-5300 locally or 877-678-7447 (toll-free)

Honolulu Freight Service
Web: HFSNet.com
Phone: 808-531-0258

Young Brothers Limited (Hawaii interisland moves only)
Web: HTBYB.com
Phone: 808-543-9311

The cost of shipping a car from California to Hawaii through Matson is about $1K for a standard vehicle. This means within these measurements: 21' 8" long x 8' wide x 7' high. As you can see – there is wide leeway and most vans, trucks, and cars fall within that range.

Moving You to Hawaii

Check whatever airline has a hub in the airports near you. Hawaiian Air also serves some mainland cities – and has some great fares at times.

There is a website that specializes in finding really cheap fares from around the USA to Hawaii here: BeatOfHawaii.com

Checklist Before Going

1. Sell your house, or figure out what to do with it. Rent it out?

2. Make a list – what can you not live without in Hawaii – and what can you sell or give away? I really think you should not bring everything you own – there is no point. Buy what you need when you arrive in Hawaii. Your lifestyle may change significantly… mine did, every time I moved!

3. Call your accountant – will any portion of the moving expenses be deductible on taxes? Work moves can be written off substantially.

4. Start researching jobs – if you plan on working in Hawaii – well before you leave. In fact, this is one of the major determinants of whether you will end up "making it" in Hawaii or not. Your job should pay enough, and be a good match for your personality. There are some awesome jobs in Hawaii – I've had three. Of course, there are hundreds more; you just have to find them.

Finding a job will be difficult before you arrive – but check out the scene. Find a company you want to work for. Find an area you want to live. Find a career field that has frequent job openings. Do your research before you arrive.

5. Choose an island and an area to live. Saying you'll live on Oahu or Maui, isn't enough. The locales differ remarkably from each other. Kapolei versus Hawaii Kai – the differences are enormous. Again, research for many hours to find the place you want to live. This, in addition to your job, will be crucial in the outcome of your move.

Use Google Earth to see a satellite view of different areas of the islands. This has helped me a lot over the years!

6. If you or your family members will be attending school – do your research! There are good and bad schools in Hawaii – and the good ones charge a high tuition. Punahou on Oahu, where

President Obama went, costs way over $1K per month in tuition. Yes, I'm talking about high school!

7. Have a plan for the day you arrive, and the days after as you transition into a permanent residence. There are condo's available all over Oahu, but less so on the other islands. There are, of course, hotels everywhere, but they are very expensive to stay during your transition.

8. Notify all friends and relatives of your move.

9. Complete change of address at the post office.

10. Get a bank account in Hawaii. Mainland banks do not exist in Hawaii, so get a local account as fast as you can - on vacation in the islands would be ideal before you arrive.

11. If you already have a house, condo, or apartment you're moving into – turn on the utilities – electric and water a couple days before you leave for Hawaii.

12. Turn off your utilities at your old home.

13. Research mobile phone service and Internet if it will be essential when you arrive.

How long will it take you to find a home?

I recommend you spend a lot of time thinking about exactly what you want, and compare that to what is available in Hawaii on the island you want to live. Housing is different on each island. Have a real clear idea what you want to spend, and which area you will likely work, before you go.

It's quite possible to find a house and move into it within about two months of arriving. Or, it could take you more than six months. You can almost always find an apartment (condo) in a couple of days. You should already be familiar with the island you're moving to – and you should have a list of homes you want to see that you found on the Internet.

You should contact a Realtor before you go – if you plan on using one, because they can line up a group of homes to show you that fit all your specifications. Sometimes in housing listed online you won't have any idea what a neighborhood looks like. A realtor living in Hawaii can tell you what the area is like – though they are limited by what all they can tell you.

There are people who move to Hawaii and rent with just $4K in their pocket as they get off the plane in Honolulu.

Others are going to buy a home and will need to spend weeks or months looking. If that is your situation, you should budget about $12K for you (with family) to get through sixty days of living in Hawaii without income.

If you're going alone – budget about $7K to $10K. If you and a spouse, then more like $10K to $20K.

You'll likely be eating out for all of your meals unless you feel inspired and want to rent a room with a kitchen and create your own meals. With the time you'll spend on the road you are probably better off just to plan to eat at restaurants during your house-hunting period.

If you require something better than a $100/night room – budget accordingly.

The Long Airplane Flight to Hawaii from Mainland USA

Though it's not anything like a 24-hour flight, like it was for me coming from the USA to Thailand, the flight to Hawaii can still be quite long for those not used to being in the air for five to ten hours at a time. New Jersey's Newark airport has a direct non-stop flight that takes about ten hours going straight to Honolulu.

Flying for that many hours – especially with kids – can be traumatic!

I've flown about 120 trips on passenger planes, and here is how I get through long flights. Some of these tips come from a time when I've had kids, so those tips are in this section as well.

IPhone - If you have an iPhone, or other 'smartphone' you're going to make it with a minimum of boredom. Load your phone up with mp3's first. You'll need about twenty songs per hour – at three minutes per song. If you're flying from New Jersey straight through – you'll need two-hundred songs minimum – and that's if you just want to play them all and not choose from among them. You'll need four-hundred if you want any sort of choice in the matter.

Grab some videos from YouTube. There are free services that allow you to download whole YouTube videos and play them on your phone when you want, without an Internet connection. Usually you just copy-paste a YouTube website address (URL) into a box on the download site and then choose what quality video you want to download to your computer. If you have a computer with Macintosh software, you'll have to transfer it to your phone through Apple's convoluted and ridiculous system. Meaning, upload to iTunes and then download it back to your phone, but hey – you bought their products! I did too and love them for most everything but this silly feature of theirs.

If you were smart, you bought an Android phone, and can just transfer files easily from your computer straight to the phone. Saving about five hours of trouble.

Angry Birds – is a great way to pass the time. Make sure you have a lot of levels to play – over thirty or so. You can buy many different editions to keep you and your kids entertained. You probably won't pass all the levels by the time you reach Hawaii, so you'll have something to do for the trip back home. Hopefully you're so exhausted by your action-packed Hawaii trip that you sleep the entire flight back, but it's good to have options.

If you have kids – teach them how to play Angry Birds and as many other games as you can on your portable device before you leave, that way they'll be overjoyed when you hand it to them to play for nine hours straight! If you have more than one kid, you might buy the cheap iPod, which can do everything the iPad or iPhone does, except use mobile phone services. You can still make calls using SKYPE or a VOIP service that requires Wi-Fi Internet so, it's a pretty good deal to buy an iPod for all the kids in the family.

EBooks – Smart phones and tablet computers are great ways to read Amazon Kindle eBooks or books purchased from the iBook store at Apple. To read Amazon's Kindle books on any device, just download the free Kindle software for Amazon and register your device with your Amazon.com account. This way, you can purchase eBooks from your device – or anyone's computer – by logging into your account at Amazon. After you purchase your eBook, you can choose which device to send it to. The eBook is automatically sent to your preferred device the next time you're connected to the Internet. The books you buy are downloaded automatically and it's all very seamless. Amazon knows how to create a nice experience for buyers.

If there is something else you want to read – an article, a TXT file, a PDF, a MS Word file, or something else, you can have Amazon send it to your phone also.

They just came out with new software you can install on your computer which will allow you to send any document from your computer to your Kindle (whether you use the Kindle software or hardware reader) by right clicking the file on your computer and choosing, "Send to Kindle." The name of the software is also called, "Send to Kindle." The location for it at present (12/2013) is:

Windows PCs
www.amazon.com/gp/sendtokindle/windows

Mac PCs
www.amazon.com/sendtokindle/mac

Movies - You can rent whole movies from Netflix and view them on your computer. Keep in mind your plane to Hawaii will likely have a couple in-flight movies play for you at your seat. Amazon also has a video download service that will allow you to use your smart phone to view them, or iPad or other tablet computer.

Sleep the Entire Flight - If you are traveling alone, or in a group of adults – you can always try the "get a little hammered before you board" trick. For this I only need one or two beers, which I drink fast before I get on the plane. I get very sleepy when I have any alcohol, so it isn't long before I'm zonked out for at least three to four hours; sometimes I make it the whole way to Honolulu International Airport when I'm lucky!

Flying With Children - Flying to Hawaii from the mainland is a long flight made even longer if you have a kid screaming for even a fraction of the time. If you are bringing one or more kids, I can't emphasize this trick enough:

Sleep deprive them! Make sure the kids are ready to sleep as the plane climbs to altitude. If it makes you feel any better, you're not really depriving them of sleep, look at it like you are preparing them for the big time difference, so they can get used to it easier!

Bring With You On the Plane:

Long-sleeved shirt, socks, and some clothes you can bundle up into a pillow. They give out pillows on the plane, but usually it isn't enough for me and I bundle some shirts around it to make it thick enough. I also have this odd aversion to putting my head on anyone's pillow other than my own.

Earplugs. If it isn't your child screaming, it will be someone else's. One problem is that some children on the flight invariably have a sinus condition, a cold, or allergies, and their sinuses build up pressure and it feels like they will explode. It hurts a

LOT. I had it very bad one time, and I thought I would start screaming myself. If your children have a head cold, make sure to give them something to clear up their sinuses good – or, don't take them on the flight – the pain can be unbearable.

Lip balm – to keep your lips moist, the air is dryer than the Sahara Desert on a long flight. You might also bring some drops to keep your eyes moist.

Anti-bacterial wipes or lotion if you can get it on the plane, but I think that's been eliminated as a possibility lately. What hasn't?

Bandana to tie around your eyes, eye-patches, whatever you can use to cover your eyes from the person in front that leaves their window slide open for the 90°F sun to shine right onto your face, while the rest of the plane is entirely dark.

Deck of cards if you're traveling with someone, or heck, even if you're not – everyone knows how to play '21' or poker – right? Make some friends, but be careful not to lose your money!

Pad of paper. I always write farewell letters to my mom and wife when I fly on a plane. It's just a good way to pass the time! I also bring some blank sheets that I can draw ideas on. For some reason, sitting on a plane with nothing to do but think for half-a-dozen hours, really brings out some creative ideas.

Diapers, milk, wipes, snacks, toys that don't make noise, children's books and their favorite stuffed animal – or whatever is necessary to help them sleep.

6 – AFTER YOU ARRIVE

You'll need to include in your start-up costs the amount for turning on your utilities. The costs vary by island, and your credit report might play a part in whether or not you'll be required to put a cash deposit down or not.

Water - Deposits range from $50 - $100. Your deposit can be refunded after a year of continuous service. Sometimes there is a reinstallation fee of $60 if it was turned off and turned back on again.

Natural Gas - Fee to start service, the connection fee, is $25 - $50. Deposit ranges from $75 -$100. Refund of deposit is possible after a year of on-time payments.

Electricity - Fee to start service is $15 -$40. Deposit between $50 - $100. Deposit refunded after year of continuous on-time payments.

Phone - No deposit required. You're likely better off with a mobile phone unless your mobile carriers don't cover the area you live in very well.

Sewage - On Oahu this is included in the water bill. On other islands, it ranges between $25 to $40 every other month.

Hawaii State ID Card - You need an original Social Security card, and one of the following:

• Certified Birth Certificate issued by the state repository in the state where you were born

• Document for a Child Born Abroad of American parents

• Certificate of citizenship or naturalization

All changes in status or name due to marriage, divorce, annulment, adoption, or citizenship must be supported by certified legal documents.

Call 808-587-3111 for current fee (cash accepted only).

Web: State.HI.US/hcjdc

Motor Vehicle Registration and Licensing

Oahu: 808-532-7700 ext. 222

Maui: 808-270-7840

Molokai: 808-553-9067

Lanai: 808-565-7878

Hawaii: Hilo - 808-961-8351, Kona - 808-327-3543

Kauai: 808-241-6577

Health Insurance (for Hawaii State Employees)

The State of Hawaii employee health insurance plan is subsidized and not a bad deal. Individuals will pay between $50 to $100 for Medical, drug, chiropractic, vision, and dental. Family contribution is between $215 and $285 (per month).

Hawaii Auto Insurance

By law, your Hawaii auto insurance coverage must cover:

• Damage to Property

- PIP – Personal Injury Protection

- Bodily Injury

Public Transportation – The Bus

They call it "The Bus", on Oahu (thebus.org) and a trip costs $2.25. On Maui (www.co.maui.hi.us), it's "Maui Bus" and runs $1 per ride. On Kauai (Kauai.gov) and Big Island (www.HeleOnBus.org) they also have a bus service they call "Hele-On Bus."

The Bus is a great way to get around if you do not have a car, or if you have one but do not want to face the traffic through Honolulu or some of the other heavily traveled cities on other islands. Oahu has programs you can join for ride–sharing which also helps put a dent in traffic, and keeps you sane because you won't have to drive every day through bad traffic.

Taxi

Taxis are available on the major islands – not usually the yellow cabs that are easy to spot, all kinds of cars are taxis.

Molokai and Lanai Buses?

They don't have buses.

7 – GEOGRAPHY OF HAWAII

Hawaii is located quite far from major landmasses. In fact, the Hawaiian Islands are located 2,390 miles from California, and 3,850 miles from Japan. Besides Easter Island, the Hawaiian Islands are the furthest from any other landmass.

You might be surprised to learn, there are 132 Hawaiian Islands, reefs, and atolls stretching over 1,500 miles and earning it the title of the longest island chain in the world. The largest of the islands – Hawaii (Big Island) – is the one the state is named after, obviously.

The 8 main islands are:

- Oahu

- Maui

- Hawaii

- Kauai

- Lanai

- Molokai

- Niihau

- Kahoolawe

Birthed from Volcanoes

All the Hawaiian Islands were created by volcanic action. Each island we can see is the top of a mountain that goes deep into the ocean. Formed by undersea volcanoes. Those islands in the southeast part of the chain are youngest – and on Hawaii you can see new land being created daily as the volcano eruptions continue to spew lava out of the ocean.

Though Mauna Kea Volcano on the Big Island is 13,803 feet high above sea level, when measured from the sea floor it is more than twice as high as Mount Everest mountain's 15,260 feet in elevation, and is 33,100 feet high!

8 – POPULATION & DEMOGRAPHIC INFO

Some quick stats about the population of the islands. This data represents all populated islands.

- State Population, 2013 estimate - 1,362,184

- Persons under 18 years old, percent, 2009 - 22.40%

- Persons 65 years old and over, percent, 2009 - 14.50%

- Female persons, percent, 2009 - 49.50%

- White persons, percent, 2009 - 30.20%

- Black persons, percent, 2009 - 3.20%

- American Indian and Alaska Native persons, percent, 2009 - 0.60%

- Asian persons, percent, 2009 - 38.80%

- Native Hawaiian and Other Pacific Islander, percent, 2009 - 9.20%

- Persons reporting two or more races, percent, 2009 - 18.00%

- Persons of Hispanic or Latino origin, percent, 2009 - 9.00%

- White persons not Hispanic, percent, 2009 - 25.10%

- Housing units, 2007 - 506,737

- Housing units, net change, April 1, 2000 to July 1, 2007 - 46,195

- Housing units percent change, April 1, 2000 to July 1, 2007 - 10.00%

- Homeownership rate, 2000 - 56.50%

- Median value of owner-occupied housing units, 2000 - $272,700

- Households, 2000 - 403,240

- Persons per household, 2000 - 2.92

- Median household income, 2007 - $62,613

- Persons below poverty, percent, 2007 - 8.50%

- Personal income per capita, 2006 - $37,023

- Unemployment rate, 2007 - 2.60%

- Employment in government, 2006 - 175,081

Source - U.S. Census Data.

Population Size

Back in the 1980's I remember the population of Hawaii had not yet reached a million. The census shows 964,000 in Hawaii in 1980. In 2004 there were 1,263,000 people living in Hawaii. The estimate for 2013 is that there are 1,362,184 living here. You're not the only one moving to paradise!

Though it seems like a huge increase, the population of the U.S. mainland on average is outpacing Hawaii, so there isn't any real need for concern. Of course, the available land area is shrinking steadily. Some say it's completely gone and that there is no new inhabitable land that can be created in Hawaii.

In 2000 Hawaii had 189 people living per square-mile on average. In the mainland U.S. the population density was only eighty people per square mile.

If looking solely at Oahu, there were 1,467 people per square mile!

If you live, work, and play in town on Oahu, you can get the feeling that you're very crowded and always surrounded by people. This contributes to the idea of island fever that eventually gets to Hawaii residents and pushes them away from living in the islands.

If at all possible, plan some time away from Oahu and see the other islands or visit the mainland or other countries when you can.

9 – WEATHER

Picture the ultimate weather... mostly sunny, not too hot. Gentle breezes blowing. Never too cold. Cool nights. Some rain, but not usually too much.

Welcome to Hawaii!

The funny thing is that on the islands the forecast for each part of an island is often quite different. Surf, sun, rain, wind - are all variable and change constantly.

Many locals say – if you do not like the weather, wait five minutes it will change. That's about right. It changes very fast.

Once I went up in a little Cessna plane with my roommate in the Air Force. He had just received his private pilot license. I paid the $50 for gas and we hit the skies in a little propeller engine plane from Dillingham Airfield on the north side of Oahu.

We had been up in the air for about twenty minutes when massive storm clouds started rolling in. We wanted to land but the air traffic controllers said to land in Honolulu where it was still sunny. We flew down there to find it rained out. They redirected us to the north again. We landed in a horrible rainstorm with forty mile-per-hour wind gusts and absolutely zero visibility.

I learned then, and never forgot, Hawaii weather changes in the blink of an eye.

On the big island of Hawaii, you can ski at the top of Mauna Kea's peak. A helicopter will need to drop you off – but it's possible. You can get a deep tan reclining on a towel on the beach that same day when you're finished. Mauna Kea is a dormant volcano with such a high summit that it gets snow. Maui too has a very high dormant volcano, Haleakala Volcano which goes over 10,000 feet and gets quite cold, with snow at times too – but it quickly melts.

How Much Sun Does Hawaii Get?

Here's a breakdown of the average number of days with sunshine per year in the main cities on each of the four major islands:

- Hilo, Big Island: 168

- Honolulu, Oahu: 271

- Kahului, Maui: 276

- Lihue, Kauai: 240

Source – National Climatic Data Center.

Year Round Heat

It's warm all year. Some would call Hawaii "hot." I never would, having lived in Miami, Tampa, and Thailand for a combined total of fifteen years. Those places are hot. Hawaii is the perfect weather for me, but you may find it hot all the time. I know people who sweat continually in Hawaii. They're not doing anything physically, but they just sweat constantly. If you're one of those people, Hawaii may not be the right place for you to live. If you think you can get used to it, make the effort, I'm sure you can, many people do.

No Seasons?

I like to say there are no real weather seasons in Hawaii. Only warm, balmy weather and that's about it. Sure, once per year you might get to breath fog on a cold December or January day, but it doesn't happen often. Not even every year.

There are technically two seasons in Hawaii. *Kau* wela – the summer, goes from May to October. This is a warm, fairly dry time, but there are still many occasional rain showers coming through. *Ho'oilo* – the winter is from November to April and is characterized by slightly cooler temperatures and more rain.

Perfect Weather?

Hawaii gets many sunny days each year. The weather in Hawaii is typically about 80 degrees and with a slight breeze called "trade winds" that blow from the northeast to the southwest. In fact, local Hawaiians often tell directions in relation to which side of the island gets the most wind. The northeast side of Oahu is also known as the "windward" side. The opposite is the leeward side.

Hawaii's Blazing Sun

Hawaii is close to the equator so the sun is stronger here.

You'll feel the sun's intensity is different from when you lived in the mainland USA, even if you lived as far south as Miami, Florida. I sure did. The sun is more like a radiation heater than just a source of convection. It feels as though you're being cooked from the inside. Sunburns can be especially nasty, I remember peeling thick layers of skin off my forehead and upper back when I got burned badly a few times. It only takes a few times to learn!

On clear sky days, the sun can be especially intense, so it is recommended you use hats and sunscreen to avoid negative effects. If you accidentally end up with sunburn, the local aloe plant cut open and applied directly is a soothing remedy.

Air Humidity

Though not usually stifling, the air humidity in Hawaii can be something to get used to if you do not have wet air in your current home. You'll notice it as you exit your air-conditioned plane if it's especially hot and humid that day. You may even pass-out. Seriously, I know someone that did!

For most of us though, it isn't that bad, and you'll get used to it. The heat and humidity of Hawaii is tempered by the near constant trade winds that blow most months of the year. Trade winds are stronger during the summer and weaker through winter months.

Along with trade winds are the Kona winds, which come from the southeast. These occur during the winter months and bring rain with them.

Average Relative Humidity Range in Percent (Annual):

- Honolulu, Oahu: 58 - 70

- Kahului, Maui: 60 - 72

- Lihue, Maui: 70 - 74

- Hilo, Hawaii: 71 - 76

Source – National Climatic Data Center.

Frequent Rain

It rains often on all the islands. Not all at the same time over all islands, but at different times in different areas.

On average each year, the islands of Hawaii get seventy inches of rain. That's almost eight trillion gallons of rainwater falling each year. Seems like a lot, right? It doesn't seem like it, most of the rain falls in certain areas of the islands. It isn't like you wake up to rain everyday!

The wettest island is Kauai – and this island also has the distinction of having the wettest spot on the entire planet. An average of 486 inches of rain falls there each year. Do you know how much SNOW that would be if it fell instead? Me neither, but it's a lot of rain regardless. More than an inch of rain per day. That's a lot!

Hilo on the Big Island Hawaii gets 130 to 200 inches of rain per year and is the wettest city in the United States.

There are some very dry spots in Hawaii too. Some places get less than six inches of rain per year!

There is a lovely type of rain the Hawaiians call "Kilihune" – it's the soft misty rain that falls and cools you off on a hot day.

So, no matter which Hawaiian Island you choose to be living on – it rains often – but usually in short bursts. Some find that annoying. If you ride a motorcycle or bicycle a lot, you should be prepared for heavy showers occasionally. It happens, that's Hawaii.

Rain is at its worst during the winter. Rain virtually stops in June and July – but there is sometimes the occasional shower anyway.

Hawaii is incredibly lush. There is a reason for that; it is raining every day somewhere on the islands. That's a given. Even though the sun is shining very brightly and the rest of the sky is blue – there might be a rain cloud up over the mountains, dumping large amounts of rain on it. You can see this quite clearly, and nearly daily if you live in or near Lahaina, Maui by the West Maui Mountains.

If you live in Hawaii, you'll get used to the rain. It's almost daily, and yet it doesn't usually last more than thirty to sixty minutes. A few times per year it will rain for hours or days at a time. That's bearable, right?

Tropical Storms and Hurricanes

Just four hurricanes have hit the Hawaiian Islands over the years since 1957. Hawaii is on the border of a tropical zone and can get very strong winds at times, and even a tropical storm once or twice per year.

Storm effects are giant ocean swells, torrential rains, fast gusting winds – sometimes seventy miles per hour gusts or even faster. And of course, storms generate some gigantic waves.

Flash flooding can occur during heavy rain. Some tourists and locals alike have lost their lives while exploring normally placid streams or waterfalls. In particular, sea caves, and waterfalls like Maui's Oheo Gulch (Seven Sacred Pools), should be very carefully explored or better – avoided, when there is rain upstream. Several times people died at this stunningly beautiful attraction.

A special note to those walking along sea-cliffs. Rogue waves are more common than you'd think, and you never know when they will hit. This is why those familiar with Hawaii's waters will tell you to keep your eye on the ocean at all times. Waves might be two to three feet high for the majority of the day and then one comes "out of the blue" that is twelve feet or bigger. It happens. People die sometimes because of it. Often, death and injury are preventable just by keeping one eye on the water at all times.

Climate Zones

In the entire world, there are thirteen climate zones. Hawaii has eleven of them. Each of these zones has its own set of weather characteristics, flora, and fauna. Hawaii's topography consists of high and low elevation, pressure changes, rain, winds, and surface qualities that combine to produce these different climate zones.

10 – WHICH ISLAND IS RIGHT FOR YOU?

The islands are quite diverse. If you like nightlife, you can only live on Oahu. If you like quiet, intimate gatherings on the weekend, you could live on just about any of the islands.

You'll need to visit all the islands if you want a big choice, otherwise try Oahu, Maui, and Big Island. Few can live on Kauai, Molokai, or Lanai. These islands have small populations and, though beautiful, they are not usually something most people can handle. The solitude becomes too much!

Maui

Over 140,000 people lived on Maui as of the 2000 census. When I lived there I felt like there were far less than this because the majority live in the central and southern Maui region. I was on the west side of the island and there aren't very many residents or tourists there in comparison.

Jobs?

Jobs are predominantly in the tourism area, and as on all islands there are some in construction. Healthcare is picking up as elderly Californian's buying homes on Maui, move to the islands to retire and need nursing and other periodic care.

The best places to live for nightlife and other activities?

Kahului (central), Wailea (south), and Lahaina (west).

There are daily flights to Oahu and the other islands, and sometimes they are even cheap. In the past there have been airfare wars in which fares dropped to $25 to $50 per flight! Don't count on this though; the typical fares are between $100 - $200 for interisland flights.

In my own opinion, Maui is the ultimate island to live on if you have the money to fly to Oahu often for shopping, nightlife, or other things you crave that you won't get on Maui. Maui is filled with good people, and the most beautiful scenery. There is less to do on Maui than Oahu but, that's OK because the lack of crowds at the most beautiful spots make it all worth it.

The Big Island of Hawaii

By far this is the biggest island, and able to hold all the other islands within its boundaries if placed on top. The Big Island has active volcanoes, world-class big game fishing, and a whole lot of land to explore if that's what gets you excited.

The island is enormous in comparison to any of the other islands - over 4,000 square miles. The road around the perimeter (Highway 19 and 11) takes you 222 miles, but it is not a complete perimeter tour.

You'll pass through a lot of different topography on a drive around the island. The Big Island is diverse and impossible to see all there is to see in a month's time.

Jobs?

Tourism, some construction, and agriculture are what you'll find here.

The population is just 148,000+ and people are spread out quite a bit. There are two main towns – Hilo (east) and Kona (west), and each is very different from the other.

Kona Side

Kona is very dry and rugged terrain. It is the focus for tourists to the Big Island of Hawaii for a few reasons. One being that the rain is not as abundant as it is in Hilo. Kona gets around twenty-five inches of rain per year on average.

Kona's beaches and bays are ultra beautiful and are relatively easy to access.

Some major resorts have opened in Kona over the last twenty-five years, resulting in billions of new dollars coming into the economy.

This side of the island gets a lot of sunshine. As a result, the place is built up much more than Hilo – and there are so many things to do in Kona you'd not run out of adventures anytime soon.

Facing the leeward (windless) side results in Kona's mild waters. Swimming, bodyboarding, snorkeling, surfing, bodysurfing – any water sport - can be enjoyed daily. The water is said to be the clearest in the state at Kona beaches.

The beaches are perfect – some of them making it into the yearly top 10 of America's beaches often. Hapuna is one such beach!

Vog – volcanic fog, results from the open vents on the volcano – and affects the Kona side much more than the Hilo side. Some residents and visitors report really being bothered by it – others, are not. Some residents think that people often confuse allergies with vog – and blame the vog instead. There is a completely different set of flora than wherever you came from – in Hawaii. You might have allergies affect you more or less on the islands. Do keep that in mind.

Hilo Side

Hilo is the world's wet weather capital with over 125 inches of rain per year on average. Yes, that is over ten-inches per month! Most of the rain falls at night (thankfully), but during the day, brief and intense showers can pop up at any time.

Could you live with that? Many people cannot and choose Kona instead.

However, because of the rain, Hilo is the greenest part of the island. Flowers, fruit, and vegetation abound. It's like the green side of Kauai – truly beautiful flora. The waterfalls are amazing on this side of the island – and there are no waterfalls at all in Kona.

The beaches in Hilo are also beautiful, but not so easy to access. There are black sand beaches that should not be missed on a trip here. If you're coming for the beaches, you could visit Maui instead, and see black and pink sand beaches too.

Hilo is akin to old-Hawaii. It is ultra-laid-back, and in contrast with the up and coming Kona side of the island. Hilo is for those that love nature, quiet, and that can deal with the near constant rain. Native Hawaiians choose to live in Hilo more than Kona. It's a rather private and simple place that looks a lot like the Hawaii of long ago.

Some say that visitors in Hilo are just tolerated – and not really welcome. Of course, business owners wouldn't say that, but those that have lived here for years see any advancement of the area toward increasing tourism – as a step backward.

Most people moving to the Big Island live in Kona and visit Hilo when they can for the waterfalls and different beaches.

Kauai

Kauai's population is just over 63,000. Tourism is the main support.

Kauai is a lush, green, flower-covered island with many birds, turtles, and fish varieties.

If you chose to live on Kauai, you should probably make friends quickly because people are quite spread out across the island. I have a friend living there now that moved to Kauai on a whim. For the first year or so he seemed like he was almost regretting it. At times he loved it, the natural beauty of the place alone sustained him. Now he seems to be doing much better. He is happy whenever I speak to him, and he looks like he is there for the long-term.

Two other guys I know living there have an Internet marketing business that is based on their holistic living approach. They seem to be loving it, and their business is thriving.

Kauai is probably what you picture Hawaii as being like if you've never visited the islands. When you disembark from your plane and walk across the tarmac, marveling at the tiny airport – you'll imagine immediately – living there for the rest of your life. Everyone does! I sure did. I think few can make it work though.

I don't imagine many of you reading this book will ultimately choose to make Kauai your home. Honestly, in my opinion, I wouldn't recommend that you do, because I just think it's not a match for what most people want long-term. But of course, you might be different.

Feel free to prove me wrong and send me email with how you're getting along so well there! I'd love to hear it!

Molokai and Lanai

These two islands are beautiful, and almost barren. There are few people on either. Molokai boasts 7,000+ inhabitants, and Lanai has less than half that number. Molokai usually has Hawaii's highest unemployment rate.

You might decide to live on Molokai or Lanai if you are a writer, or need solitude daily to keep you happy. There is plenty of it! I have to say; I've considered it myself.

Molokai Island is located between Maui and Oahu.

Molokai is thirty-eight miles long and ten miles wide and has a land area of 260 square miles. Molokai is well known as the place where Father Damien de Veuster, a priest originally from Belgium, lived and cared for those with leprosy.

Today there is no contagious leprosy, though there are still some patients with the disease living on the island and being treated.

More info is available at Molokai-Hawaii.com, Molokai's official site.

Lanai is a smaller island than Molokai and is basically a large pineapple plantation. There is one town, Lanai city, with about 3,200 people living there. The island is controlled by Maui County.

If you're planning to visit the island you will need to rent a four-wheel drive vehicle because most of the sites worth seeing are located down long and bumpy dirt roads.

Oahu

The island of Oahu is only about 44 miles long and about 30 miles wide, with 111 miles around the perimeter. Oahu has the most people (estimated at 953,207 for 2013) by far, of all the Hawaiian Islands, and even more than the rest put together. Most people choose to move to Oahu for the variety of things to do, as well as the ease of finding part-time or full-time work. Oahu's beaches are every bit as lovely as most of those on Kauai and Maui, and living there you'll have access to world class shopping and entertainment on Oahu.

On Oahu is Honolulu, the capital of Hawaii, as well as Diamond Head Volcano, Pearl Harbor, the "North Shore", and Waikiki – all of which I'm sure you've heard of already.

Oahu has more jobs, more roads and highways, more shopping, more tourists, and more things to do, than any of the other islands. With all that, comes a price. I've heard someone refer to Waikiki as New York City on a beach. That's close, but I think Waikiki still has its charm.

There are many hotel high-rise buildings in Waikiki and in Honolulu in general. Waikiki is space-limited so construction goes up vertically, not horizontally across more land.

Jobs on Oahu are more plentiful in these areas:

• Tourism

• Government and Military

• Construction

• Agriculture

• Healthcare

• Retail

Living in Waikiki

Waikiki is the center of Oahu, the place where most tourists choose a hotel, and there are many activities centered here. Prices are high for nearly everything, as you might expect.

If you are fond of nightlife, you'll love Waikiki, as the major clubs are all located here. Restaurants of every variety are here, like in every big city, but with an emphasis on Hawaiian and Asian foods. You can probably find a German restaurant if you look for it, but I don't remember there being more than a few Indian restaurants. If you like Korean, Chinese, Japanese, Vietnamese, Thai, Italian, fusion-style restaurants, or sandwich places – you'll feel right at home in Waikiki.

Shopping for food in Waikiki is very expensive. Sometimes you won't even feel like eating.

There are few grocery stores in Waikiki the one that I frequently visited was near Ala Moana Shopping Center and behind 747 Amana Street. It was always crowded, and there is a limited selection of foods. The other alternative is to shop at the local ABC or Long's Drugs stores, but they are very high priced – and again, with a limited selection.

The entire population of Hawaii is cost-conscious when it comes to food shopping so find out from friends where they shop for the best deals. There are outdoor food markets on all the islands.

Living Elsewhere on Oahu

There are many sections of Oahu in which you can live. Waikiki is great for those that like action and things to do. Everything is within walking distance, bus distance, or bicycle distance. Many people ride bikes to get around so they don't need to worry about paying for parking and sitting in traffic.

Living in "Town"

Waikiki, Manoa, Punchbowl, Makiki, Kaimuki, Pali, Diamond Head, China Town, are all considered the town area. Town is crowded, but packed with things to do. There are many high-rise buildings packed into this small space, and almost all of them are places to house residents and visitors.

Town is the most expensive area for shopping outside of Waikiki, and the one locals usually prefer to avoid living in because it is nothing like the "real Hawaii" they know and love.

Life on the Windward Side

Kaneohe, Waimanalo, Kailua.

In my own opinion this is the nicest area on Oahu, next to the North Shore. There is lush foliage, thanks to the rain that comes almost daily in this area. The water is crystal clear, and there usually isn't that much traffic (Kaneohe being the exception at times). Still, nothing like Waikiki or Pearl Harbor traffic.

Kailua Beach Park is nice, and a locals favorite. It has now been exposed to the world with a recent ranking of "Best Beach in America".

Kailua has some outrageously priced real estate for sale. One of my former co-workers owns nearly twenty homes here, and he isn't selling.

In the last couple of years more and more business has come to Kailua and it is now, in addition to a world-class beach, a quaint shopping district.

Kaneohe has also grown considerably, and has a new mall. Some of the homes are astounding, and on the whole Kaneohe has never looked better. The Ko'olau mountain range and cobalt blue ocean views are spectacular. The waves are small and there is little coral in the area, making it ideal for bringing the family.

Waterskiing, fishing, kayaking, kite surfing (surfing with a kite to lift and power you around) are all activities you can enjoy not just in Kaneohe, but also all over the northeast of Oahu.

Laie, Ka'aawa, Hauula are all very small areas on the way toward the north shore from Kaneohe. They are very quiet and if seclusion is your ideal, you can live here and you may love it.

Homes are expensive, and there is very little in the way of apartment or room rentals. If you live here and need to commute into town you can count on about an hour average each way.

Living in East Oahu

Hawaii Kai, Kahala, Aina Haina, Diamond Head areas.

If you are at Waikiki's "The Wall" and driving toward Diamond Head you'll enter into another world where there are less condos and the focus is more on residential living. The homes have a little more land, and it's probably a lot like where you live now – assuming you have palm trees, flowers, fruit trees, and a view of an extinct volcano in your neighborhood.

Once you get through the residential section you'll hit the H-1 freeway and there are some businesses along there, under the H-1, including Kahala Mall, Starbucks, and some great pizza places.

Hawaii Kai is the area with a view of Koko Head crater, right before the road climbs the lava cliffs leading to Hanauma Bay, Sandy Beach, Makapu'u, and other great beaches. Hawaii Kai is a large, well-planned residential area with canals on deep water for those of you with boats you want to be able to take out on the Pacific Ocean.

There is quite a procession of cars moving from Hawaii Kai to Waikiki before 9 am., and at rush hour in the late afternoon. If you live here you can count on forty to sixty minutes of commute in stop and go traffic daily, during the week.

Many people who move from the mainland USA to buy a home on Oahu, choose to live in Hawaii Kai, as it resembles the type of residential neighborhood they are familiar with. It looks mainland-ish in a way, and yet the beauty of it will knock you over. It really is a great place to live, I have a couple of friends that live there now, and I don't get tired of visiting them!

Average price of a home in Hawaii Kai, is around $630K (12/2013).

West of Pearl Harbor

Ewa (Eva), Kapolei, Makakilo.

Ewa is a very local area, but there are quite a few transplants that end up buying homes there. A local guy I worked with in the Air Force years back was from Ewa and he used to talk about it like it was one of the ultimate places for Hawaiians to be from.

Target (store) came to Ewa, there are numerous little shopping centers and a brand new mall is being built at the moment. The west side is not filled with tourists. You might see no tourists except at the gas stations and big water park in Kapolei.

Kapolei and Makakilo are residential apartment neighborhoods that are rather affordable and within an hour's commute of town. There are many new buildings in Kapolei, and my girlfriend had a two-bedroom apartment with dining room, family area and large back porch for $220K back in 2004. Not bad right? Many people agree, and the housing market in this area is always teeming with life.

Leeward Side

Makaha, Nanakuli, Waianae.

The leeward side is opposite the windward side. The leeward side is Waikiki side, where the wind blows from the interior of the island, toward the beaches. The beaches and coast of the west side of Oahu are beautiful, though it is nowhere near as lush and green as the windward side. The homes in this area are truly "locals only", and I have had a couple of bad experiences driving through this area. Once when I had taken a wrong turn, in an area I wanted to explore. There were four locals with knives showing them to me as I drove in.

Needless to say I reversed and drove right back out.

Housing in this area is dirt-cheap. The locals say "cheeep" in a funny way - you'll notice it someday.

You'll want to think hard about moving into the Waianae area, and possibly even Nanakuli or Makaha.

Makaha does have a nice golf course with some newer custom homes that you might like.

Central Oahu (Mililani, Wahiawa)

As you drive up into the mountain over the H2 freeway toward the North Shore from town, you will see Wahiawa and Mililani. Mililani is a nicely planned city that has a great residential atmosphere to it. Plenty of people live in this area – there are many new and old homes to choose from if you choose to live here.

Housing costs are cheaper than town and there are some good schools in Mililani if you have children. Mililani has a military base and there is a large population of military living around the base. Mililani and Wahiawa can be cooler because they are up in the mountain a bit. There are breezy sections, and also areas where the wind is blocked by the many trees.

You should have a look at this area if you're considering moving to Oahu; many find the atmosphere more in line with what they are looking for.

Pearl City, Pearl Ridge, Aiea, Halawa

Pearl City is like town outside of town. It's located near Pearl Harbor, to the west of Waikiki and the airport. It has a rather large resident population and there are many condominiums and houses to choose from if you want to live here. The area is rather dry, and the roads are in good condition.

Homes are a little older – 1960-1970's usually, though some are beginning to tear down the older homes and replace them with newer construction these days. Houses usually have a small yard in this area.

The commute from here to town is about an hour each way during weekdays.

If you like, you can get a home up on the hill – and have a view of Pearl Harbor, or even to Diamond Head Volcano.

Aloha Sports Stadium is here, as is Pearlridge Mall – a giant shopping center with all sorts of businesses. If you need it, you can probably find it at Pearlridge. Surrounding the mall are many other stores so you can find what you're looking for, whatever it may be.

There are a couple of hiking trails that I've explored in this area. One I remember in particular is a short one - the Aiea Loop. Oh, and the Aiea Ridge Trail too. I remember finding wild strawberry guava to eat, as well as mountain apples (rose apples).

North Shore (Haleiwa, Sunset Beach, Pupukea, Waimea)

As you crest the mountaintop and look down on Haleiwa and the coast of the North Shore you will be glad you "stay Hawaii." The view is magnificent and if you catch it on a clear day you can see the different blue hues of the Pacific Ocean. Locals call this area "country" and "up country." The North Shore is magical when it comes to surfing. The Pipeline is a place where the wave curls into a perfect tube, one of the few places on earth where big waves turn into near perfect tubes.

It is great fun to watch a professional surfing event at the North Shore. The power of the waves, the grace of the surfers, is humbling and a great experience to see live.

Homes on the North Shore are expensive, and either small or gigantic. Most homes are older and small, and packed with people living in them because the location is so idyllic. Many pro surfers from around the world are welcomed into homes of residents living on the North Shore, sometimes staying for free!

The coast is rugged, and the waves, world class during the winter and flat during most of the summer.

If you hear about thirty+ foot waves on the north shore, you should jump in your car and immediately head up to Pipeline Beach, Sunset, or Waimea Beach to see how big they get. I've been there during fifty-foot waves at Waimea and it's quite a site. The only other place that regularly gets bigger waves than Waimea Bay is "Jaws" in Paia on Maui where they sometimes reach over seventy feet high.

Living on the North Shore is probably not for you if you'll be in town often. With no traffic you can reach town in forty minutes. With traffic – over an hour. There is little on the North shore except a small grocery, some coffee and pizza shops, and the clothes shops in Haleiwa for t-shirts, surfboards, and world famous Matsumoto's Hawaiian Shave Ice shop.

11 – EMPLOYMENT

Each year MoneyRates.com looks at best and worst states in the USA to make a living based on some criteria: Average Income; State Tax Rate; Cost of Living; and Unemployment Rate.

They use these to compute an adjusted average income amount.

Is living in Hawaii all it is cracked up to be?

According to them, the state isn't doing so well. Hawaii ranks worst out of all fifty states.

For the second year in a row Hawaii has the distinction of being worst place in the US to make a living.

They rate Hawaii as having the highest cost of living of any area in the USA too. Surprised?

Me neither.

That all said, if you can make $50K - 60K per year in Hawaii for yourself, or even you and your spouse, you'll be OK if you are frugal. You won't own a nice house, chances are, but you'll be able to continue on living in Hawaii.

Employment is tough to find for most people. Jobs exist in certain career fields. If you're a waiter-waitress, nurse or other healthcare worker, or you have worked in the travel industry, you can probably find a job in Hawaii. If not, it's a serious struggle finding jobs for most people who move to Hawaii to live. The entire island is built on tourism. If your specialty is not sales, customer service, waiting tables, or selling retail you might want to reconsider living in Hawaii if you need to work. Or at least do a lot of research before you arrive.

It's a very tough job market, and you shouldn't let the unemployment figures lull you into a false sense of security about the place. The jobs most often open are in those areas I mentioned above. Bring a whole lot of savings to support you if you do not have skills in one of those fields.

Someone wrote me recently and said she and her husband were thinking of moving to Maui. They didn't have jobs yet. What would their chances be of getting something in construction?

Finding a job on Oahu might be quite difficult if you're looking for something specific. When I moved back in 2002 I knew I wanted a job working in the Internet marketing area since that was my specialty. I knew I wanted to make $50K minimum, but hopefully $70K. I was willing to wait a year or so before making it to $70K. The online business world was going very strong at that point and I didn't have trouble within two weeks of arriving lining up a great position with an up-and-coming dotcom business.

The jobs available in Hawaii are, of course, mostly based on tourism. The second biggest area is either construction or in healthcare. The figures are not accurate when describing construction job availability since many workers are working under the table and off the record.

The available jobs are most often in these areas. If you can work in either of those two industries, you probably won't have any trouble at all finding a job on Oahu.

That's just Oahu. Oahu has about one million residents and there is some variety in the tourism area. You could even start your own unique tour business if you wanted. Oahu is not that difficult to find jobs on, and you'll probably be fine if that's where you want to live.

Now, on to the other islands…

I've spent a year plus on Maui working as a Marketing Manager for a resort firm there. Maui is heavenly. It was a perfect match for me. Many people who visit Maui think the same thing. Maui is high on the list of people wanting to move to Hawaii, but few have the money or job skills needed in order to make it there.

In my case I started on Oahu and from here, found what I thought might be the perfect job on Maui. It's much easier to start on Oahu and transition to another island. Much easier because you are now "in Hawaii" and can interview for positions on other islands. As you probably know it's very difficult to secure a position in Hawaii without first already living in Hawaii. A necessary catch-22 for most businesses looking to hire full-time staff. They want to meet you first. Go figure!

If you're coming straight to one of the smaller (in population) islands – Big Island, Kauai, Maui, or worse, Lanai or Molokai, you'll want to have your ducks in order. *Ducks*, meaning dollars. Cash savings. You'll want to have a lot of reserves because the reality of moving to one of the smaller Hawaiian Islands without a job is that you're going to spend a lot of your cash reserves just on basic living expenses until you find a job – which might take a year in some cases.

Finding a job on Maui, if I just moved straight over there, would be quite difficult. I can do a dozen different jobs related to Internet marketing, but it's quite possible that when I arrived, nobody is hiring. The job market is very small for everything except tourism related jobs, and healthcare (or retail).

If you have job skills in an area that doesn't relate to tourism or construction or something that relates directly to positions needed in Hawaii – on Maui, or one of the other islands besides Oahu – you might have a REALLY tough time of finding a job.

On Big Island, there are two population centers, but there are only 190,000 people living there. Cost of living is cheaper than Oahu or Maui, but still – the number of job openings must be pretty weak. Especially during this time of economic flat-line.

Kauai would be worse than Maui for job hunting. Finding a job outside of hotel staff, waiting tables, pineapple picking, or retail, on Molokai and Lanai would be virtually impossible. And then, if you did – could you afford to live there?

So, to wrap it up I would say this about moving to Hawaii and finding a job…

Moving to Hawaii if you *need to find a job* can be difficult. The expenses you'll face, and the difficulty you may have in landing a job, are things you need to take under careful consideration. If it were me I would try desperately to find a couple of companies that are hiring for what my specialty is, before I moved. That way at least there's a chance I could have a job quickly and not use all my savings as I ran all over the islands to find a job that fit me.

In this case too, I'd not recommend moving directly from the mainland to any other island except Oahu, unless you have a lot of savings and you do not mind blowing it.

Medical Career Field

The huge "medical" field or health field appears to be the best career field in Hawaii. *Best* meaning lots of opportunity and a competitive salary to match Hawaii's high cost of living.

Today at Craigslist.org there are 195 jobs listed in the medical field just over a three-day span.

Hawaii has an aging population. It's a place where many people from California, Michigan, and countries all over the world go to retire. The cost of medical care for elderly on an outpatient basis is very high. Often families will choose to hire their own in-house personal care aide to help their elderly parents to save some money and allow the flexibility of keeping the parents at home and not in a much too expensive seniors' facility.

Medical transcription is one job that has surfaced, and is paying about $25 per hour. If your vocabulary and typing skills are up to it you might try that as a career. Nearly all the jobs on Craigslist.org are for telecommuters so you can live in Hawaii and work with any number of medical facilities across the USA. I saw an online course among the ads that said it certified people for being medical transcriptionists. Seems like a good job.

Hawaii business is focused on a couple things, and if you work in one of these areas you can likely move there and find a job quickly:

Tourism – If you want to do sales, answering phones, or working in the hotel industry and have experience you'll find a job quickly. If you sell condominiums or time-share and want to make your mark on Maui or one of the other islands - there is ample opportunity to do so.

Sales – If you sell anything – you can find a job on the islands quickly. Everyone needs to sell something, and when there are millions of tourists arriving each year, no matter what the economy looks like – businesses in Hawaii need to sell all the time. One thing Hawaii will always be in need of – are more sales people. The jobs are plentiful and pay well if you can sell!

Healthcare – There are lots of aging people on Oahu and the other islands. They need in-home care, but not necessarily nurses. There are many live-in opportunities for those that want to trade some hours of taking care of a person in need in exchange for a room and sometimes food. There are also plenty of counseling jobs and jobs working with veterans or those that need mental health services. Plenty of jobs.

Construction – There are many jobs working with construction and home renovation firms. People are putting a lot of money into rehabbing their homes and need help. Tilers and roofers are always in demand.

Those with skills they can use online to make $ can move to Hawaii easily. If you can do web development or writing or have some other valuable skills that enable you to cyber-commute you can build up a couple of jobs (gigs) and move. You'll have money until the projects run out, and by then you'll have worked hard enough to get more to replenish them and stay in Hawaii.

Information Technology – There are many IT jobs available on the islands, usually they are for web site developers and network technicians, but, the whole gamut is present on Oahu. Programmers, FLASH developers, Internet marketers, and graphics designers can all find work in the islands without too much trouble. Many work on their own doing odd jobs, or working on their own projects.

The Internet in Hawaii is every bit as fast as your home network on the mainland. There is no difference between internet you can access in Hawaii vs. mainland. There are plenty of entrepreneurs with their own Internet businesses online. If your skill-set is in the IT field you won't have a problem finding someone that needs what you do. I found three IT jobs on Oahu and Maui very quickly, as I needed them. IT is one of those areas you just might be able to land a job from the mainland without being in Hawaii, as some companies allow IT staff to work from home – even on the mainland.

My IT Jobs

"How did you get your IT job in Hawaii" is a question I get asked by many people through email at my website.

First of all I had a lot of IT credentials. I had CompTIA's A+ certification, Microsoft's MCSE, seven Microsoft MCP certifications, and about two dozen hardware certifications for fixing DELL, IBM, HP, and Compaq desktops, notebooks, and printers. I already had four years of experience working in break-fix and network management, and I was an SEO expert on top of it. I knew how to develop websites, and I knew a lot about Internet marketing.

IT jobs in Hawaii are not so hard to find.

I landed at Honolulu International Airport on Oahu on January 21, 2002. I had a great IT job within eight days. I interviewed for four different positions. Two of them I didn't like. Two of them offered me the job. I took a job with a Hawaii email spam king. He was, and still is quite undercover. He didn't do anything blatantly illegal, but it was a balancing act.

We were a three-person office before hiring two more. In a year, we grossed $5,000,000 and cleared over $3,000,000 after tax.

Such was life for a dotcom spam email organization in 2002.

How did I find the job?

After I got my Hawaii driver's license, or Hawaii State ID – I can't remember which I got first – I went to the Workforce Development office in downtown. I signed up and told them all of my skills. They were excited to have someone with skills come in to apply, and they really helped me a lot. They took the time to go over many possible jobs with me that I might qualify for. There were about thirty jobs I was qualified for that they had on the books, and they were getting more in daily. It was really easy. Within a couple days I had interviews, and I chose a job making $50K per year because I knew I could advance quickly in the organization and make more.

Back then it seemed like there were a fair number of companies looking to employ people who knew something about internet marketing and search engines. They didn't quite know what we were worth, and we didn't either. Some companies didn't know how to go about integrating an Internet marketing expert into their traditional hierarchy of staff that never needed such a person.

When I left the job with the spam king I moved to a position as "Marketing Manager" for a resort management firm that had four properties – two on Big Island and two on Maui. I didn't know much about traditional marketing at all. Print advertising and the travel industry, bookings, and the rest of it were all new to me. But I learned a lot while I was there on Maui.

Is it easy to find an IT job in Hawaii today?

I'd say yes, it's easy.

Might you have to take a job you don't necessarily want to remain in for a long time in order to give yourself some more time finding the perfect IT job?

Yes, quite possibly. I think a lot of people do this.

Here's the thing about getting jobs in IT on the islands…

There has been a large-scale brain drain in IT, and in the medical field, but I really saw it in IT. Information technology whizzes tend to leave Hawaii immediately if they're not entrepreneurial, to look for work on the mainland. California is full of tech companies that need people with IT wired brains. They're paying approximately five times what jobs in the same area pay on Oahu.

One way of looking at it is that anyone with half a brain that knows his or her way around IT in Hawaii leaves as soon as possible.

The rest of us?

We stay! If you love Hawaii, you're not moving to California, Arizona, Utah, and Washington. You're staying in Hawaii. There's a trade-off in Hawaii between working for peanuts and getting to live in the ultimate place on earth. To me, it's quite worth it. I could have moved to California and made a lot more per year, but I moved to Hawaii instead. It's the price of staying in paradise. One of the prices anyway.

There always seem to be jobs available for IT professionals on Oahu. I have never had a problem finding a job, and nobody I know in the field had much trouble either. Even today as I look at job openings, I find many. Seems like companies have finally realized they need either an on-staff Internet marketing manager, or to hire a consultant for fifteen to twenty hours per week part-time.

I had a neighbor in my Waikiki condo that was a C programmer. He worked for a company in California, but worked in his room about five hours each day, and was out surfing the rest of the day. If you can swing one of those deals, wow… that is probably the ultimate way to work in Hawaii. Find an out of state position where you can work online. Or, create your own and be a consultant for your own business.

Honolulu Magazine had some interesting charts full of demographic information. One showed the average income for people living in Hawaii is just $75K per year per household. Now, what they didn't say was exactly how the US Census takers qualified these totals. Household income, loosely defined, could be taken to mean everyone's income in a house. We all know that mother, father, adult kids, and grandkids live in the same house often times because housing is just so expensive. If the chart above was just husband and wife and included singles as well, that would make sense, but if it includes everyone – more than two adults at the most – that's really saying something.

Income of $75K per year for two unmarried people living in the same household is $37,500 each. Twelve thousand of that goes to taxes from each. This leaves $25K each, $50K total for two people. That isn't so great at all.

Fully one-quarter of all households are pulling less than $35K per year in income. That's plain unlivable.

I really think that anything over $50K per person is 'enough' to live in Hawaii - any island. If you're making any less than that you're going to be too stressed that you aren't making enough.

12 – STARTING A BUSINESS

Hawaii is not a great place to start a business in my personal opinion. Many people try, but I think the failure rate is higher in Hawaii than other places. There is a lot of competition in areas that matter, like tourism. If you don't already have a successful tourism focused office open in another part of the world, to come to Hawaii and make it work is going to be very difficult.

The cost of business space, employees, and the high tax rates are prohibitive.

Before you attempt to start a business in Hawaii, at least plan on living on the islands for a year first. I think a lot of valuable insight can be gained into the mindset of both Hawaii residents and tourists visiting the island. You have to know your customers and you have to know what the competition is doing. Hawaii is a very different population than anywhere in the USA and the world. It is very hard to guess what locals and tourists are going to like, and buy on a regular basis. I have seen so many companies start, and fail in Hawaii that I just expect that when one starts, it fails within a year. Probably well within a year.

If you're interested in starting a new business go to this website, they cover it pretty well:

Business.gov (click)

and

Small Business Administration - Hawaii (click)

13 – STATE TAXES

Hawaii collects personal income taxes from its residents at the following rates.

For single taxpayers:

- 1.4 percent on the first $2,400 of taxable income

- 3.2 percent on taxable income between $2,401 and $4,800

- 5.5 percent on taxable income between $4,801 and $9,600

- 6.4 percent on taxable income between $9,601 and $14,400

- 6.8 percent on taxable income between $14,401 and $19,200

- 7.2 percent on taxable income of $19,201 and $24,000

- 7.6 percent on taxable income of $24,001 and $36,000

- 7.9 percent on taxable income of $36,001 and $48,000

- 8.25 percent on taxable income of $48,001 and $150,000

- 9 percent on taxable income of $150,001 and $175,000

- 10 percent on taxable income of $175,001 and $200,000

- 11 percent on taxable income of $200,001 and above

Hawaii Income Tax Comparison

- A minimum wage worker earning $15,000/year pays $1,050.00

- A worker earning the median salary of $45,000 pays $3,600.00

- An upper class worker earning $100,000/year pays $8,000.00

Hawaii Income Tax Law

The Hawaii income tax is based on a bracketed system, with different rates applicable to individuals with different salaries.

Hawaii effectively doubles bracket widths for married couples filing jointly. Other states with this policy include AL, AZ, CT, ID, KS, LA, ME, NE, and OR.

Hawaii Standard Deduction

The Hawaii standard deduction is $2,200.00 for individuals and $4,400.00 for married couples filing jointly from 2013 forward. The standard deduction may be chosen instead of filing an itemized deduction, and taxpayers generally choose whichever deduction allows them to pay the least amount of income tax.

Hawaii Personal Exemptions

Hawaii's personal income tax exemptions include a single exemption of $1,144.00 and a dependent exemption of $1,144.00. Dependent exemptions can be claimed for children, relatives, or others who live with and are supported by the taxpayer as described Section 152 of the IRC (Internal Revenue Code).

14 – SCHOOLS

Hawaii has a single statewide public school system. It has one centralized school board, located on Oahu, which governs schools across the entire State of Hawaii – all 284 public schools. Funding for each school is fair and balanced.

Bringing Your Kids to Hawaii

Bringing your school-aged kids (keiki) to Hawaii to live might seem like a great idea… 'Let them breathe the clean air and soak up the sunshine… swim with the dolphins!' Sure. They can do all that. But, they'll still have to endure the school system. For mainland kids arriving in Hawaii for public or private school it is often traumatic.

I'll catch flak for this – but, speaking from the heart - I wouldn't recommend that anyone bring their kids to Hawaii to live if they'll be attending the public schools. I just wouldn't. That's me. I've considered at length whether I would want my daughter to grow up in Hawaii and attend Hawaii's schools. I've decided – no, definitely not.

In Hawaii, homeschooling might seem like the best option. I do think Hawaii would be a great place for a child to grow up, I am just unsure about the school system.

Does that mean that all kids going to public schools in Hawaii grow up with problems? No. Personally I know a dozen kids or more that grew up fine, respectful of their parents, are hardworking, and just all-around good kids. I know kids that went to Punahou and that went on to Yale, and Berkeley. They are great kids, as far as I can see.

I also know some kids that grew up like local hoodlums and are breaking into cars for a living.

It's a tough call, and I'd say that whom your child befriends is probably the biggest predictor of whether or not he or she will have a childhood experience that is in line with your expectations for your child. Problem is – we rarely choose our kids' friends?

The Best Schools?

Some residents with kids personally recommend:

Koko Head School, Aina Haina Elementary, Mililani Mauka Elementary

Honolulu Magazine does an annual review of Oahu's public schools. The article, if you're interested in finding it online, is called, "Grading the Public Schools."

Though the reviews don't cover the "dirt" like they should, you'll have some idea, which schools are at least trying to provide the best experience for kids.

The Top 10 Primary Schools on Oahu (in order, best are first):

- Momilani Elementary

- Mililani Mauka Elem

- Liholiho Elementary

- Manoa Elementary

- Noelani Elementary

- Wilson Elementary

- Aina Haina Elementary

- Maemae Elementary

- Hokulani Elementary

- Koko Head Elementary

Where your child goes to school is dictated by where you live.

I don't think there are real problems with the teachers in Hawaii. I know they are trying very hard to raise the standards. I do know that there is a serious lack of facilities and funding for some schools.

I think a big part of the problem with Hawaii's schools, isn't the schools at all. It's the social situation that kids find themselves in. There are plenty of kids that are coasting through life and not interested in school at all. Their parents aren't that interested either. They have a view of life that doesn't coincide with my own – of working hard and accomplishing things for themselves.

As I've said many times already, the Hawaii lifestyle is one of ease and no stress. Many kids are copying their parents in this regard. This sets up examples for your kids to see in school. The local kids are fun to be around. I don't know where they get it from, but there are some really hilarious kids. The Pidgin' – local dialect – is really quite funny, and most kids want to speak it well and make everyone laugh too.

The kids that speak pidgin' instead of proper English for the most part, are probably not the ones that are knocking themselves out to learn at school though.

The social situation for kids in Hawaii is opposite of what you as a parent probably want for your child. Though you might love the laid-back atmosphere of Hawaii, you will probably be fighting the influence it has over your children.

Hawaii Private Schools

Nearly 20% of school children in Hawaii attend one of the 130 private schools. These schools have, on average, better reputations than the public schools, but can be very costly.

The percentage of kids in private school taken in comparison with other states in the USA – is the highest in the nation.

Some private schools focus on college-prep, so your child can get into a good university upon graduation from secondary school. Others focus on creativity and the artistic side of development – while not neglecting traditional curricula.

Here is some information about select private schools; tuition has been updated to reflect the **2013 – 2014 school year**:

Punahou School

Barack Obama graduated from this private school and became president. This is considered by many to be the ultimate private school in Hawaii. There are over 3,800 students running the entire age range from kindergarten to 12th grade. The focus of Punahou is on college preparation, and it is considered one of the best schools in the entire nation.

Punahou has an excellent athletic program. Facilities include a heated Olympic-size swimming pool and an eight-lane Mondo running track surface. Students can choose from twenty-two sports!

In addition to a stellar athletics program, students can study dance, drama, and music – all nationally recognized programs. Other programs include jewelry, photographic darkroom facilities, and glass-blowing studio!

Cost per year for tuition: $19,950

Iolani School (ee-o-lan-ee)

Iolani School is a private school with over 1,800 students from pre-school age to grade twelve. Iolani School is affiliated with the Episcopal Church in the United States.

Iolani School is in Honolulu on the island of Oahu. The school focuses on college prep as well as athletics. More than two-thirds of all attending students are part of an Iolani athletic team – covering thirty-two competitive sports.

Cost per year for tuition: $18,900

Schools with Religious Affiliation

Maryknoll School is a private Roman Catholic school with 1,400 students in pre-school to twelfth grade. Located in Honolulu.

Annual Tuition

- Grades K - 5 = $13,850

- Grades 6 - 8 = $14,500

- Grades 9 - 12 = $14,500

Sacred Hearts Academy is a private Roman Catholic school for girls only. Students served are from kindergarten to twelfth grade.

Annual Tuition

- Grades K - 6 = $8,892

- Grades 7 - 8 = $10,325

- Grades 9 - 12 = $12,071

Damien Memorial School is a private, Catholic school for boys located in Honolulu. This school teaches students from seventh to twelfth grades.

Annual Tuition

- Grades 6 - 8 = $9,675

- Grades 9 - 12 = $11,375

Other Private Schools

Honolulu Waldorf School is a private school serving about three-hundred students from pre-school to twelfth grade.

Annual Tuition

- Early Childhood half-day program = $8,500 – 11,750

- Grades 1 – 8 = $13,400

- High School Students = $15,450

Montessori Community School is a private school providing a Montessori education for children ages two through twelve.

Annual Tuition

- K – half day = $9,621

- 6 yrs. to 9 yrs. = $11,187

- 9 yrs. to 12 yrs. = $11,691

Hawaii Preparatory Academy is located on the Big Island of Hawaii and is a private school, teaching students from kindergarten through twelfth grade. On campus boarding is available for grades six through twelve. Students are international including those from Hawaii, fifteen other states, and fifteen foreign countries.

Annual Tuition

- Grades K - 5 = $17,300

- Grades 6 - 8 = $19,100

- Grades 9 - 12 = $22,300

There is also boarding available starting at $38,300 annually.

Island School is a private in Lihue on the island of Kauai. This is a college prep, which has students from pre-school through twelfth grade. Tuition per year for Pre-Kindergarten is $8,700. Kindergarten through eighth grade is $12,700. For high school aged children, $13,300.

Hawaii Universities

The University of Hawaii (UH) with main campus at Manoa, is a public university that offers bachelor, master, doctoral, and post-doc degrees. It is of course, accredited by the Western Association of Schools and Colleges.

List of Universities

- University of Hawaii at Manoa, Hilo, or West Oahu

- Community Colleges

- Hawaii Community College

- Honolulu Community College

- Kapiolani Community College

- Kauai Community College

- Maui Community College

- Windward Community College

Graduate Schools

- John A. Burns School of Medicine

- William S. Richardson School of Law

Private Universities

- Hawaii Pacific University (HPU)

- Brigham Young University Hawaii (BYU Hawaii)

- Chaminade University of Honolulu

- Argosy University

- Hawaii Tokai International College (HTIC)

- Honolulu University

- The International College and Graduate School. Christian affiliation

- Remington College

- Heald College Honolulu

- Trans-Pacific Hawaii College

15 – VETERANS SERVICES and BENEFITS

Office of Veterans Services
Tripler Army Medical Center
459 Patterson Road
E-Wing, Room 1-A103
Honolulu, HI 96819

Phone: (808) 433-0420
Fax: (808) 433-0385

A good site to have a look at before you move to Hawaii is Hawaii.gov. The following information about Veteran benefits and services comes from there.

List of services for veterans, active military personnel, spouses and dependents of veterans:

Assist in preparation of VA claims

Assist with burials of indigent veterans

Employment and Re-employment

Hawaii Veterans Newsletter, Roster, Website and Memorial Fund

Help individuals file VA Appeals

Support various Grant-in-Aid requests for veteran related items, for example veterans' cemeteries, Arizona Memorial, Aviation Museum, Veterans Centers statewide etc.

- Governor's Liaison to veterans

- Assist with legal name change

- Legislative Advocate for veterans – State & Federal

- Maintain discharge documents

- Obtain veteran birth, marriage, divorce & death certificates nationwide

- Provide notary services

- Refer individuals not qualified for VA benefits to other agencies

- Represent veterans at VA hearings

- Tax Exemptions for totally disabled veterans'

- Review medical service records

- Validate Service Credit for the State Employees Retirement System

- Yukio Okutsu Hilo Veterans Home – development & oversight

16 – SENIOR CITIZEN AGENCIES

The best website for information on Aging and Disabilities in Hawaii is:

HawaiiADRC.org

The Executive Office on Aging (EOA)

The Executive Office on Aging (EOA) is the designated lead agency in the coordination of a statewide system of aging and caregiver support services in the State of Hawaii, as authorized by federal and state laws.

The federal Older Americans Act establishes an Aging Network and provides federal funding for elderly support services, nutrition services, preventive health services, elder rights protection, and family caregiver support services. Chapter 349 of the Hawaii Revised Statutes establishes the Executive Office on Aging as the focal point for all matters relating to older adults' needs and the coordination and development of caregiver support services within the State of Hawaii.

To learn about EOA's efforts to develop comprehensive and coordinated systems to serve older adults and family caregivers in the State of Hawaii, please read the Hawaii State Plan on Aging: 2008-2011.

Programs and Services

Healthy Aging Partnership

A statewide public-private partnership committed to improving the health and well being of residents. The partnership offers evidence-based health promotion and disease prevention programs: the Enhanced Fitness (EF) Program on Kauai and the Ke Ola Pono Disease Self-Management Programs-Chronic Disease Self-Management (CDSMP), Arthritis Self-Management (ASMP) and Diabetes Self-Management (DSMP). Ke Ola Pono classes are open to adults 18 and older.

For information on accessing these services in your local area, please contact your county office on aging:

- Honolulu: (808) 768-7705

- Hawaii: (808) 961-8600

- Maui, Molokai, Lanai: (808) 270-7774

- Kauai: (808) 241-4470

Senior Medicare Patrol Hawaii (SMP Hawaii)

A volunteer-based program to ensure Medicare is not billed for health care services, medical supplies, and equipment not received. If you suspect fraud or errors when reviewing your Medicare statement, please contact SMP Hawaii at 586-7281 on Oahu and toll-free at 1-800-296-9422 from the neighbor islands.

Hawaii's Fraud Prevention & Resource Guide is designed to help residents protect themselves against fraud. The 134-page guide provides information about different types of fraud, including identity theft, securities fraud, marketing fraud, and healthcare fraud.

Sage PLUS Program

This program provides free health insurance information, education, counseling, and a referral service for people with Medicare. Volunteers are trained and certified to assist members and their families with questions about Medicare benefits,

Medicare Advantage Program, Long-Term Care financing, and Medicare Part D - the prescription drug benefit. For assistance, please contact Sage PLUS at 586-7299 on Oahu and toll-free at 1-888-875-9229 or 1-866-810-4379 (TTY).

The Long-Term Care Ombudsman Program (LTCOP)

This program provides information, outreach, and advocacy for residents of long-term care facilities. If you have a problem, complaint, or question regarding services provided at a long-term care facility, please call the LTC Ombudsman at 586-7268 (Oahu).

To ensure that all long-term care residents are aware of the services provided by the Long-Term Care Ombudsman, volunteers are trained and certified by the LTC Ombudsman Volunteer Program to regularly visit licensed LTC settings. To become a certified volunteer, please complete the LTCOP Volunteer Application and mail it to the LTCO Volunteer Coordinator at Executive Office on Aging, 250 South Hotel Street, #406, Honolulu, HI 96813.

In-Home and Community-Based Services

Services are available to assist older adults in remaining independent and active. Types of services provided: adult day care, assisted transportation, attendant care, case management, chore services, congregate meals, home delivered meals, homemaker/housekeeper, information and assistance, legal assistance, nutrition education, personal care, and transportation.

Family Caregiver Support Program

Support services are available to family caregivers such as: information, assistance, individual counseling, support groups and training, respite, and supplemental services.

Hawaii Department on Aging and Elder Services

Older Americans Act

In 1973, an amendment to the federal Older Americans Act (OAA) required states to separate their aging planning and service areas and to designate Area Agencies on Aging (AAAs) to implement programs and services for older Americans at the local level. The local Area Agencies on Aging offices serve certain counties and implement the elder service programs within their geographic boundaries. The quickest way to find out what services a senior may qualify for and what senior programs are available is to contact the Area Agency on Aging office serving the county where the senior lives. A few states have websites which provide information for the entire state and other states provide a county lookup on their website to find the correct area office to contact for senior services.

What State Senior Services are Provided?

Area Agencies on Aging provide assistance with senior benefit programs, social security, Medicare, eligibility for low-income senior programs including home and community services (some states will provide part-time care giving in the home through their home and community services program), along with:

- Transportation

- Home-delivered Meals

- Prescription Drug Programs

- Healthy Aging Programs

- Case Management

- Caregiver Training

- Senior Activities

- Support Groups

- Volunteering

What services are offered by the Senior Health Insurance Program (SHIP)?

SHIP is a free counseling service for seniors and pre-retirees and is part of a federal network of State Health Insurance Assistance programs located in every state. SHIP counselors answer questions about Medicare, Medicare Supplement Insurance, Medicare Advantage and Medicaid along with prescription coverage and low-income assistance. You local Area Agency on Aging will have information on SHIP and many provide SHIP counselors to give group presentations.

Find Your Local Area Agency on Aging Office:

Hawaii.gov/health/eoa/

State Senior Services Help Line: (808) 586-0100

State Senior Services Email Contact: eoa@doh.hawaii.gov

Elder Abuse Hotline: (808) 832-5115

17 – SOCIAL ENVIRONMENT

Sure, everyone works in Hawaii. Well, most do. But, even though everyone is working, there is an underlying attitude that life is not about work. The people living in Hawaii understand well that the secret to a happy life is about what you're doing outside of work. Work-style is a little more laid-back. There is less intensity about it. People get their work done – but, it's not a pressure-cooker environment unless you're working in sales and your income depends on it.

I told you about a friend that sold insurance over the phone in Hawaii and he did not enjoy his working conditions. I knew another couple that sold time-shares on Maui. They made a lot of money, but nobody could really stand them as they were far too motivated and concerned about making money off those they knew and were introduced to.

People living in Hawaii like it laid-back and want to keep it that way. After all, that's why they're living in Hawaii in the first place. To be surrounded by a like-minded group of laid-back people is really invigorating and gives one a great feeling. If you don't feel like you fit in, you won't enjoy it, and people won't enjoy you much either.

Cultural Experience

There are a variety of cultures to be experienced while living in Hawaii. As I mentioned, the Japanese and Filipinos are the predominant groups, and of course there is the Hawaiian culture, parts of which most groups have adopted as their own.

There's a large variety of food to choose from. I mentioned the McDonald's breakfast I liked most had Portuguese sausage, rice, and soy sauce. There are Korean food restaurants, Hawaiian restaurants, Japanese restaurants; every group has their own restaurants. Thai, Burgers, Filipino, Italian, it's like the best foods from all over the planet assembled on Oahu.

Quite a nice experience if you like a variety of food. The best is when you befriend some locals and they ask you to picnic with them somewhere on the weekend. You'll get introduced to some amazing local-style foods like lumpia and Kalua pig!

Making Friends

This topic isn't covered in most books about moving to Hawaii. I believe it is one of the crucial factors in whether you will stay long-term or leave sooner than you intend.

A big problem is when a couple moves to Hawaii and one has friends at their new job – and the other either doesn't work, or doesn't like the people at work, and doesn't make new friends.

This happens so often in Hawaii.

Many people will say, after a year or two, they "don't like Hawaii." When in fact it has nothing to do with Hawaii. It's a lack of developing new friendships. Having some friends in Hawaii can be the difference between enjoying your stay, and not. You should take some time to make new friends even if you think – 'ahhh, they'll come later.' Better now than later when you're unmotivated and would rather just hate Hawaii for it instead.

How to Make Friends in Hawaii?

First, get active in something. There are Buddhists, Jehovah's Witnesses, Mormons, Christians, and the whole lot, in Hawaii. You an easily join whatever group you choose. All of them have activities going on.

There are many sports and outdoor related activities in Hawaii, of course, and you're probably interested in some of them because you are moving to an island that seemingly revolves around outdoor activity.

There are running, fishing, rugby, Frisbee, running, hashing (hash house harriers have three groups on Oahu alone), drinking, social, boating, writing, computer, authors, and dozens of other groups and clubs that you can join which will help you make friends.

Alternatively – just go out and do what you enjoy – and try to meet people who are doing the same thing. If you bike, try the bike shops to see about weekly or daily rides. Seek these things out because they might not just come to you, and you might not know intuitively what to do to find friends that are like you are.

I myself have a difficult time finding friends I like to hang out with. In Hawaii within the first couple weeks I already had a few friends that I enjoyed immensely. In Hawaii it's easier to make friends than in other places I believe. See if you find that to be true also.

Moves to islands other than Oahu can be a little tougher. There are less people, so there are less people like you. There isn't as much to do on the other islands. Still, there are thousands of people on each island that need friends, like you do, so go find them.

The Shaka Sign

Originally it may have started out to be a fist with your thumb and pinky finger extended – as if waving (palm out), but, if you watch the locals do it – they don't do it that way. It is more of a shake back and forth – twisting the wrist by pivoting at the elbow…and it is done palm facing in toward your body.

The Shaka sign means "hang loose", and people give the sign usually when they are saying goodbye to each other or posing for a photo.

The Origin of the Shaka Sign?

Good question – and it has not been definitively answered, and it won't be. Just accept that!

Some say the shaka sign was shown in the 1940s as a symbol of blessing by a local Hawaiian folk hero named Hamana Kalili from Laie who had lost his three middle fingers in a sugar-mill accident.

Some say it started when Kalili waved his deformed hand to shoo children away from jumping trains.

Some say the symbol started when one of the first surfers in Hawaii raised a shaking pinky and thumb out of the water after having his middle fingers bitten off by a shark.

Yet another possibility is that it began with the Spanish that immigrated to Hawaii. They would fold the middle three fingers in and brought the thumb to their mouth to symbolize drinking with the native Hawaiians they met.

To me, this is the most plausible since Hawaiians use it often while drinking and to symbolize drinking and good times.

If you drive, you might see the shaka sign used in traffic as you let someone enter the stream of traffic in front of you, or someone does something stupid, and throws up a shaka to calm your hot head.

The shaka sign is a tradition empowered symbol reminding locals and visitors of the way people look out for each other in the islands. It's also a way to spread the aloha spirit, the spirit of love between people.

Hawaiian Flower Leis

Upon landing in Hawaii – if you know someone here, or were part of a tour group, you might be leid with a necklace of fragrant pikake lei flowers around your neck, and even a kiss if you're lucky.

This Hawaiian tradition is a really lovely way to welcome newcomers to the islands, and you'll be doing it for others that come to visit you after you move too. It's contagious!

There are many types of leis and they can be made not only from flowers, but feathers, leaves, shells, candy or whatever else someone wants to put in them.

18 – HOMES

Space on the islands is at a premium. It's no wonder then that Oahu, with nearly a million residents, seems a bit small. There are other reasons the islands seem small.

Parts of Hawaii are uninhabitable. Some hills have loose rock – and homes cannot be built there. Quite a bit of the islands are comprised of mountainous area.

Living on an island is a little different than living in downtown Boulder, Colorado. The Hawaiian Islands are not large. Oahu is about sixty-five miles on the long side and less than forty on the short side. Can you imagine living in a 2400-mile square? The only way you go further than 60 miles is on a plane or in a boat – which sounds interesting, but there's another set of issues there I'll talk about in a minute.

Island Fever

Defined as the feeling that one is stuck on an island, and doesn't have the freedom to just go somewhere and drive for a few hours to 'get away' for a while.

In Hawaii you are, in fact, isolated in the middle of the Pacific Ocean. You're thousands of miles from any major country. If you're anything but Japanese or Filipino you are probably feeling like a minority – because you are. Hawaii is a multicultural melting pot. It's not easy to pick up and fly away to a neighboring state for the weekend. There are no more road trips to other states as you did in the mainland. Hawaii is a bit confining – especially if you do not have the money to visit the other islands often, and visit the mainland once or twice each year.

Island fever usually hits first timers that moved to the islands after six months or a year. The sudden realization that – this is all there is. Sure, Hawaii is beautiful. It has awesome natural scenery and fun things to do, but this is it. This is home, and it's not a big home, it's a little island.

There are parts of the island you wouldn't want to go see, and parts you shouldn't see. There is a lot of private property on Oahu and the other islands, and you will never see a good portion of the island. So in reality, you're stuck living and exploring the public places – whatever the government has declared as such.

Island fever is one of the big sources of discontent among new Hawaii residents and it shouldn't be overlooked because if you move to Hawaii to live it will likely hit you at some point in time and it might be the cause of leaving paradise.

House and Condo Prices (Buying)

From June through October 2013 the average sale price of a single-family home in Hawaii was $509K, this was 39% below the list price. Condominiums averaged selling for $395K, just 1% below asking price.

Rent on Oahu – even for a one room studio far away from downtown is very high - $900+.

For two people living in Waikiki or downtown Honolulu on Oahu you would spend $1K to $1,500 for a studio or 1-bedroom with no-frills.

For $445K in Clearwater, Florida you can have a very nice four or five-bedroom home on a deep-water canal and park your deep-sea fishing boat in the backyard at your own dock.

Not so in Hawaii!

Hawaii is one of the most expensive places to live in the USA. If you're going to buy a house you can count on paying over

$500K no matter what the housing market looks like at the moment. Likewise, for a decent condo – over $300K and much more in a good area and in a good building.

Before buying a home, you should take the time to visit the neighborhood during the weekdays and weekends, days and nights. See who lives there, ask people if there are any problems in the neighborhood. Go without your Realtor and get a good feel for the place before deciding to buy.

You could start your search by using the advanced search function at the online Hawaii MLS – Multiple Listing Service – the real estate listings for Hawaii:

MLS Hawaii

Cost of Rentals

If you plan on renting in Hawaii it might come as a shock to you a little bit unless you're currently living in California or New York City. A one-room studio will run between $1,000 to $1,500 per month. You will have a ½ kitchen in studio rentals, and maybe one or two closets, but for the most part all your things will need to be in the same room. Studios with a balcony are great because you get some extra storage space, and maybe a view.

At 1720 Ala Moana Blvd in Waikiki is a condominium where I paid $750 per month for a one bedroom place. I had a large balcony and a swimming pool, so I was quite happy with the arrangement for a couple months while I was transitioning into a better place. I found the condo by looking in Craigslist.org. The owner was living in California and she had a couple units at that location. I transferred money to her through PayPal to cover the first and last months rent, and paid a deposit equal to a month's rent. This is the typical fee (3 months rent) up front when renting in Hawaii.

In and around Waikiki, nice one-bedroom apartments typically start at $1,200 or higher, and two bedroom apartments and very small homes, start at $2K or more per month. At 400 Hobron Lane in Waikiki, "Eaton Square" (by the Ala Wai Canal) I found a studio with a nice ocean view for $875. It had no balcony, and a very small kitchen, but what it did have were excellent barbeque facilities and a large swimming pool on the top of the building. We had many friends over at night so it was the perfect arrangement. We ended up moving into a bigger unit in the same building. We really enjoyed the place.

On Maui, I mentioned that my girlfriend and I lived on the west side near Kahana. There are no large apartment buildings or condos, so we had to rent an "ohana" unit, next to a large 6-bedroom house on Mahinahina Street. We had a kitchen, small family room, bedroom with some closets, and a very small restroom. We paid $1,100 for it per month – and were happy to get it since we didn't want to rent a room in someone's house and live with them.

So, housing will be a challenge for those of you that are used to paying $500 per month rent, like you can in still do across much of America.

Because living in Hawaii is viewed by employers as a perk itself, salaries are lower than the cost of living suggest they should be.

I've seen it said that the average 2-bedroom apartment for rent isn't affordable by two-thirds of Hawaii's renting residents. I can believe that.

And forget about buying a house – which is out of the question for most residents these days.

What many locals do to avoid paying high rent prices is rent with many people, or even buy a home with many people. It is not uncommon to find four different families living in one house and sharing expenses.

19 – THINGS TO DO

On Oahu, there are quite a few things to do. There are many shopping malls, concerts to see, and many different sporting matches to attend. If you don't enjoy watching as much as you like participating, every sport imaginable is available to take part in. There are beaches everywhere – with all those fun things to do at the beach: snorkeling, swimming, diving, surfing, bodyboarding, bodysurfing, looking for crabs, playing cards & backgammon, sleeping, etc.

During my years in Hawaii I often had trouble figuring out each day what I wanted to do for fun after work. There was just *so much* to do that my head was always spinning.

I'm an outdoors and adventuresome type. If you are too, you'll probably never ask yourself what there is to do, you'll just be doing it. There are amazing mountain hikes with different levels of difficulty. There are scores of great beaches on each island. There are so many things to explore. There is more shopping than you could ever want.

There are out of the way places that are amazing to explore… the tide pools at Dillingham Air Field on the North-West shore is one such place that is just amazing to behold. Most visitors never see it. Whether or not you surf or bodyboard, you can learn to bodysurf. Bodysurfing in Hawaii is excellent because there are areas designated for bodysurfing only. Point Panic in Kaka'ako is one such break located within a short distance of Waikiki that I used to visit at lunch. Bodysurfing is a lot of fun, and pretty safe.

There are hundreds of touristy things to do, and many ways to enjoy Hawaii's natural beauty. Here are a few things you might enjoy doing if you're bored.

Snorkeling

Hanauma Bay is one of the best snorkeling places on the planet, but it is not the only one! Honolua Bay and Molokini Island on Maui are also spectacular for snorkeling, and so are a handful of other spots. Ask around and find the best places – people are happy to share their favorite spots. On Maui I used to walk to the beach from our home and jump in and snorkel for hours when the water was calm.

Surfing, Bodyboarding, Body Surfing

There are usually surfable waves available somewhere on the islands at all times. Surfable, meaning one to two feet or bigger. The waves are very strong in Hawaii – that much you probably know. You might see many people enjoying them – and think that you can enjoy them too. Keep in mind that if anyone is in waves bigger than about three feet, they likely live in the island and have experience playing in waves that big.

The waves are big – and the riptide currents are strong at some beaches –and depending from which direction the waves are coming. Take some time to learn about the ocean's amazing waves in Hawaii by going slowly and not jumping into a situation that can prove dangerous, or even fatal.

In the winter the north shores of the islands have the bigger and more consistent waves. In the summer, it's the south shores where everyone goes for the best waves.

Ocean temperatures are usually between 70 - 80 degrees Fahrenheit. Yes, it's similar to bath water if you take cold baths!

Bodysurfing is a past time enjoyed by most of us, when we've forgotten our boards. It's really a blast to slide down a wave using nothing but 'you' as a board.

Rainbow Gazing

Anuenue' in Hawaiian, rainbows can be seen frequently, and sometimes daily in Hawaii. You can often see two or three rainbows at a time.

Don't stop looking at night either – there are *moonbows*, believe it or not. After food shopping in Kahana, Maui one time at about 10:30 pm. we looked up to see the most incredible rainbow at night, it was illuminated by the bright full-moon! I hadn't known there was such a thing... but, if you use Google images (images.google.com) you can find many photos of moonbows in the Hawaiian Islands.

Explore Lighthouses

There are lighthouses on all the islands. The Makapu'u lighthouse near Makapu'u beach is a nice hike up a winding and windy path and gives great views once you arrive. There is also an exceptional lighthouse and viewpoint on Kauai – Kilauea lighthouse – that I've visited a couple of times. You can see rare birds there like the red-footed booby!

Wilderness Trails

There are many great hiking trails on Oahu, Maui, Kauai, and Big Island. Hiking trails on the islands almost always have scenic views where you can see all the way to the ocean. In particular, some of the Ko'olau mountain trails that reach the ridge halfway between southern Oahu and the windward section of Kailua and Kaneohe – are just stunning.

Biking

Buy or rent a bike. Outside of Waikiki many areas are easy to ride in. I especially like to ride past Diamond Head by the ocean, and back into the residential area back there. It's quite a nice ride.

Photos or Videos

Set off on a day trip on the bus or your own vehicle and see what photos or videos you can come up with. Share them on Facebook, YouTube, Flickr, and Twitter.

Diamond Head Volcano

There is a path up the side that is a little strenuous –but well worth the trip when you arrive at the top and are treated to panoramic views. Well worth the trip.

There are so many things you can do if you live on the islands. When you think you've seen all an island has to offer – start exploring the other islands.

As a resident, you'll find things to do that tourists never thought of. The blowholes remained like that for a long time, they were kind of hidden, and tourists didn't usually get to see them much. Locals sure did! I remember making many trips to the blowholes on Oahu, as well as the toilet bowl – which was even more hidden.

20 – WHAT DO PEOPLE LIVING IN HAWAII DO?

I'll tell you a bit of what I do and then I'll add some about what others are doing with their time.

Life on the islands is not 100% stress-free living. Life on Oahu especially, is sometimes a bit of nerve bender with things like traffic, high costs, and crowds of people to get you down. There is frequent petty crime, theft, and vehicle break-ins. There is a methamphetamine epidemic on the islands and people on drugs often steal things they can sell for cash. So, vehicle break-ins and theft of your money from your shoe while you're surfing, unfortunately happens often. It will likely happen to you. Welcome to the club. So, there is stress to deal with on the islands, just like there is where you're living at now.

Weekdays

Weekdays are filled with w-o-r-k. If you're not retired and living on a cushy pension, then you're probably working hard to pay the bills and to afford some of the nice things your neighbors have. Many, and I mean MANY residents on Oahu and the other islands work more than one job. Some work three. It's a fact of life that if you can't make more than minimum wage working in Hawaii, then you're going to either get used to living like that, or work more to be able to afford more. There are a lot of ambitious people on the islands, and working two or three jobs is considered, in some circles, *normal*.

If you don't live in close proximity to your job, you might have to fight traffic to get there and home every day. That's no fun, right? Though you're living in Hawaii, one of, or *the* most amazing place on the planet, it doesn't matter if you have to deal with bumper-to-bumper traffic every morning on the freeway. If you're going from the west side of Oahu to town side, you're going to be in this situation. Some people can deal with it and it hardly raises their heart rate, others suffer near meltdowns every morning they drive to work. Traffic on Oahu is horrendous during rush hours. It isn't getting better in the foreseeable future, only worse. Just another reason to work online - right?

For a long time I worked in Kailua and lived in Waikiki. That wasn't a bad arrangement. Traffic was light and I couldn't have been happier. For a while in the Air Force I lived in the Ala Moana area and drove up to Hickam AFB in the morning. I was going against the majority of traffic, so again, it was not too bad. I have never had to fight the really bad Oahu traffic going to work, and only on Oahu occasionally other times during a special event like a concert or football game where traffic gets bad. Now that I work online I am so happy not to even leave the house if I don't want to. It makes moving back to the islands a lot more appealing at this point.

Hawaii workplaces are usually quite laid-back. Everyone knows the traffic sucks. Most of your co-workers have also dealt with it. Some may have run you off the road on your way to the job! Lunchtime consists of a brown bag brought from home in many cases. Most people would rather save money than eat out. If you go out to eat, you will have to face traffic again. Or, maybe you will be lucky enough to be able to walk to a lunch cafe or the Foodland Deli for some ahi poke with shoyu.

Anyway, you probably work for eight to ten hours on the weekdays and head home, fighting traffic again.

Oh, I almost forgot. One thing that is cool about living in the islands is that many employers are *surf conscious*. What I mean is, they understand that if there is an incredible swell happening on one of the shores, and you are a diehard addict, they will sometimes allow you to stagger your hours to accommodate some extra hours in the water. Being in the water keeps many of us happy, and if your employer is as cool as this, you will probably stick with the job for a very long time. Many people take off the entire day and make it up by working a weekend day to compensate the boss. I was able to work out some early morning work hours with time off in the mid-afternoon to hit the waves. It really does take the stress out of life to be able to do something like this when the Hawaiian Surf Gods start churning out the big waves.

If you're really a water nut and need to get your surf on more often – as in daily – you'll get up early before work and head out for the daybreak sessions with your other surf-addicted pals. There is the same group of people out there before 6 am. every single weekday. Some give it a break on the weekends, and some are there at that hour just the same. There is a magical stillness about the water during those early hours. It grows on you. Surfers that meet at the same place every morning are usually all friends or very tolerant of each other, and it's a great way to start the day. Keep in mind if you're going to break into someone's group. Do it lightly and with the utmost care to remain respectful until they start to accept you. Really, it is just good practice.

Back to the schedule. You arrive home after work. If you have kids you take them where they need to go, you go shopping at the Wal-Mart or one of the other shopping areas, you watch TV, cut the grass, change the plasma in the Lamborghini Aventador, you go to the park and run or ride your bike, maybe even fit in a late afternoon surf session, and then grab some dinner – usually at home, and hit the bed. You wake up and do it again.

The Weekend!

This is what Hawaii residents live for. I know, we all do, no matter where we live. But, people living in Hawaii really know how to make the most of a weekend by doing the least. The weekends almost always include at least one day gathering with friends and family at a beach for a picnic-type get together. For some families, both Saturday and Sunday go like this. It's tradition, and one that everyone loves. The opportunity to try local food and get in touch with those that mean the most to you, is one favorite thing to do when the weekend rolls around. Even if someone has other plans that day, they usually still make an effort to stop by the beach to see their friends and family at least for a short time. Some favorite gathering places for these picnics are Ala Moana Beach Park and anywhere along Waimanalo Beach. The water is usually gentle enough for swimming in-shore, and with some waves for anybody that wants to venture out. These gatherings happen all over, but you'll see many families at these two spots on Oahu and at beach parks across all the islands.

There are so many things to do on the islands on the weekend, that you shouldn't get tired of the options available. If you find yourself bored, you should probably be asking yourself if living in Hawaii is right for you in the long-term.

I think the problem for most people who arrive in Hawaii and then become disillusioned by it, is that they don't have enough friends. You have to put some time into finding new friends; they don't just show up at your door with a fruit-basket and an offer to join them for a luau. You have to really make an effort in Hawaii to make good friends. It's like anywhere, but I think those moving to Hawaii sometimes have this idea that it's much easier and they won't have to make the effort. You do have to make a lot of effort or you will find yourself sitting at home in the evenings and on the weekends. Hawaii is a much more fun place to be when you know more people and enjoy hanging out with them. It can be a very lonely place for people without many, or any friends. In my case, I tend to isolate myself a bit and just do things I want to do like biking, running, surfing, and hiking. I'm happy doing those things alone or with others. When in Hawaii I made a conscious effort to find new friends to share these activities with so I didn't become bored by myself. If you also are a loner – *make the effort!*

There is more shopping on Oahu than you could ever need – in my own opinion. (See Chapter 24 – Shopping)

If you're used to shopping in New York City or LA, some other big city, you will probably find the offerings pretty meager. If you're not a big shopper, like me, you'll probably find everything you could want. What you can't get, you can order online, but there is an extra charge for shipping to Hawaii sometimes. This is an unfriendly reminder of just how remote you are in comparison to the rest of the world.

What you do on the weekend will depend on what type of person you are, and what you like to spend time doing. If you move to Hawaii, you should know that the overall focus of most people is on being outdoors. You won't find too many groups that meet in a shuttered building and turn the lights low. It's an outdoor state, with outdoor-minded people. If you don't like being outdoors, you probably won't like life in Hawaii and you're better off to save yourself the money and aggravation of moving.

Three and Four-Day Weekends!

Yes, such things exist, and they are well taken advantage of in Hawaii. Personally, I like to go to the other islands on a long weekend because it gives me more time for my money. Robert's Overnighters (RobertsHawaii.com) are short trips to other islands with hotel and car that I enjoyed a lot. Though the islands are similar in nature to each other, each one also has a different feel. All are worth experiencing, and eventually I'll get to the couple I haven't visited. If you haven't seen them all, make some plans for the next long weekend to see something new. I like Maui and Oahu best, but who knows, you might find Kauai or Big Island Hawaii more to your liking. A visit may even prompt a move on your part. For an exciting way to go, take a small boat to one of the other islands. There are affordable trips like this on small yachts and trimarans that give you more than just the another island experience, you get to experience being on the immense Pacific Ocean in a tiny boat. You can probably fish from the boat, and you'll make friends with some of the other passengers. It's more of a social trip than a quick airplane trip.

Camping is a great activity for a long-weekend. On the coast of Waimanolo is some of the best public camping you'll find. If you want remote camping, you might try hiking Kauai's remote "Kalalau Trail", which according to some videos I've seen, is absolutely breathtaking. It is quite a hike, eleven miles over sometimes slippery and dangerous terrain. You wouldn't want to take small *keiki* with you on that trip.

There is a lot more eating outside, and meeting outside when in Hawaii. Many restaurants are open-air. Everyone seems to love a picnic or barbecue, whether at the beach or someone's home. The food possibilities are endless. If you haven't tried ahi poke, seared ahi at Roy's, or a grilled mahi-mahi sandwich at a barbecue on the beach or an oceanfront restaurant, you must.

Outdoor exercise and sports activities are very popular among locals and visitors, as you might imagine. There are aerobic groups all over that just meet at a spot daily for an hour or so of high-intensity jumping around. There are bike clubs, running clubs, surf clubs, walking clubs, mountain hiking clubs, motorcycle clubs, car clubs, archery groups, yoga of every sort, Tai che, Taikwondo, Jeet Kun Do, stargazers, you name it, Hawaii has it.

At least Oahu has it. Some of the other islands have less to do. For instance, I couldn't for the life of me imagine living on Molokai or Lanai – or even Kauai for that matter. There just isn't enough going on to keep me happy. Think about such things before you leave. This is why I recommend that most people move to *Oahu* first so they can live here a bit and see if it fits them. If not, try one of the other islands. It's easy to go visit another island to see if it has what you require to live before you go. You'll save money this way and probably have a more enjoyable experience than just moving straight from somewhere else in the world to one of the less-populated Hawaiian Islands.

What do people who live in Hawaii – *do in Hawaii*? They live life! It's probably a very different lifestyle from what you are accustomed to, but, if you are someone that enjoys the outdoors and you can put in the effort to make friends and try doing new things, try new food, and embrace a new culture, Hawaii living might be right for you. You'll never really know until you try it.

What is holding you back from giving it a try?

Here's my own response to what an average day looked like for me while living on Oahu. Followed by what an average day looked like for me living on Maui.

My Day-to-Day Life On Oahu

I had just arrived on Oahu and already had my first IT (information technology) job. I was making $50K per year, but it felt like nothing. Luckily I also had some online businesses that were giving me some money every month. I like to eat out often, and $50K wouldn't have worked for me. Keep that in mind, meals are so expensive in the islands.

I lived in a small 1-bedroom condo with a nice lanai that gave partial ocean views. The roof had a stunning Waikiki ocean view, so I spent a lot of time up there washing clothes in the laundry room and working on websites.

I was renting for $750 per month on Kapiolani Blvd in Waikiki on the island of Oahu. I was on the fifth floor, and there was an elevator in my building. There were about ten condos per floor and seven floors. We had an outdoor conference area beside the 20′ x 40′ swimming pool, a small library, and a place with computers for residents to use. We paid an extra $100 per month for a guaranteed parking space beside the building because street parking could be hit or miss. Before paying for the parking spot we sometimes had to park two blocks away from our condo!

We had a locked gate that opened with a magnetic card. The building was about thirty years old and looked it, but structurally it wasn't in bad shape, it just needed some updating. The maintenance fee we learned later was something like $450 per month. That was outrageous because we didn't even have security in the building! Hawaii maintenance fees on condos are through the roof. Keep this in mind if you're planning on buying a condo when you move to Hawaii. Usually you should rent first and figure out all the little things that will affect your purchase decision.

Getting to Work in Kailua, Hawaii (Oahu)

I worked in Kailua, so I woke up about 5 am., showered and got in my Honda for the short drive over the Pali Highway to Kailua.

Traffic sucks getting out of Waikiki and up to the Pali Highway. Once there, it's all good. Kailua is a very small town on the northeast side of Oahu. Kailua has some of the nicest beach areas in the world.

On the way to work I'd stop at one of two places to grab a big breakfast – Starbucks, or McDonalds. If Starbucks, they had these giant dark chocolate muffins with chocolate bites in them. I'd get two of those and a big blueberry muffin, along with a giant quad-shot espresso latte.

If I grabbed McDonald's through the drive-thru I'd have the rice, soy sauce, Portuguese sausage type thing, and scrambled egg. I'd get the hash browns and a big coffee. Sure the coffee was nothing like Starbucks – but sometimes I craved the scrambled eggs. Occasionally I was running late and McDonald's was faster than waiting in the line at Starbucks.

Kailua Workplace

Work started at 6 am. I was never late. The boss's brother-in-law, a giant Japanese guy, always arrived later – about 8 am., but we figured the boss had cameras installed, or at least saw when we logged into the computers.

I sat in the air-conditioned office in my shorts, bare feet, and t-shirt from 6 am. to noon and then headed out for a sub sandwich, ahi-poke from the grocery across the street, or something else quick – even Taco Bell. It always felt so amazing to hit the open air and feel the wind. Kailua is exceptionally beautiful. Kailua Beach is usually ranked very high among world beaches, and is considered the best beach in Hawaii by many.

Traffic is a bit crazy all over the island at lunchtime. Waikiki is just insane at this time.

I usually ate at a park on the beach, or just back at the office. My office mates were cool enough and it was great to eat on the steps leading up to the office, look out over traffic and people walking around looking for something to eat. The cool trade winds were always blowing. The sun was usually shining with clouds floating by.

There was little stress at the office, the boss was also local. Then there were two of us from the mainland. We worked on the computer and phones all day and got off about 3 pm., a couple hours before rush hour, which was nice.

After Work Activities

From work I usually headed straight to the beach. I had my surf stuff in the car and would pick one - Bellows, Makapu'u, Sandy's, or even down to Waikiki if I felt like hanging with all the tourists. If waves were good on the south end I'd go to Ala Moana Beach and hit Magic Island break, there were some nice waves there at times.

About 6 pm., I'd get hungry again and go off in search of pizza or other Italian food usually. I ate soup and other things occasionally, but usually pizza was my dinner. I ate pizza slices every day for a couple years in New York City while walking around as a freelance photographer. I never broke the habit.

I'd eat with a friend I met, or by myself – no matter. The weekdays were basically just for me. I would hit a bar on the beach if I wanted to hear music and watch the waves roll into Waikiki. I lived in Waikiki, so I walked most places after dark. It is entirely safe, and a nice way to get around town.

Sometimes I ran at the Ala Wai Canal – to Diamond Head Volcano. It's a nice run along the sidewalk with Plumeria (Frangipani) blooming on the many trees there.

I'd be home around 10 pm. most nights and working online to see what I could do with my online businesses… answering email and things like that.

I worked five days per week and had weekends free.

Life in Hawaii… is Low Stress

That's basically life on a daily basis in Hawaii for a working guy with a job in IT. There was enough money to go do some things… no need to work a second or third job. It was a very stress-free way of living, and you would probably enjoy it, like I did.

Many people fill their time living in Hawaii with television and drinking at the bars. I filled mine with eating great food, exercise, and working on my websites to see them do better. There are all sorts of people in Hawaii, living all sorts of lifestyles. There are many distractions available, drugs primarily, but you need not partake if it's not your style. You'll be offered pot and other things often, on the street and maybe socially, but there's no real problem about it if you choose not to get involved. To each his own in Hawaii… to each, her own.

An Average Day Living on Maui

I lived with my partner on the far west side of Maui, in an area known as Honokowai. We lived on Mahinahina Street. My family and friends all laughed at that street name, not sure why, it was pretty par for the course in Hawaii - many strange names!

We lived in a little ohana. This is an in-law suite, a separate structure away from the main house where the in-laws could stay in traditional Hawaiian culture. The tradition continues today because it's a way for people who own a home to rent out yet another place to live on their property.

We paid $1,100 per month for a very small (< 400 Sq. ft.) bungalow type accommodation. Electricity, water, and garbage, were all extra charges - and amounted to another $150 per month. We ran the air conditioner a lot while home because there was no insulation in the place and the afternoon sun heated it up quite a bit while we were at work.

Weekdays

We woke up, showered, shaved, had some bagels with butter and jelly in the toaster, Kona coffee, and headed out the door. We had shipped my Honda over from Oahu. Having a car while living on the west side of Maui - is essential. Things are rather spread out on the island. You could also make do with a motorbike or scooter if you didn't want a car.

We drove into Lahaina where we both worked across the street from each other. She worked as an accountant at a small firm. I worked at Classic Resorts, a property management firm as a marketing manager. Sometimes we'd sit under the palm trees and eat a packed lunch together. Other times we'd walk down to Front Street and eat at one of the delicious restaurants there on the ocean.

Her office had a very relaxed atmosphere. There were only about four employees and they all got along well, joked a lot. The owner was a retired tennis pro and I think the other workers were also transplants from the mainland USA.

Maui has a whole lot of Americans, Canadians, and others living and working there. I didn't really feel like a minority.

Our work hours were 8 am. to 5 pm. I got to run around the island to the different properties, and for meetings and comped activities - like helicopter tours around the islands, so I was out of the office a lot. My wife was in the office in front of the computer, doing spreadsheets - but, that's what she really enjoyed.

After work we usually went home first and headed back out right away for some exercise. A walk along the beach or the sidewalk alongside the beach was our usual daily routine. Maui sunsets are to die for, and I still remember the fire in the skies and ocean during some of those walks.

We then showered and headed out to find something to eat. We usually ate out and spent a ton of money doing so. It was a fair trade off for us. We were both food junkies. We enjoyed every minute on the island of Maui. To me, this is the ultimate place on the face of the earth to live! It fit my lifestyle and personality very well.

Weekends

There were so many things to do on the weekend, and there was no stress to do any of it - it was all just relaxing time. Maui is nice because most people don't work too hard during the week, then they don't work at all on the weekend. So, there are a whole lot of laid-back people on the island. People aren't stressed. Everyone is either making enough money, or retired and living on pensions. The beauty of the island is breathtaking. Everywhere you look there is something to make you stare in amazement.

Usually we would head to one of the morning fresh fruit and vegetable markets around the island. There was one in Lahaina, one in Kahana, they are found all over the island. Locals grow food in their backyards and sell it at very reasonable prices at these little markets. It's a great place to get local Filipino and Hawaiian food. We loaded up on fresh produce and usually grabbed something with noodles and chicken for a picnic later in the day.

We'd go home, drop off the food, and then head back out to a beach to meet up with friends and co-workers usually. There was always someone to be found at a beach somewhere on the island and it's just a nice way to spend some downtime.

Lunch would be a picnic at a beach, or wherever we happened to be - the top of Haleakala Volcano, on the road to Hana, in Paia watching the giant waves at Jaws, or just a ride around the perimeter of the island. The west coast is really something special, and if you go to Maui, you must make the drive around at least once, stopping along the way to see the blowholes and various beaches.

We'd usually go home, shower, and head back out for dinner and a movie on Saturday night and just dinner and drinks on Sunday night. There are so many great restaurants on Maui, it's hard to choose, but we always seemed to find one with something delicious. Ka'anapali in particular has a number of great restaurants on the beach that we really enjoyed.

Sunday during the day was typically the same as Saturdays. On one of those days we might spend cleaning up around and in our home, washing the car, going to Costco and Sam's Club. Sometimes we took a flight over to Oahu or Kauai to see something new for the weekend.

I think when you have enough money on Maui; you're really as happy as can be. We weren't saving much money, but still we were able to enjoy ourselves a lot without thinking too much about it. That's the key to living on Maui - make enough that it doesn't matter how much you're spending, because you will want to spend a lot of time in the restaurants!

21 – RELIGION

Mainland immigrants to Hawaii are usually either Christian or without a chosen religious preference. Those who move from the Philippines are predominantly Roman Catholic. Chaminade University is mostly Mormon students. Japanese, Chinese, Thai, Korean, and Vietnamese residents are mostly Zen, Mahayana and Theravada Buddhist. Indonesians and Malaysians are mostly Muslim.

Hasidic Jews, Jehovah's Witnesses and others all have a presence in Hawaii. There is no one dominant religion, and however you choose to worship, there is probably a group for you - at least on Oahu where most faiths are represented.

Nearly half of Hawaii's residents practice some form of Christianity, meaning Catholic, Christian, Protestant, etc. Nearly any denomination existing in the mainland also exists here in Hawaii.

Far east religions play an important role – Buddhism, Shinto, Hinduism, Islam, and other spiritual practices are all found on the islands.

A surprisingly large number of Mormons live in Hawaii. Many attend Chaminade University. Jehovah's Witnesses, Jewish, Pagan groups, are all here.

Religious followers in Hawaii are distributed as follows (data self-reported by religious establishments):

• Christianity: 351,000 (28.9%)

• Buddhism: 110,000 (9%)

• Judaism: 10,000 (0.8%)

• Other: 100,000 (10%)*

- Unaffiliated: 650,000 (51.1%)**

* "Other" in this data are religions other than Christianity, Buddhism, or Judaism; this group includes Bah?' Faith, Confucianism, Daoism, the Hawaiian religion, Hinduism, Islam, Sikhism, Shintoism, Zoroastrianism, and other religions.

** "Unaffiliated" refers to people who do not belong to a congregation; this group includes agnostics, atheists, humanists, and the irreligious.

22 – FOOD

You can find most of the food you're used to eating in the mainland US, but there is also an incredible variety of food that you have probably never seen before. When I walked through the Chinatown market, or the Filipino market in Waipahu, I was always amazed at the variety of foods there were to choose from. Local Hawaiian, Japanese, and Filipino foods are easy to come by, and you are sure to find some new favorite foods as you sample them over your time in the islands.

Must try foods:

Ahi Poke - This is a local dish with chunks of freshly caught raw yellow-fin tuna, tomatoes, garlic, sesame seeds and oil, shoyu (soy sauce), pepper water, chili pepper, sea salt, inamona (relish made of roasted and mashed kukui nuts), and bits of limu seaweed. There is Limu Poke that has a lot of seaweed, and there are about ten different styles of poke you can try in the islands. I used to wake up early on Saturdays when I lived on Oahu, and drive all the way up to Kahuku Superette to get their poke. I thought it was the best on the island.

Seared Ahi - I really love tuna. I could add "Ahi on the grill" too, but I won't. If you get the chance though, throw some ahi and marlin on the grill on a skewer with some tomatoes, and douse it liberally with shoyu as it cooks. I don't think you'll be disappointed. Seared ahi is best done at one of the Roy's restaurants on the islands. On Maui it's located in Ka'anapali on the 18th hole of the Ka'anapali Kai South golf course, and was one of my favorite restaurants for nearly everything they made. Each month I made sure Roy's got enough of my money, so they stayed in business!

Taro (Colocasia esculenta) - this is a very popular paste that accompanies meals as a dipping paste usually. Taro chips are also made. It is almost like purple potato. The taste is mildly sweet or even tasteless when made into the paste.

Mahi-mahi (Coryphaena hippurus) - an excellent tasting fish that is common in Hawaii restaurants. A mahi-mahi sandwich is a must try. These fish are commonly speared by locals jumping off kayaks. I've seen this on the West side of Oahu a couple times.

Ono (Acanthocybium solandri) - Ono means "delicious" in Hawaiian, and it certainly is the best tasting fish I've ever had. The fish is called "wahoo" more commonly. It is a type of Spanish mackerel, but without the harsh oil taste in the dark meat found in that fish. I had wahoo with walnut sauce in a great little restaurant on Kauai overlooking the Pacific Ocean, and I have to count that as among the best meals I have ever had in my life. *Ono!*

Lomi salmon - Small cubes of high grade salmon with Maui onion, tomato, and chili peppers.

Kalua pig - If you're in Hawaii, you might as well pay the fee and go see a Luau. There you will most definitely have succulent Kalua pig. The pork is tender, soft even. It is stringy because it is pulled off in strings. It is marinated and comes with cabbage. One of the simplest, and yet most delicious meals in Hawaii. Don't miss this if you're a meat eater.

Opihi - These are cone shaped shells that stick solidly to rocks in the tide. You will only find them (alive) where the water is splashing them every so often to keep them wet and provide them with nutrients. They are scraped off with a flat-edge blade and put in a bucket. They can be eaten raw, and that was the only way I've ever had them. They are every bit as delicious as any raw shellfish I've ever had. I like them mixed in shoyu (soy sauce), sliced ginger, garlic, and something spicy, I think it was wasabi mixed into it. *Delicious!*

Huli-huli chicken - Grilled chicken cooked on a rotisserie (turned) and marinated in a mixture of brown sugar, ginger, and shoyu (soy sauce).

On the windward coast next to Waimanolo Beach is a place called Bellows Air Force Station. It's a lovely beach and picnic area that I frequented a couple times each month. At the entrance to the park was a mobile huli-huli chicken truck. They served it with scoops of rice, shoyu, and a macaroni salad. Anyway, if you see a sign for it on the side of the road, get yourself some, it's quite good.

Monapua - A steamed, oval shaped white bun with reddish meat paste filling inside. The filling can be pork, chicken, Kalua pig, yams, hot dogs or whatever else they want to throw in there. You can find it fresh at roadside stands, or frozen in the markets.

Dragon fruit - Pink, roundish fruit larger than oranges and apples at their biggest. These have a lightly-sweet white or pink flesh with thousands of tiny seeds suspended throughout that are edible. The taste is similar to mulberries. This is one of my favorite fruits. The other is next.

Rambutan - Pink, red, or green golf-ball sized fruit with fuzzy green tentacles covering the exterior. The inside is like a large grape with one seed in the center. The flesh is absolutely delicious like no other fruit I've ever had.

Other Foods

Of course, you can have whatever fast food you usually do in the mainland, all the usual ones are in Hawaii too. Taco Bell, McDonald's, Burger King, Pizza Hut, KFC, etc. There are also a number of island specific restaurant chains that have sprung up. I treated myself to the calorie-filled grilled chicken at Jack in the Box every now and then.

Average Eating Out Costs Per Person

Average Hawaii breakfast cost?

Super cheap for $6-7. Average about $9.

Average lunch?

Super cheap for $10. Average about $15.

Average dinner?

Super cheap about $12. Average about $20-30.

23 – GOLF

Golf on Big Island

Big Island Hawaii has some of the best golf in the entire world.

It is the number one destination in Hawaii for golfing enthusiasts. Some of the most beautiful courses on the planet are to be found here, and anyone who loves golf should get to play here at least once in their life. There are expensive green fees for many of the well-known private courses on the island, but there are also some cheaper options available.

Some visitors make a special trip to this island just for the golfing. Most of the golfing is on the Kailua-Kona side and north of the city. The views from some of the courses are spectacular. Bring your cameras and don't forget to take photos as you golf. While the golfers are busy, the rest of the family can go "Shopping on the Big Island!" – see the next chapter for shopping on all islands.

There is an impressive selection of stunning golf courses to choose from on Big Island including:

Makalei Golf Club

72-3890 Mamalahoa Highway, Kailua-Kona, HI 96740
Website: Makalei.com
Yelp Rating: 4 stars (based on 1 review)
Email: Info@makalei.com
Phone: (808) 325-6625
18-Hole Course: Par 72

Makalei Golf Club is located in the hills above Kona. The name 'Makalei' means peacock, and this course is unique because it has so many of these birds wandering around – it is sometimes referred to as Peacock Place. There is very little flat ground on this course and most of the holes require playing uphill. For this reason, it is considered to be one of the most challenging courses to play on Big Island. The fact that it is located in the Hualalai Mountain means there are some spectacular views of the surrounding countryside to be enjoyed. Dick Nugent & Associates designed the Makalei Golf Club, and they did a great job of creating a course that fits in perfectly with the local environment.

The facilities at the Makalei Golf Club include a restaurant, pro shop, and practice area. The Peacock Grille is open from 11 am. to 2:30 pm., and they offer a good range of snacks and hot meals. There is also a well-stocked bar. It is possible to hire the Peacock Grille for special events such as weddings or corporate events. There is also a beverage cart available at those times when the Peacock Grille is closed. The pro shop offers a good range of golfing equipment and apparel, and they also sell some interesting gift items. The practice facilities include a driving range, and two practice greens.

It costs non-Hawaiian residents $85 to play on the course any time before 11 am. The price falls to $55 if people want to play after 11 am. If visitors only want to play 9-holes they need to pay $65 during peak-times. A set of clubs costs $50 per day to rent or $165 for one week. If you intend to be staying on Big Island for a long time, it might be worth considering some type of membership. The Gold package membership costs an initiation Fee of $99 and $79 per month – discounts are available for seniors and families. Unlimited use of the practice facilities costs $25 initiation Fee and $22 per month (prices correct as of late 2013).

Big Island Country Club

71-1420 Mamalahoa Highway, Kailua-Kona, HI 96740
Website: BigIslandCountryClub.com
Yelp Rating: 3.5 stars (based on 4 reviews)
Email: info@bigislandcountryclub.com
Phone: (808) 325-5044

18-Hole Course: Par 72

The Big Island Country Club (previously known as Big Island Muni) is another hilly course that is built on top of a volcano. The temperatures here are lower than down by the coast, and there is usually a refreshing light breeze. The course is well maintained but players shouldn't be too surprised to find goats or wild turkeys wandering onto the fairway. Holes 17 and 18 are the toughest to play. The Big Island Country Club is under the control of a new manager, and there are ongoing efforts to bring improvements to the course.

There is currently no clubhouse at the Big Island Country Club, but this will hopefully change in the future – there are apparently plans to build a new facility soon. At the moment, players will need to go elsewhere for post-game drinks and dining.

The green fees at Big Island Country Club are very affordable, and this is what attracts many visitors to the course. It costs $65 to play here before noon and $55 after this time – the price also includes a two-person shared cart. If people only want to play 9-holes, they will only need to pay $35. Large groups who book here (more than 17 players) only need to pay $45 for each person. If visitors have a preferred player card (these are handed out free at many resorts and condominiums), they can get further discounts on the prices at Big Island Country Club.

Waikoloa Village Golf Club

68-1792 Melia Street, Waikoloa, Island of Hawaii, HI 96738
Website: WaikoloaVillageGolf.com
Yelp Rating: 3.5 stars (based on 4 reviews)
Email: wvagolf@hawaii.rr.com
Phone: (808) 883-9621 (24-hour reservations)
18-Hole Course: Par 72

The Waikoloa Village Golf Club is the second oldest course on Big Island, and it is located in a particularly beautiful area. Players get plenty of stunning views as they make their way around this course – including glimpses of five of the most famous volcanoes on the island. The course was designed by Robert Trent Jones junior who has designed over 250 courses during his career to date. It can sometimes get a bit windy here, but this can add a bit of spice to the game. The Waikoloa Village Golf Club is suitable for all levels of player.

The amenities at Waikoloa Village Golf Club are good enough that you will probably want to spend an hour or two here after you have finished your game. The clubhouse restaurant opens seven days a week, and there is indoor and outdoor seating available. The large bar has five HDTVs, so this can be a nice place to watch sporting events. It is possible to rent a room in the clubhouse to host private functions. The golf shop has been newly renovated, and they offer special deals on golfing apparel and equipment. They also sell items with the famous Waikoloa Village Golf Club logo – this can make a nice memento or gift. The staff members who run the golf shop are qualified for Ping iron fitting.

It costs $83.50 for visitors to play here before 2:30 pm. and $50 after this time. People who are staying at the Village Resort only need to pay $72 before 2:30 pm. Residents of the island pay $40 before 2:30 pm. and $25 after this. It costs $40 to rent a set of clubs – $20 if playing in the twilight hours. Prices correct as of late 2013.

Hualalai Golf Course

100 Kaupulehu Drive, Kailua-Kona, HI 96740
Website: HualalaiResort.com
Yelp Rating: 5 stars (based on three reviews)
Phone: (808) 325-8480
18-Hole Course: Par 72

The Hualalai Golf Course is part of the Four Seasons Hotel, and the legendary Jack Nicklaus designed it. This is not only the most gorgeous golf course on Big Island, but it is arguably one of most beautiful in the world. The Hualalai Golf Course is used as part of the PGA Champions Tour, but anyone can get to enjoy the unforgettable experience of playing here. Jack Nicklaus did a superb job of planning this course, and it his technical know-how has been combined with the natural beauty of the location – for example, he makes great use of lava formations in the middle of the fairway. Players are also treated to some wonderful views of the ocean.

The amenities at Hualalai Golf Course are second-to-none. The clubhouse provides plenty of space, and there is a great selection of food available Keolu Restaurant. Players are provided with free drinks and fruit during their game – there is even a cookie jar at the halfway point on the course. The Keolu Golf Shop has a full selection of golfing equipment, clothing for men and women, as well as golfing accessories. The professionals at the club provide complimentary clinics two times every week – private lessons are also available. Hualalai Golf Course also has an impressive 9-acre practice area.

The green fees for Hualalai Golf Course are about $195 – people who are staying at the resort can expect a discount. It is highly recommended that anyone who wants to play at this golf course books in advance (this is possible one week before). Lessons are available with one of the pros for $55 for half-an-hour. It costs $60 to rent a set of clubs and $10 for a pair of shoes.

Volcano Golf and Country Club

Hawaii Volcanoes National Park, Volcano, HI 96785
Website: VolcanoGolfShop.com
Yelp Rating: 2 stars (based on six reviews)
Email: par@volcanogolfshop.com
Phone: (808) 967-7331
18-Holes: Par 72

Volcano Golf and Country Club has been open since 1922. This is a suitably challenging course that is located at an elevation of 4,200 feet. It has also been described as the most unusual golf course in the world because it is located on the rim of an active volcano. One of the nice things about playing at this high altitude is that the weather is much cooler, and there are plenty of spectacular views to enjoy as well. Beginners are likely to find this golf course to be a bit difficult to play – even low handicappers are going to be tested here.

The facilities at Volcano Golf and Country Club include a restaurant and a pro shop. The restaurant can get busy because it also caters for tour groups as well as players. The portion sizes in the restaurant are now ample (this may have been in response to previous reviews where customers complained that the portion sizes were too small). The pro shop has a full selection of products including things like caps, balls, towels, and clothing with the Volcano Golf and Country Club logo.

It costs $56 to play a round of golf at Volcano Golf and Country Club – this includes tax and the cart fee. A set of clubs can be rented for $20.

Mauna Kea Golf Course

62-100 Mauna Kea Beach Drive, Kohala Coast, HI 96743, United States
Website: PrinceResortsHawaii.com/mauna-kea-golf-course/
Yelp Rating: 5 stars (based on 10 reviews)
Phone: (808) 882-5400
18-Holes: Par 72

Mauna Kea Golf Course is part of Mauna Kea Beach Hotel. Laurance S. Rockefeller created the resort and the golf course, and he is known for only accepting the best at anything he did. He brought in the best golf architect of the time who was Robert Trent Jones Senior (his son designed Waikoloa Village Golf Club), and they created something really special. The Mauna Kea is a superb golf course, and it is famous for having the hardest par-3 hole in the world – the eleventh hole. The grass here is a lush green, and the course provides outstanding views of the Pacific Coast – you will probably want to bring along your camera as well as your golf clubs. Some of the most unique challenges of this course include lava flow hazards and giant sand bunkers.

The facilities at Mauna Kea Golf Course are top class and include a restaurant, locker facilities, fully stocked pro shop, shower facilities, driving range, and putting practice area. The Number 3 Restaurant is open every day from 11 am. to 5 pm. (lunched served 11 am. to 3:30 pm.). It is located mid-course, so it can be nice for players to stop here before returning for the final nine. The menu has a good selection of sandwiches, gourmet pizza, and desserts. There are a number of highly respected golf pros working at this course, and they are able to provide private instruction as well as group clinics.

The standard green fee for playing 18-holes at Mauna Kea Golf Course is $225. This price falls to $175 between 11 am. and 1:30 pm. and $155 after 1:30 pm. It is also possible to play nine holes for $110. If players want to play more than once a day it only costs $110 for a replay. The junior rate for playing at Mauna Kea Golf Course is $95. It costs $50 to rent a set of clubs and $15 for a pair of shoes (all prices as of late-2013). The driving range if free and this includes unlimited balls.

Hapuna Golf Course

Highway 19, Hapuna Prince Beach, Island of Hawaii, HI
Website: PrinceResortsHawaii.com/hapuna-beach-prince-hotel/hapuna-golf.php
Phone: (808) 880-3000
Yelp Rating: 4 stars (based on 1 review)
18-Holes: Par 72

The Hapuna is a link-style golf course. It was built in 1992 by Arnold Palmer and Ed Seay. It has been designed in such a way as to disturb nature as little as possible. The first nine holes here are played uphill, and the second nine are downhill – the highest level of the course is 700 feet above sea level. The fairways are lined with high grass. It is a great option for beginners and intermediate players because it isn't too challenging, but the goats that tend to wander onto the course may put off some serious players. It's a fun place to pay, and this is what makes it so charming.

The facilities at Hapuna Golf Course include locker rooms, shower facilities, pro shop, a fitness center and spa, driving range, putting greens, and practice bunker. The driving range is open every day from 7 am. to 4:30 pm. and it is completely free with unlimited balls. The full-service pro shop opens every day between 6:30 am. and 5 pm. There are also PGA professionals who are able to provide private lessons and group clinics.

The standard cost of playing at Hapuna Golf Course is $125 for 18-holes. The price falls to $75 after 1 pm. If players wish to go for another round on the same day, it costs only $45 for a replay. The junior rate at Hapuna is $50. At the moment (late 2013) there is a special package at the course, which costs $375 and includes two rounds here and one round at Mauna Kea Golf Course. It costs $55 to rent clubs and $12 to rent shoes. Hapuna Golf Course also has a half-day ""Master the Mental Game" package, which costs $195.

Hilo Municipal Golf Course

340 Haihai Street, Hilo, HI 96720
Website: N/A
Yelp Rating: 4 stars (based on 2 reviews)
Phone: (808) 959-7711
18-Hole: Par 71

If visitors are looking for somewhere cheap to play a few rounds, they are not going to do much better than Hilo Municipal Golf Course. This venue is not as fancy as many of the private clubs, but it offers a surprisingly high quality golfing experience – more than what you would expect at a Municipal venue. This is where local people tend to go when they want to play, so it can get busy at the weekends. Willard Wilkinson designed the course in 1951. The people who work here are friendly, and they keep the course in good condition. The one odd thing about this course is that there are no bunkers – this is due to the fact that Hilo gets so much rain that this would not be practical. The course is relatively flat, and it is hard to play here if it has been raining hard.

There are a modest number of amenities at Hilo Municipal Golf Course. The pro shop has a reasonable selection of equipment and apparel. There is also a restaurant and snack bar. Practice facilities include a driving range.

Visitors to Hilo Municipal Golf Course pay $44, and this included a cart. Residents of Big Island can buy a monthly card for $40, and this means they can play as much as they want – although there is a $3 surcharge at weekends. People are allowed to use the course for free after 5 pm.

Mauna Lani Golf Resort Courses

(North, South, and Keiki Courses)
68-1310 Mauna Lani Drive, Island of Hawaii, HI 96743-9704
Website: MaunaLani.com
Yelp Rating: 4.5 (based on 12 reviews)
Phone: (808) 885-6655
North and South Course, both 18-Hole: Par 72
Keiki Course 9-hole: Par 33

The Mauna Lani has three different courses to choose from. The 9-hole Keiki Course has been designed with junior golfers in mind, but it will also be suitable for complete beginners. The North Course and South Course are both provide an international standard experience with Bermuda grass greens and exceptionally beautiful views – particular the South Course, which provides nice views of the ocean. The two courses are about equal when it comes to difficulty level, and there are plenty of hazards including lava flows on the sides of the fairways. Everything at Mauna Lani is well maintained, and people who play here will have an unforgettable experience because it is one of the best golf courses in the world (it was also awarded this distinction by Golf Week Magazine in 2013). Tournaments are played at Mauna Lani on a regular basis.

Mauna Lani is part of the golfing resort, and the facilities here are of a high standard. There is a pro shop, locker rooms, bar, and restaurant. There is a decent practice area, which includes a putting green and driving range. There are also private lessons as well as golfing clinics.

It costs $215 to play 18-holes at Mauna Lani. If people are staying at the resort, they will only need to spend $165. Club rental is $55, and it costs $15 to hire a pair of golfing shoes. Children who wish to play on Keiki course need to pay $25, and this includes free clubs. Adults who wish to join in need to pay $35.

Sea Mountain Golf Course

Hwy 11 & Nino Ole Hawaii, Pahala, HI 96777
Website: TheHawaiiCondo.com
Yelp Rating: 2.5 stars (based on 2 reviews)
Phone: (808) 928-6233
18-Hole: 72 Par

The cheapest round of golf on Big Island can be found at Sea Mountain Golf Course. This belongs to Hawaii Beach Condo, and Arthur Jack Snyder designed it. Sea Mountain is located in an area of great natural beauty, and it can be best described as rugged. It is close to Punaluu Black Sand Beach, and there are some nice views of the ocean. Players who come here expecting the same experience as they would at one of the popular private clubs are going to be disappointed. It is a good option for people who are in the Pahala area and just want to enjoy a no-frills round of golf. The facilities at Sea Mountain Golf Course are limited but include a pro shop and driving range.

The best reason to play at Sea Mountain Golf Course is price. People staying at the Hawaii Beach Condo only need to pay $35. Visitors can play here for $46.50 (as of late 2013) – this includes a golf cart. There are sometimes special promotions on here, and the green fees can be further reduced – sometimes as low as $20.

Golf on Maui

Playing golf on Maui is sure to be an unforgettable and almost surreal experience. Some of the most prestigious courses in the world are to be found here, and it just sounds impressive to say you have played golf on this Hawaiian Island paradise, doesn't it? The golf courses on Maui have a reputation for being expensive, but if you look, there is actually something to suit every budget.

Some of the Best Golf Courses on Maui include:

The King Kamehameha Golf Club

2500 Honoapiilani Highway, Wailuku, Maui, HI 96793
Website: KamehamehaGolf.com
Yelp Rating: 4 stars (based on 5 reviews)
Email: info@kamehamehagolf.com
Phone: (808) 249-0033
18-Hole Course: Par 72

The King Kamehameha Golf Club was designed by Ted Robinson (aka the King of Waterscapes) in 1991, and is located in idyllic surroundings – just beautiful Hawaiian terrain and no traffic or signs of habitation for miles. This is the only private 18-hole golf course on Maui, and it is par 72. The course is located in-between two inactive volcanoes (one that formed the West Maui Mountains, and the other being Haleakala), and the greens are maintained in always-perfect condition.

The clubhouse at King Kamehameha Golf Club is considered to be one of the most innovatively designed in the world. Frank Lloyd Wright created the original plans for this building in 1949, but it wasn't actually completed until 1988. The clubhouse covers an area of 74,000 square foot, and it contains a fully stocked pro-shop, a member's dining area (Wai Kahe Room), Kahili Restaurant, hot tub, sauna, luxury spa, Jacuzzi, gym, lounge areas, and the locker room. The Ho'oheno Room (capacity 100) and Kahalawai Terrace (capacity 150) can be rented for special functions such as weddings.

This is a members-only club but visitors have the option of 'Guest for a Day' membership, which costs $170 (as of mid-2013) – this includes a golf cart to use for the day. Members of other private golf clubs around the world may be able to play here as a 'reciprocal club member' – they just need to contact the club manager to see if they are eligible. Unlimited membership costs $24,500 with $5,335 annual fees – this means you can use the course whenever you like. Part-time membership costs $21K with $2,940 annual fees – this entitles you to 20 rounds of golf per year. There are also membership packages for the spouse of existing members and for children.

Waiehu Golf Course

Lower Waiehu Beach Road, Waiehu, HI 96793
Website: N/A
Yelp Rating: 2.5 stars (based on 2 reviews)
Phone: (808) 244-5934
18-Hole Course: Par 72

Waiehu is an 18-hole public golf course that was built in 1945. Players here get to enjoy some splendid views of the sea and Waihe'e Reef. The par-72 course itself isn't too challenging, so highly skilled players may feel a bit underwhelmed. It can also get busy here with groups of up to six taking their time on the greens, so you can expect it to be slow going during these times. Players may notice a different feel to the course between the first nine holes (along the coast) of the course and the second nine (beside a mountain) – this is because the latter were not added until 33 years later. Waiehu Golf Course has hosted a number of amateur championship matches. It opens weekdays at 6:30 am.

and on weekends and bank holidays at 5:30 am. – the course closes every day at 5 pm.

Waiehu clubhouse offers a reasonable number of amenities, all of it on par with typical public courses. There is a pro-shop, which is fully stocked with clubs and other golfing paraphernalia. The restaurant is open to the public, but it is also possible to book it for private functions. There is also free parking close to the clubhouse complex.

The greens fees for Waiehu Golf Course are affordable. Residents and active military personnel can play here for $10 on weekdays and weekends. Non-residents need to pay $55. It costs $20 to hire a golf cart (all prices correct as of mid-2013). Waiehu Golf Course also has a lighted driving range that is open to the public.

Elleair Maui Golf Club

1345 Piilani Highway, Kihei, HI 96753
Website: ElleairMauiGolfClub.com
Yelp Rating: 3.5 stars (based on 9 reviews)
Email: mseki@elleairmauigolfclub.com
Phone: (808) 874-0777
18-Hole Course: Par 71

Elleair is another public golf club, which has been open since 1987. The course here is suitable for players of different skill levels – even those with a low handicap should find that there is plenty here to keep them challenged. The fairways are nice and wide. There are some nice views of the Pacific Ocean from a couple of the holes, and you also get to admire the West Maui Mountains. The greens (made from Bermuda turf grasses) here are kept in excellent condition. A game at this course starts off easy with a par-4 hole going downhill – overall the course is par-71. This course becomes more challenging when the trade winds are blowing, as you might imagine!

The facilities at Elleair have an excellent reputation – the staff members here are very friendly and helpful. Kono's on the Green functions as the nineteenth hole. It offers some nice views of the course, and it is possible to dine and drink inside or outside. They have a fully qualified chef who is happy to serve up local dishes as well a good selection of burgers, pizzas, and pastas. The pro-shop is fully stocked with all the well-known brands, and they are also able to arrange golf club repairs.

Elleair Maui Golf Club has a lighted driving range and other practice facilities. They are also able to provide lessons with one of their four golf pros – it costs about $60 for a half-hour lesson (as of mid-2013).

The Elleair Maui Golf Club has a special offer at the moment (mid-2013) whereby people who register with them will receive a free round of golf on their birthday. They have a number of different packages available such as six rounds for the price of five ($300), Aloha Fridays ($55 for a round), weekday 9 holes ($15), and a two-round package ($110). Junior players get to play here for free if they are accompanied by a paying-adult.

Maui Country Club

48 Nonohe Street, Spreckelsville, Maui, HI 96779
Website: MauiCountryClub.org
Yelp Rating: N/A
Phone: (808) 877-7893
9-Hole Course: Par 36

Maui Country Club is a private 9-hole golf course (par-36). Players can enjoy a full game by going around the course twice using a different tee. The layout makes this a great walking course, and it takes about two hours to do 9 holes an easy pace. The grounds here are well manicured and the greens are made from Bermuda grass. There are regular amateur tournaments played here each year, as well as weekly tournaments for men and women.

The facilities at Maui Country Club are top notch. The dining area in the clubhouse offers a nice view of the ninth hole. It is possible to eat or drink indoors or outdoors. It is also very family-friendly. Their menu includes specialty burgers made from Maui Cattle company beef. The pro shop is run by Mark Shimamura – he is not only a professional golfer, but he is also a certified club fitter and club repairer. Maui Country Club also has a large swimming pool, fitness gym, and six tennis hard courts.

Visitors to Maui Country Club pay $40 for 9 holes, or $70 for 18 holes (this includes the price of a cart). They have a special price on Mondays when it costs $24 for 9 holes, and $45 for 18 holes – this can only be booked the day before. Guests of a member of Maui Country Club pay the Monday price every day.

Ka'anapali Kai Golf Course

2290 Ka'anapali Parkway, Lahaina, Maui, HI 96761
Website: KaanapaliGolfCourses.com
Yelp Rating: 3.5 stars (based on 27 reviews)
Email: emailus@kaanapaligolfcourses.com
Phone: (808) 661-3691
18-Hole Course: Par 70

Ka'anapali Kai benefits from some amazing local scenery, and it is set in what used to be a sugar cane plantation – it is still possible to catch glimpses of the sugar cane steam train. This par-70 course has something to offer every level of player. The boundaries are marked by lava rock, and there are a number of natural canals that now act as water hazards. There are also plenty of colorful exotic flowers and coconut trees on the course, and this just adds to the attraction of the grounds.

Ka'anapali Kai has a Hawaiian-style clubhouse overlooking the green of the 18th hole. There is a restaurant for those who wish to eat a meal, and there is also the Mango Café, which serves snacks and beverages. The pro shop has a nice selection of clubs, logo shirts, golfing shoes, and balls. There are also locker facilities and shower rooms. Ka'anapali Kai Golf Club has a driving range beside the clubhouse, which stays open between 6:30 pm. and 4:30 pm.

Anyone staying at the Ka'anapali Resort usually pays $150 for a round of golf. Those who are not staying at the resort need to pay $195. It is possible to get a cheaper Twilight rate ($95) if players book to tee-off after 2 pm. All prices are correct as of mid-2013.

The Dunes at Maui Lani Golf Course

1333 Maui Lani Parkway, Kahului, Maui, HI 96732
Website: DunesAtMauiLani.com
Yelp Rating: 4.5 stars (based on 16 reviews)
Phone: (808) 873-0422
18-Hole Course: Par 72

Robin Nelson designed the Dunes at Maui Golf Course – he also designed a number of other popular courses in Hawaii and South East Asia. The 18-hole course is designed in a very traditional way, but it benefits from all the latest technology. This is a challenging course (72-par), especially the back nine, but this is also a fun place to play golf so it will be suitable for beginners as well as experts. The winds can be strong here, and this tends to spice up both the long and even the short games, depending on how hard they're blowing.

The Dunes Clubhouse looks like a plantation-style mansion – it covers an area of 40,000 square feet. Most players will retire to the Cafe O' Lei after they have completed a round. This bar and restaurant is tastefully designed and is large enough to seat up to 250 people – there is both indoor and outdoor seating. The bar is fully stocked and they have a good selection of snacks and meals created by Dana and Michael Pastula (they are both the chefs and the owners). There is also a pro shop in the clubhouse which stocks a good range of men and women's golfing apparel along with clubs and other equipment.

The standard greens fee for Dunes Golf Course is $112. If players are willing to brave the midday sun (teeing-off at 11 am.), they only have to pay $99. There is also a twilight rate of $70 (after 2 pm.). Players who wish to book another round only have to pay $50. They charge $30 for rental of a set of golf clubs and $10 for a pair of golfing shoes. The practice range at Dunes Golf Course opens daily from 6:30 am. until 7:30 pm. (except on Wednesdays when it doesn't open until 8:30 am.).

Pukalani Country Club

360 Pukalani Street, Pukalani, Maui, Hawaii 96768
Website: PukalaniGolf.com
Yelp Rating: 2.5 stars (based on 11 reviews)
Phone: (808) 572-1314
18-Hole Course: Par 72

Pukalani Country Club is located right on the slopes of Haleakala Mountain (an inactive volcano, towering some 10,000 feet above). The course enjoys a 1,100-foot elevation above sea level, so this is one course where you can look forward to some nice scenic views of the valley. Pukalani has a reputation for offering the right combination of an enjoyable golfing experience with reasonably priced green fees. The course was designed by Bob Baldock who has designed almost seventy courses around the US.

The old clubhouse at Pukalani was destroyed by a storm a few years back, but the new facilities are pretty good. They have an open-air dining area, which offers a super view of the ninth and tenth holes. There are special events here throughout the week – Friday night is prime rib night, and they have live music on the first Tuesday of the month. The bar has a happy hour between 3 pm. and 6 pm. The pro shop opens between 6:30 am. and 6 pm. and sells the usual golfing equipment as well as branded apparel for men and women.

It costs $61 for visitors to play golf here before midday. The rates go down at twilight (12 pm. to 2:30 pm.) to $35 and there is also a super-twilight rate (after 2:30 pm.) of $31. Residents of Hawaii get a discount on these rates. It costs $25 to hire a cart and a set of clubs costs $35 before 2:30 pm. and $25 after this. There is also a driving range, which opens from 6:30 am. until 6:30 pm. and it costs $4 for a full bucket of balls.

Makena Golf Course and Resort

5400 Makena Alanui, Wailea-Makena HI 96753
Website: MakenaResortMaui.com
Yelp Rating: N/A (previously 4.5 stars based on 20 reviews)
Phone: 800- 321-6284 (toll free) or (808) 874-1111
18-Hole Course: Par 72

Makena Golf course is currently closed for extensive renovation. It is due to reopen in early 2014.

Golf on Oahu

Golfing on Oahu is about what you'd expect – awesome. One of the most impressive things about golf on Oahu is that there are just so many courses to choose from. There is a course and an activity to suit every budget, and it is possible to play a round of golf here for as little as $18 for 18-holes – that's $1 per hole. Of course, the fancy courses that get to be featured in the magazines like Golf Digest are going to charge significantly more than this.

Mililani Golf Club

95-176 Kuahelani Avenue, Mililani, HI 96789
Website: MililaniGolf.com
Yelp Rating: 3.5 stars (based on 20 Reviews)
Phone: (808) 623-2222
18-Hole: Par 72

The Mililani golf course offers a good mix of fun and challenge. It is usual for people who play here to want to come back again. This club is located right in the central plain of Oahu, and there are some nice views of the Waianae and Ko'olau mountain ranges. There are many tall trees around the course which are impressive to look at, but not so nice when your ball gets caught up in them. The grounds are kept in pristine condition, and it is a good course for all levels of player.

The facilities at the Mililani Golf Club include a restaurant, practice area, and pro shop. Alonzo's Restaurant opens daily (Monday to Thursday 8 am. to 7 pm., and Friday to Sunday 6 am. to 7 pm. It is open to the public, and it has a reasonably extensive menu, which includes breakfast, lunch, and dinner options. It is possible to put on a banquet where there is a group of at least 40 people, and there is a three-hour limit on the time guests can stay on the premises – it works out at about $1.75 per person for a standard banquet.

Visitors pay $99 to play 18 holes at Mililani Golf Club, but the green fees fall to $75 after 11 am. Residents of the island usually pay $45, and there are also special rates for juniors and seniors (over 55 years of age). The driving range is open every day from 6:30 am. to 10 pm., and it costs $5 for a full basket of balls – $4 for a half-basket.

Oahu Country Golf Club

150 Country Club Road, Honolulu, HI 96817
Website: OahuCountryClub.com
Yelp Rating: 4 stars (based on 27 reviews)
Phone: (808) 595-6331
18-Hole: Par 71

Oahu Country Golf Club is renowned for having one of the hardest courses on Oahu – players will need to play tactically if they hope to do well. It is sometimes referred to as the 'Grand Dame' of courses in Hawaii, and it is the second oldest course on Oahu. It is home to the Manoa Cup Championship, which is the longest running golf tournament on the islands. They also have some interesting amateur championships during the year such as the Family Tournament and Battle of the Sexes. There are many hills on this course, and there can also be a great deal of wind, but this just adds to the challenge.

The facilities at Oahu Country Club are pretty good. There is a restaurant, pro shop, and driving range. There is a dress code for anyone who wants to use the clubhouse. The newly renovated restaurant has a decent reputation, and it provides a great view of the course. They have also recently appointed a new chef who is able to create an eclectic mix of dishes. Other facilities available at this course include an 80,000 gallon heated swimming pool.

Oahu Country Club is a private club and people and membership is by invitation only. The cost of regular membership is only discussed once the person has been invited but rumors are that it is expensive. Non-Resident Golf Membership is also offered, and anyone interested in this should contact the clubhouse for more information. It costs $65 to play here, and this includes a rental cart.

Ewa Beach Golf Club

91-050 Fort Weaver Road, Ewa Beach, HI 96706
Website: EwaBeachGC.com
Yelp Rating: 4 stars (based on 17 Reviews)
Phone: (808) 689-6565
18-Hole: Par 72

Ewa Beach Golf Club was designed by Robin Nelson and opened in 1992. The layout is based on a traditional Scottish links course. The fairways are lined with trees, and this makes it easier for players to hit the ball accurately. This was the first course on Oahu to use environmentally friendly turf. The first three holes of the course are the most challenging, and the rough for all eighteen holes is a bit unforgiving. This course is in the pathway of Honolulu Airport, so there is a steady stream of airplanes flying overhead.

The facilities at Ewa Beach Golf Club include a practice area, restaurant, male and female locker rooms, showers, and bar. The restaurant offers some nice views of the course as well as the ocean, and it is a family-friendly type of place. They open weekdays from 10:30 am. to 6:30 pm. and weekends from 8:30 am. to 7 pm. There is a large pro shop, which sells all the usual golfing paraphernalia as well as some Ewa Beach Club unique items. Private golf lessons are available with the club pro.

Visitors pay $160 for 18-holes at Ewa Beach Golf Club including a golf cart – the price falls to $115 after 12:30 pm. It costs $40 to rent a set of clubs and $3 for a locker. It is important to note that golfing shoes are not available for rent at this venue. There is a strict dress code and appropriate golfing attire is expected – including collared shirts.

Waialae Golf Course

4997 Kahala Avenue, Honolulu, HI 96816
Website: WaialaeCC.com
Yelp Rating: 4.5 stars (based on 35 reviews)
Phone: (808) 734-2151
18-Holes: Par 72

Waialae Golf Course is a PGA course, so one of the nice things about playing here is that you follow in the steps of some of the greatest players in the world. The Sony Open is played here each year. It was built in 1927, and holes on the course have been designed to mimic famous course around the world – for example, the 13-hole is based on the French Biarritz Course, and the 8-hole is similar to the Scottish North Berwick Course. The secret to playing well at Waialae is to keep the ball straight, but this is not so easy on windy days. The views from this course are spectacular, and it is worth playing here for this alone.

The clubhouse at Waialae Golf Course has been renovated recently, and it is considered to be one of the best in the US. The new design incorporates elements of Hawaiian culture and combines this with lavish style. The facilities include tennis courts, male and female locker rooms, swimming pool, and fully equipped gym. The pro shop is run by a team that is very knowledgeable about what they sell, and they are properly trained for fitting clubs. The shop has a good selection of souvenirs as well as golfing equipment and clothing. There are a number of dining areas at this clubhouse – some of these are members-only and some can be hired for functions.

Waialae is a private member Golf Course, but unaccompanied guests can usually play here for $250 – this includes a golf cart. Guests of a member of the club will usually pay less than this. Some of the more expensive hotels on Oahu are able to arrange access to Waialae for their guests.

Ko'olau Golf Club

45-550 Kionaole Road, Kaneohe, HI 96744
Website: KoolauGolfClub.com
Yelp Rating: 4 stars (based on 36 Reviews)
Phone: (808) 236-4653
18-Hole: Par 72

Ko'olau golf course is not for the faint-hearted, and even skilled players will need to work hard to end up with a good score here – it is considered one of the toughest courses in the world and the most difficult in the nation. There are four sets of tees to choose from, to suit different levels, so even beginner players are going to enjoy the experience. It has been listed number 7 by Golf Magazine as one of the top-100 places to play in the world. Dick Nugent designed it in 1992, and he did an impressive job of fitting the course in with the natural beauty of the place. There is a stunning mountain backdrop for many of the holes, as well as some nice views of the bay. Anyone who wants to play here is advised to take along plenty of extra balls because they are almost certainly going to lose at least a few.

Ko'olau offers a clubhouse with plenty of facilities. The pro shop is fully stocked, and they also have a selection of Ko'olau branded items to choose from. Honey's Restaurant serves up

Pacific-Asian as well as Continental cuisine. Brunch on Sundays is particularly good, and they have live music on Friday and Sunday night. The clubhouse also has banquet facilities that will be able to hold up to seventy people. The KMR School of Golf is also here, and this non-profit project is designed to foster the best junior talent around. The club also has practice facilities, which include a driving range, and seven thousand square foot putting green. The club pro is able to provide PGA standard private instruction.

Visitors to Ko'olau Golf Club pay $145 for 18-holes or $110 after noon – there is also a super-twilight fee after 3 pm. when the price falls to $55. Juniors (age 7 to 17) pay $55 to play, and there are discounts for military personnel and seniors (over the age of 55). If people want to go for another round on the course (it must be the same day), they only need to pay $25. Visitors who expect to be playing a few games at Ko'olau Golf Club can purchase a 7-day unlimited golf package for $299. A set of clubs can be rented for $50, and golf shoes cost $15 to rent – prices correct as of late 2013.

Ala Wai Golf Course

404 Kapahulu Avenue, Honolulu, HI 96815
Website: www1.honolulu.gov/des/golf/alawai.htm
Yelp Rating: 2.5 stars (based on 11 reviews)
Phone: (808) 733-7380
18-Holes: Par 70

Ala Wai is a municipal golf course close to Waikiki in Honolulu. The fact that this venue is conveniently located, reasonably priced, and popular with the local people means that it can get busy – it can be sometimes impossible to book a tee time. This is a mostly flat course that is separated from downtown Waikiki by a canal. There are some nice views of the Ko'olau mountain range and Diamond Head. It is a great course for beginners but more experienced players may feel a bit unchallenged. The greens are maintained to a reasonable level but nowhere near the same standard as the private clubs.

The facilities at Ala Wai include a cafe, pro shop, and driving range. The Ala Wai Cafe opens every day between 6 am. and 9 pm. There serve a selection of snacks and beverages as well as full meals. The driving range is open from 7 am. to noon. The club can also arrange private or group lessons.

The standard green fee for visitors to Ala Wai is $55 for 18-holes. Residents who have a golf ID pay $22 during the week and $26 at the weekends and holidays (a Hawaii Driver's License can also be used, but it costs an extra $3 with this form of ID). It costs visitors $33 to play a 9-hole game, and this price is further reduced to $16.50 for a twilight game.

Bay View Golf Course

45-285 Kaneohe Bay Drive, Kaneohe, HI 96744
Website: BayviewGolfCourse.com
Yelp Rating: 3 stars (based on 17 Reviews)
Phone: (808) 247-0451
18-Hole: Par 72

Bay View has recently undergone a bit of a facelift, and this means that the greens are in very good condition. The course was originally opened in 1963, but it underwent a major redesign in 1997 by Robert Nelson. One of the nice things about this venue is that they also provide night golfing. The back nine is where he most challenging holes are to be found, and this is also where the most scenic views are to be enjoyed. This is another good course for beginners, and the green fees are very reasonable.

The clubhouse at Bay View included a restaurant, driving range, and golf club rentals. There are also private rooms for hire that can cater for up to one hundred people – there is also ample parking outside. The Bay View Grill is open Monday to Saturday from 6 am. until 2 pm. and Sunday from 11 am. until 2 pm. – there is also a snack bar. Private lessons and golfing clinics are available from the course pro, and will be suitable for every level of player.

The green fees at Bay View are very reasonable. Visitors only need to pay $26 for 18 holes during the week and $34 at the weekends. A 9-hole game costs $18 during the week or $26 at the weekend. This does not include the cost of a golf cart, which adds another $18 onto the price ($14 for nine holes). Residents only pay $13 ($17 at the weekend) for an 18-hole game and $9 ($13 at the weekend) for a 9-hole game. There are other discounted prices for juniors and seniors.

Kahuku Golf Course

56-501 Kamehameha Highway, Kahuku, HI 96731
Website: www1.honolulu.gov/des/golf/kahuku.htm
Yelp Rating: 4 stars (based on 8 reviews)
Phone: (808) 293-5842
9 Holes: Par 36

The Kahuku Golf Course is another municipal course on Oahu, but this one only has nine holes. Players can enjoy a full game by going around twice. This is a laid-back and friendly course, and it is the type of place where you can turn up in shorts and a t-shirt – unlike many of the private clubs where there is a strict dress code. This is a relatively flat course, and it can be challenging when the wind is blowing hard. Kahuku Golf Course is located in North Oahu, and players get to enjoy some nice views of the coast. Overall, it is a nice place to go for a fun game of golf, and the cost of playing here is very reasonable. It is not as busy here as the municipal course in Honolulu, so there is usually no problem getting a teeing off time.

The facilities at Kahuku Golf Course are limited. There is no restaurant or snack bar so players are advised to bring along their own food and drink – there are some vending machines and picnic tables are available near the clubhouse. Kahuku doesn't have a pro shop, but it is possible to rent clubs and a hand cart (there are no motorized carts at Kahuku).

One of the main attractions of Kahuku golf course is the price. Visitors only need to pay $12 for 9-holes. If they wish to do the full 18-holes it costs just $18. Residents of Oahu with Golf ID pay even less to play here.

Turtle Bay Resort Golf

(Fazio Course and Palmer Course)
57049 Kuilima Drive, Kahuku, HI 96731
Website: TurtleBayResort.com/hawaii_golf/
Yelp Rating: 3.5 stars (based on 23 reviews)
Phone: (808) 293-8574
Fazio Course 18-Hole: Par 72
Palmer Course 18-Hole: Par 72

Turtle Bay is one of the most exclusive resorts in the north of Oahu. They have two golf courses to choose from – Fazio Course and Palmer Course. Fazio Course was designed by Thomas Fazio, and it is the easier of the two courses. There have been some important competitions held here including the LPGA Hawaiian Open. This course has been described as 'walker-friendly', and players get to enjoy some nice views of the north shore. The Palmer Course is considered to be one of the best courses on the island and it has received praise from the likes of Golf Digest and Travel & Leisure Magazine. This course is right beside the coast, and it passes through some stunning natural wetlands. This course was designed by Arnold Palmer, and it opened in 1992.

The facilities for the two golf courses are superb. Both Fazio Course and Palmer Course have their own practice area – this includes a driving range, putting green, and short-play area. Players get to retire to one of the many dining or bar option at the end of their game. Lei Lei's Bar & Grill at Fazio Course is very popular, and this open-air venue serves tasty fresh seafood as well as plenty of local dishes. Turtle Bay also has a few pros available to provide private lessons or golfing clinics.

There are a number of packages available for anyone who wants to play at Turtle Bay. Those who are not staying at the resort can pay $175 to play at Fazio or $195 to play at Palmer (this includes transportation to the course). If visitors can make their own way to the course, they only need to pay $160 for Fazio or $185 for Palmer. There is also a five-day unlimited golf package available to non-guests for $499. Guests of Turtle Bay enjoy a 25 percent discount on the standard price. A one-hour private lesson with one of the pros costs $85, and there are also options like a ten-minute tune-up ($20 or free for guests), full-day instruction ($350), or a golf and fitness course ($170).

Olomana Golf Links

41-1801 Kalanianaole Highway, Waimanalo, HI 96795
Website: OlomanaGolfLinks.com
Yelp Rating: 3 stars (based on 25 reviews)
Phone: (808) 259-7926
18-Holes: Par 72

Olomana Golf Links offers a good mix between affordability and a high-quality course. President Obama once played here, and he is said to have made some impressive shots. This is an old course, but it is kept in a good state of repair. Players are treated to some nice views of the Ko'olau Mountain Range as they make their way around the course. The ground here can be a bit lumpy, but overall this is a good course for beginner and intermediate players. Olomana Golf Links is on the windy part of the island, so this can make shots a bit more challenging.

The clubhouse at Olomana is pretty good. It is a family-friendly space, and the restaurant offers a good selection of dishes for breakfast, lunch, and dinner. They also offer a full range of beers and wines. The lounge area of the clubhouse overlooks the course, and there are also a big screen TV in here as well. It is possible to hire a room here for a social function, and this can be a nice choice for business gatherings, parties, or wedding receptions. Practice facilities include a driving range.

The regular price for playing at Olomana Golf Links is $95. If people intend to play here regularly, they can join the Pacific Links Golf Oahu Program for $60, and this means a significant reduction on the standard price. Holders of this card also have priority when booking, and they can use the driving range as much as they want – they will also be able to attend some free golfing clinics.

Hawaii Kai Golf Course

(Hawaii Kai Championship Course and Executive Course)

8902 Kalanianaole Highway, Honolulu, HI 96825
Website: HawaiiKaiGolf.com/e/
Yelp Rating: 3 stars (based on 21 reviews)
Email: proshop@hawaiikaigolf.com
Phone: (808) 395-2358
Hawaii Kai Championship Course 18 Holes: Par 72
Hawaii Kai Executive Course 18 Holes: Par 54

Hawaii Kai offers two courses to choose from. The Executive Course is a great option for beginners or people who have not played in a long time. It has been designed with the emphasis is on helping players improve at putting and chipping – all holes are par 3. There are many golfers who played their first ever round here, and it is perfect for this purpose. The Championship Course offers far more of a challenge. It is made up of wide fairways and large greens. The surrounding scenery is simply stunning, and it includes plenty of views of the sea as well as the Makapu'u Cliffs – it is recommended that players take along their camera with them because there will be plenty of photo opportunities. The ability to keep the ball straight when the winds are blowing is the secret to success here.

Hawaii Kai has a cozy clubhouse at the rear of the course with locker rooms, a restaurant, bar, and well-stocked pro shop. The Queen's Beach Restaurant has been newly refurbished, and they sell a good selection of breakfast items, salads, local food, and full meals. It is possible to rent a function room at the clubhouse to comfortably sit up to 250 people – they can also provide a banquet. There is also a full selection of beer, wines, spirits, and soft drinks available – a beer cart also does rounds on the course. There is also a driving range here as well.

The standard fee to play on the Championship Course is $110 for 18-holes (this includes an electric cart). Players who are willing to go out after 1 pm. only need to pay $70, but this is only available on weekdays. It costs $35 to rent a set of clubs (sets for men and women available) and $8 to rent shoes. It costs $38.50 to play on the Executive Course during the weekdays and $43.50 at the weekends. It costs $15 to rent a set of clubs suitable for this course. All prices here are correct as of late-2013.

Ted Makalena Golf Course

93-059 Waipio Point Access Road, Waipahu, HI 96797
Website: www1.honolulu.gov/des/golf/makalena.htm
Yelp Rating: 3.5 stars (based on 7 reviews)
Phone: (808) 675-6050
18 Holes: Par 71

Ted Makalena is a local golfing hero who won the PGA Tour's Hawaiian Open (now called the Sony Open) during the sixties – this municipal course is named in his honor. The ground here is mostly flat, and it is another good option for beginner players – or anyone who just wants a fun game. The first nine holes are relatively easy, but things pick up a bit on the back nine. Ted Makalena Golf Course is rarely busy so it is usually no problem booking a tee time. The staff members at this venue are good at keeping the grounds well maintained.

There is not much in the way of facilities at the Ted Makalena Golf Course. There is no pro shop and no restaurant. It is highly recommended that visitors bring along at least a couple of liters of water with them. There are some putting greens available at the course, but there is no driving range.

The standard green fee for the Ted Makalena Golf Course is $55. If players have Golf ID (they need to be a resident to get this), they only need to pay $32 – this includes a cart.

Golf on Kauai

Kauai is a great choice of destination for golf lovers who want to experience playing a few rounds of golf on a tropical island. The more exclusive golf courses can be quite expensive, but it is possible to hit some balls here for as little as $1 a hole.

Some of the Best Golf Courses on Kauai Include:

Poi Bay Golf Course

2250 Ainako Street, Koloa, HI 96756
Website: PoipuBayGolf.com
Yelp Rating: 4.5 stars (based on 16 reviews)
Phone: (808) 742-8711 or toll free (800) 858-6300
18-Holes: Par 72

Poipu Bay Golf Course served as the home of the PGA Grand Slam between 1994 and 2006. This beautiful venue offers some fabulous views, and it is what golfing in Hawaii should be all about. Every hole is designed to be unique on this course, so each one of them challenges you in a slightly different way. Robert Trent Jones Junior – one of the most admired golf architects in the world, designed Poipu Bay – so playing here really can be an unforgettable experience. The course covers 210 acres and it hugs the ocean – if you are lucky, you might get to spot some humpback whales off in the distance.

The clubhouse at Poipu Bay Golf is almost as impressive as the course. It covers an area of 21,000 square feet, and it includes a pro shop (one of the best stocked in the US), restaurant, locker area, and lounge. The Bay Grill and Bar has an open-air venue, and this can be a nice place to spend a few hours after you have completed a round. This restaurant also provides an excellent view of the golf course, so it can be a nice place for family to wait while you play.

The standard rate for visitors to Poipu Bay Golf Course is $240 for 18-holes – guests of the Grand Hyatt only need to pay $170.

If visitors wish to play a twilight game (after 12 pm.), the price is reduced to $150 – the cost falls even further to $95 after 2 pm. (there is no guarantee that players will get to complete 18-holes if they go out at this time). The green fees at Poipu Bay include the use of a golf cart with GPS tracking. It is possible to book 30-days in advance, and it is recommended that you do this to avoid disappointment. Clubs can be rented at the course for $85 and shoes can be rented for $15 – anyone who wishes to play here needs to wear proper golfing attire.

Puakea Golf Course

4150 Nuhou Street, Lihue, HI 96766
Website: PuakeaGolf.com
Yelp Rating: 4 stars (based on 11 reviews)
Phone: (808) 245-8756
18 Holes: Par 72

Puakea Golf Course offers a tropical golfing experience at a fairly reasonable price –it is probably the best option if you are on a tight budget but still want to play somewhere with special ambiance. Each hole is unique, and the front nine offers a significantly different experience than the back nine - one of the nice things about playing here is you almost feel like you are visiting two courses. The ground is hilly for most of the course, and there are some nice views of the ocean. This venue is managed by Billy Casper Golf – the same management team that also takes care of Kukuiolono Park & Golf Course (see below).

The clubhouse offers some decent amenities. The Ho'okipa Café is open from 7 am. to around sunset, and it offers a good selection of drinks and snacks – it is open to the public, and it tends to attract a nice crowd. The pro shop is rather small, but it contains all the most important items you might need to buy. There is a grass driving range, putting green, and practice sand bunker. The PGA professionals who work at Puakea are able to provide lessons on request.

It costs $99 to play at Puakea before 11 am., $85 after 11 am., and $59 after 2 pm. (prices correct as of late 2013). There are also special packages available where you can get a discount if you book more than three rounds. It costs $45 to rent a set of clubs – the price falls to $25 after 2 pm.

Kauai Lagoons Golf Club

3351 Hoolaulea Way, Lihue, HI 96766
Website: Marriott.com/golf-hotels/lihkn-marriotts-kauai-lagoons/kauai-lagoons-golf-club/5238786/home-page.mi
Yelp Rating: 4 stars (based on 9 reviews)
Phone: (800) 634-6400
18-Holes: Par 71
9-holes: Par 36

There are two main courses to choose from at Kauai Lagoons Golf Club. The 18-hole course offers some of the best views on Kauai – it also has the longest stretch of holes along the coast in the whole of Hawaii. The Waikahe 9-Hole course is inland, and this one is perfect for beginners or those who just want a quick game. The main course (Kiele Course) at Kauai Lagoons was designed by Jack Nicklaus back in the eighties. Kauai Lagoons covers an area of 750 acres at Kalapaki Bay – it is just a few minutes away from Lihue Airport.

The clubhouse at Kauai Lagoons is a great place to go at the end of the game. When you arrive back you can expect to be greeted with ice-cold towels and a warm welcome. The lobby is open-air and the rest of the building manages to combine a modern-feel with a sense of traditional elegance. There are plenty of places both inside and outside the building to kick back after a round of golf and enjoy some refreshments. The pro shop here opens from 6:30 am. to 6 pm., and it offers a good range of products including specialty logo wear. There is a driving range and putting green as well as a small free course for children.

Visitors to Kauai Lagoons Golf Club pay $205 to play in the mornings or $135 after twelve o'clock. If you are staying at the

Marriott, it costs $150 in the morning and $115 after twelve –
there is also a discount for some other up-market hotels on the
island. It costs $30 to play the 9-hole if you are prepared to walk
or $45 if you need a cart. Players under the age of 17 have to pay
$60 on the main course or $15 on the inland nine. The practice
areas are free to use and open at 7 am. It costs $50 to rent a full
set of golf clubs for 18-holes and $10 for golf shoes.

Princeville Prince Golf Course

5-3900 Kuhio Highway, Princeville, HI 96722
Website: Princeville.com/golf
Yelp Rating: 4.5 stars (based on 11 reviews)
Phone: (808) 826-5001
18-Holes: Par 72
6-Holes: Par 18

Prince Golf Course is part of Princeville Resort. The main course
is 18-holes, but there is also a nice 6-hole course where each one
is par-3 – a great choice if you just want to practice or have some
fun. The Prince Course had a $5 million facelift in 2012, and it is
now definitely one of the most attractive places to play on the
island – it is considered to be one of the most beautiful places to
play golf in the world. This is not an easy course; so don't be
surprised if you lose a lot of balls.

The clubhouse at Princeville offers a wonderful view of the golf
course and the Pacific Ocean. It has been newly decorated and
covers an area of 60,000 square feet. The design of this building
is a combination of traditional Hawaiian with modern chic.
Visitors can pick up some purchases at the well-stocked pro
shop, or spend some time at the Tavern at Princeville – this is a
great little eatery with a world-class chef.

Prince Golf Course is one of the most expensive places to play
on the island with green fees for visitors starting at $200 (prices
correct as of late 2013). It costs $45 to play the mini 6-hole
course. Guests who are staying at the Princeville Resort get to

enjoy a discount – the best deal is a package that includes accommodation and golfing.

Kiahuna Golf Club

2545 Kiahuna Plantation Drive, Koloa, HI 96756
Website: KiahunaGolf.com
Yelp Rating: 4 stars (based on 8 reviews)
Phone: (808) 742-9595
18-Holes: Par 70

Kiahuna is another golf course on the island that was created by the legendary architect Robert Trent Jones Junior (he also designed the course at Poipu and Princeville). This course is going to appeal most to those players who want to be challenged. The greens are fast and even the best players are going to need to play exceptionally well when the winds are blowing – the second hole is the hardest of all. There are some nice features on the course to admire including; lava tubes, caves, archeological sites, ponds, and a stream.

The highlight of the Clubhouse is Joe's on the Green. This restaurant opens at 7 am., and they offer a great selection of breakfast items. Food is served here right up until 7 pm., and they have live music in the evenings. The bar is fully stocked with a good selection of wines and cocktails as well as beers. The pro shop sells a good selection of equipment and it stocks all the big-name brands.

It costs $95 to play at Kiahuna in the mornings, and the price falls to $75 after midday. Players under the age of 17 only need to pay $10 so long as a paying adult accompanies them. It costs $32 to rent a set of clubs.

Wailua Golf Course

3-5350 Kuhio Highway, Lihue, HI 96766
Website: Kauai.gov/default.aspx?tabid=66

Yelp Rating: 3.5 stars (based on 9 reviews)
Phone: (808) 241-6666
18 Holes: Par 72

Wailua is a municipal golf course, so it is a good option if you are just looking for a round of golf without it being anything too fancy. This course once served as a qualifying course for the US Open (back in the thirties), but it has long been overshadowed by the private clubs on the island. The morning times tend to be when all the serious golfers turn up – things are a bit more laid-back in the afternoon.

The amenities at Wailua include: a restaurant, small pro shop, shower area, locker rooms, short driving range, putting green, practice bunker, and chipping green. At the moment the restaurant (late 2013) is closed so players need to bring their own food and refreshments if they want something to eat or drink after their game.

It costs $48 for visitors to play here on a weekday or $60 at the weekends. If you are prepared to play during the twilight hours, it is half the daily rate. There is also a special offer available whereby non-residents can purchase five rounds for $215 – these games must be played during the week and within a three-month period. It costs $20 to rent a motorized cart or $7 for a pull-cart. A set of premium golf clubs costs $35 (there is a cheaper set available for $20). If you want to use the driving range, it costs $2 for balls.

Kukuiolono Golf Course

854 Puu Road, Kalaheo, HI 96741
Website: N/A
Yelp Rating: 4 stars (based on 14 reviews)
Phone: (808) 332-9151
9 Holes: Par 36

Kukuiolono is another public golf course that another one worth considering if you are on a tight budget. There are only nine holes here, but you can play twice to make up a full game. This is a great course for beginners because the play here never gets too challenging. It's quite a beautiful place to spend the morning – it was originally an estate but it was later gifted to the people of Hawaii by the owner. This is one of the few courses on the island where you are welcome to play in shorts and a t-shirt.

There facilities at Kukuiolono Golf Course are modest. There is a small restaurant and a place where you can rent equipment. If you are going to rent clubs, you need to have them back by 3 pm. There is a nice driving range here that offers an excellent view of the ocean.

The greatest thing about Kukuiolono Golf Course is the price. You can play here for as little as $9 – that is $1 per hole. It is also important to keep in mind those visitors who only want to watch you play still need to pay. You can rent clubs and a golf cart for about $20 here.

Makai Golf Course

4080 Lei O Papa Road, Princeville, HI 96722
Website: MakaiGolf.com
Yelp Rating: 5 stars (based on 2 reviews)
Phone: (808) 826-1912
19 Holes: Par 72

Makai was redesigned back in 2009, and it is another course on the island that comes from the imagination of Robert Trent Jones Jr. It is part of the Princeville Resort who also has Prince Golf Course (see above). As well as the 18-hole course, there is also the 9-Hole Woods Course that is perfect for beginners. Makai is one of the best places on Kauai to go if you are looking for instruction as they have regular clinics and two large practice areas – there are also plenty of pros around to offer instruction on how to improve your swing.

The clubhouse at Makai is newly built, and it is a nice place to spend some time after a game. The Makai Grill is open from 7 am. to 4 pm., and they offer a good selection of snacks and beverages. It is also possible to hire the clubhouse for special events like weddings.

The standard green fee for the 18-hole course at the Makai is $225 making it the most expensive course on the island – this price falls to $149 after 12 pm. If you intend to play a few rounds at this course during your trip, you can purchase the Makai Golf Pass for $435 – this allows you to play three games. The Woods Course costs $55 for 9-holes.

Golfing on Molokai and Lanai

There is a sense of exclusivity when you arrive on either of these two islands because you are off the beaten track. You can expect a friendly welcome and the chance to enjoy some amazing scenery while playing golf in this part of the world.

Lanai has two excellent courses – *the Challenges at Manele* and *the Experiences at Koele.* You don't need to stay on the island to play these courses – you can come over on a day-trip and have plenty of time to get a game in. There are a number of tour companies offering special package deals that include ferry over and a round of golf.

There is only one 9-hole course open at the moment on Molokai. If you intend to play here, it is recommended that you bring along your own golf balls and other necessary equipment. There is no pro shop on the island, but you can rent clubs.

The Challenges at Manele

One Manele Bay Road, Lanai City, HI 96763
Website: FourSeasons.com/manelebay/golf.html
Yelp Rating: 4.5 stars (based on 13 reviews)
Phone: (808) 565-2000
18 Holes: 72

The Challenges at Manele is part of the Four Seasons resort on Lanai, and it is known as one of the most beautiful courses in the world. It was designed by Jack Nicklaus, and it benefits from a perfect location overlooking Hulopoe's Bay. Bill Gates was married here on the 12th hole - the couple couldn't have picked a nicer spot for their nuptials. This is a challenging course with unforgiving fairways. Even golf pros are likely to struggle on the seventeenth hole. You can expect to lose at least a few balls with most of them ending up in the sea, but it is still going to be a worthwhile experience. This is the type of course that everyone should play at least once in their lives. The Challenges at Manele also has a driving range and putting green.

It is worth visiting the Challenges just to spend a bit of time in the clubhouse. This venue is located right beside the cliffs, and this means you get to enjoy a perfect view of the Pacific Ocean. You may even get to see some dolphins. The restaurant opens every day from 11 am. to 3 pm., and it is one of the best places to eat on the island. They serve a good selection of salads, seafood, burgers, wraps, as well as some local dishes. There is also a pro shop in the clubhouse, and it is also possible to arrange lessons.

The Challenges at Manele opens every day from 6:30 am. to 4:30 pm. The standard price for playing here is $225 including a cart. Weekend prices remain the same. Guests of the Four Seasons can get a reduction on this price. If you are arriving on the island for a day of golf at the Challenges, you can pick up the free shuttle service from Manele Harbor.

The Experience at Koele

One Keomoku Highway, Lanai City, HI 96763
Website: FourSeasons.com/koele/golf.html
Yelp Rating: 4.5 stars (based on 10 reviews)
Phone: (808) 565-4000
18 Holes: par 72

The Experience at Koele is also part of the Four Seasons Resort, but it manages to provide a very different experience than

Challenges at Manele. It is well worth playing both if you can afford it when visiting Lanai. The Experience at Koele is in a mountainous area of the island (610 meters above sea level), and it benefits from the cooler climate. The course is surrounded by pine and eucalyptus trees, and the lush greenness of the surroundings make it visually stunning – there are also seven lakes on the course. The Experience at Koele was designed by Greg Norman and Ted Robinson. This is an easier course than the Challenges, but even the best players will need to play in top form to do well here.

The Experiences at Koele clubhouse isn't as impressive as the one at Challenges at Manele, but it's still a nice place to visit after a strenuous round of golf. They are only open for lunch and offer a reasonably good selection of snacks and light meals. You can eat on the terrace or inside in the beautifully furnished restaurant. There is also a fully stocked bar. The clubhouse also has a pro shop, and it is possible to arrange private golfing lessons.

It costs $225 to play 18-holes at the Experiences at Koele – price includes a golf cart. Players who are staying at the Four Seasons resort pay $210. There is a driving range and practice area close to the clubhouse.

Ironwood Hills Golf Club

Kalae Highway, Kualapuu, HI 96757
Website: MolokaiGolfCourse.com
Yelp Rating: N/A
Phone: (808) 567-6000
9-Hole: Par 34

Ironwood Hills Golf Club is a relaxing venue that offers enough challenges to make it suitable for the more skilled player as well as the beginner. There are nine holes here. This is a plantation-style golf course that is surrounded by eucalyptus trees – the course is located in a beautiful part of the island that benefits from a nice cool breeze most of the time. One of the most interesting things about Ironwood Hills is that there are dramatic elevation changes, which makes playing here all the more exciting.

There is a small clubhouse at Iron Hills Golf Club. It is possible to hire some equipment here. It is run by Darrell Rego, the resident pro. Darrell is there to answer questions and make players feel welcome. There is no pro shop or restaurant, so players are advised to take everything they need with them. Iron Hills also doesn't have a driving range. This course is popular with the locals, so it can be a good idea to phone ahead to make a booking.

It costs $36 to play at Iron Hills Golf Club in the mornings – this includes the price of a golf cart and 9-holes. If you want to go out in the afternoon, the price is reduced to $20.

Kaluakoi Golf Course

Kepuhi Beach, Maunaloa, Molokai, Hawaii 96770
Website: N/A
Yelp Rating: N/A
Phone: N/A
18 Holes: Par 72

Kaluakoi Golf Course is currently closed (November 2013), and the course is in a state of disrepair. This was the only 18-hole course on the island, and it was fairly popular because of its beautiful location. It is expected that Kaluakoi will reopen at some point in the not-too-distant future.

24 – SHOPPING

The best shopping in Hawaii is found on the island of Oahu. The city of Honolulu is the most obvious destination if you have money to spend, and here you will find huge markets, high-end boutiques, and shopping malls. All of the usual US department stores (Costco, Wall-Mart, Best Buy, and Radio Shack) have outlets across the city, and there are also plenty of unique options as well. Other rewarding shopping experiences are to be found elsewhere on the island in places like Kailua, Haleiwa, and Kapolei. A visit to a farmers' market is a must during a trip to Oahu if you wish to enjoy an authentic shopping experience.

What to Buy on Oahu?

It is nice to pick up some local products when visiting somewhere exotic like Oahu. You are going to be bombarded with shops selling things like Hawaiian shirts and Aloha t-shirts, but there are also plenty of unique gifts available as well. Some of the local products you can choose from include:

• Hawaiian Coffee – try Waialua Estate Coffee

• Shell jewelry

• Hawaiian salad dressing

• Ukulele

• Objects made from monkey pod wood (Albizia saman)

• Koa wood ring

• Fresh island fruit (such as papaya, longan, Lychee, pineapple, star fruit, and mango)

• Macadamia Nuts

- Local jams

- Traditional clothing

- Hawaiian print bags

- Hawaiian teas

- Hawaiian Leis

- Paintings or other work by local artists

- Hawaiian style chili sauces

- Surf boards – you will find plenty of small shops in the main surfing areas of the island such as Haleiwa.

Main Shopping Areas on Oahu Include:

Honolulu Downtown

Honolulu is the largest city and capital of Hawaii – it has a population of one million people. One of the best places to go shopping in the downtown area would be the Ala Moana Shopping Center (see below). There is a Chinatown to the east of the downtown area, and this is a good place to go for exotic fruit and Asian groceries. The area close to the intersection at Nuuanu and Pauahi is good for things like antiques and art. The Aloha Tower Marketplace (see below) is located down by the waterfront.

Waikiki

Waikiki is the main tourist area in Honolulu – it is to the east of downtown. There are many resorts and hotels here and plenty of great opportunities to go shopping. The International Market

Place is on Kalakaua Avenue (see below), and there are also plenty of malls to choose from such as the Royal Hawaiian Shopping Center, DFS Galleria, and Waikiki Shopping Plaza (see below). If you are looking for an old fashioned grocery store, you might want to check out the Food Pantry (2370 Kuhio Avenue, Honolulu, HI 96815).

Kailua

There are a few notable shopping opportunities here such as the Kailua Town Center Mall (see below). Global Village (539 Kailua Road 104, Kailua, HI 96734) is a 'mom n pop' boutique which sells locally crafted jewelry as well as clothing for men, women, and children. The East Honolulu Clothing Company is a good option if you are looking for cool clothing that you won't find anywhere else on the island.

Kapolei

Kapolei is becoming a real jewel when it comes to opportunities for shopping. This town has undergone a great deal of development in recent years, and local commerce is really starting to blossom. The best selection of outlets is to be found at the Kapolei Shopping Center (see below).

Haleiwa

Haleiwa (Hale'iwa) is a small town on the north of the island. There are some charming looking shops (plantation style buildings) here where you can pick up things like surf boards. It's a laid-back kind of place, and most of the visitors who come here spend their time riding the waves. If you have a sweet tooth, you will want to check out the North Shore Chocolate Factory (66-470 Kamehameha Highway, Haleiwa, HI 96712). There are a number of art galleries in the area where you can pick up some interesting items to take home. There is a farmer's market here on Thursdays between 3 pm. and 6 pm. (see below).

Best Malls on Oahu

There are some excellent indoor and outdoor malls to choose from on Oahu.

Ala Moana Shopping Center

1450 Ala Moana Boulevard, Honolulu, Oahu, HI 96814
Hours: Monday to Saturday 9:30 am. to 9 pm. and Sunday 10 am. to 7 pm.
Website: AlaMoanaCenter.com
Ala Moana is the largest shopping center in Hawaii and the largest outdoor mall in the world. This is a shopper's paradise with over 300 stores and restaurants to choose from. You could walk around Ala Moana for hours and still only scratch the surface of what is available here – it covers an area of 2,100,000 square feet. There is a good mix of shops selling luxury goods (e.g. Tiffany & Co., Prada, and Lacoste) as well as plenty of mid-range shops and places selling local crafts and souvenirs. There are four department stores including Macy's, Shirokiya, Nordstrom, and Neiman Marcus. Other popular stores at Ala Moana include Banana Republic, Longs Drugs, ABC Stores and GameStop. There are also many dining options such as the California Pizza Kitchen, McDonalds, Chinatown Express, Subway, and the Steak & Fish Company.

Kahala Mall Shopping Center

4211 Waialae Avenue, Honolulu, Oahu, HI 96816
Hours: Monday to Saturday 10 am. to 9 am. and Sunday 10 am. to 6 pm.
Website: KahalaMallCenter.com
Kahala Mall Shopping Center is the largest indoor mall in Hawaii. It is a bit less intense than Ala Moana because it tends to be less crowded – the fact that it is indoors with air-conditioning means it is a good place to go to escape the heat. There is a good range of shops to be found here including the big names like: Macy's, the Whole Foods Market, Banana Republic, Longs

Drugs, Radio Shack, Sunglass Hut, T-Mobile, The Walking Company, and Verizon. Anyone who wants to work on their physical fitness can check out Core Power Yoga or the free Tai Chi lessons available at the center court on Mondays, Wednesdays and Saturdays (8 am. to 9 am.). Diners get to choose from plenty of great options like Aloha Salads, California Pizza Kitchen, Chili's Grill & Bar, Taco Bell, Panda Express, and Pizza Hut.

Mililani Shopping Center

95-390 Kuahelani Avenue Building 2, Mililani, HI 96789
Hours: Twenty-four hours for some businesses
Website: MililaniShoppingCenter.com
Visitors to Mililani will find a much better selection of shops in the shopping center than they will in the nearby town center. It can sometimes be difficult to find parking outside of here but a free space will always become available if you are patient. There are about seventy shops and restaurants to choose from here including: GameStop, Jamba Juice, Jack in The Box, T-Mobile, and Foodland. There is also a branch of 24 Hour Fitness.

Royal Hawaiian Shopping Center

2201 Kalakaua Avenue, Honolulu, HI 96815
Hours: Monday to Sunday 10 am. to 10 pm.
Website: RoyalHawaiianCenter.com
The Royal Hawaiian Shopping Center is the largest mall in Waikiki. There are 110 shops and restaurants here to explore. Big spenders will be able to burn off some money by visiting high-end places like Rolex Kaimana Kea, Ferrari, Cartier, Hermès, Marciano, or Salvatore Ferragamo. This is not the best place on the island to go if you are looking for a bargain, but this venue does provide a nice shopping experience. The food court here is particularly good with a wide selection of options. The Royal Hawaiian Shopping Center provides a complimentary cultural program which includes things like live Hawaiian music and dancing, ukulele lessons, hula dancing, lei-making, and

Hawaiian quilting – check out their website for the events on this week.

Waikiki Shopping Plaza

2250 Kalakaua Avenue, Honolulu, HI 96815
Hours: Monday to Sunday 10 am. to 10 pm.
Website: WaikikiShoppingPlaza.com
Waikiki Shopping Plaza is another shopping destination where the focus is on tourists with plenty of money to spend. There are a number of specialized shops here such as Victoria Secret's, Armani, and Alter Ego. Waikiki Shopping Plaza is divided into three different buildings, so it can get a bit confusing to get around if it is your first time. The food court here has a good variety of options, but it is not as good as the one at the nearby Royal Hawaiian Shopping Center. They have nightly shows here in the lobby, and they also offer free Hawaiian quilting lessons on Tuesdays and Fridays at 5:30 pm. – although anyone who wants to take part will need to purchase a $32 quilting kit (as of late 2013).

DFS Galleria

330 Royal Hawaiian Avenue, Honolulu, HI 96815
Hours: Monday to Sunday 10 am. to 11 pm.
Website: DFSGalleria.com/en/hawaii
The DFS Galleria is the place to go for duty free shopping. There are thousands of products here to choose from, and the fact that there is no tax (for foreign tourists) to pay means that it is possible to pick up some good bargains including top brands like DKNY, Burberry, Coach, and Ray-Ban. One of the really nice things about this place is you can pick up plenty of free samples, and they also have a DJ here every Saturday between 8 pm. and 10 pm. – one option if you are looking for a cheap night out.

Kailua Town Center Mall

609 Kailua Rodd, Kailua, HI 96734
Hours: Individual shops have their own set hours
Website: KaneoheRanch.com/explore-home/
Kailua Town Center Mall is part of Kaneohe Ranch and spread
out over a number of streets (all of the properties are owned by
Harold K.L. Castle and Alice H. Castle). This is a pedestrianized
area with and the architecture of the buildings based on a modern
Hawaiian style. Shops here include Longs Drugs, Whole Food
Market, Foodland Super Market, Bookends, Game Stop, Macy's,
and Radio Shack. There is also a good selection of dining options
such as Bob's Pizzeria, Jamba Juice, K & K Barbecue Inn, Maui
Tacos, Teddy's Bigger Burgers, and Subway.

Aloha Tower Marketplace

1 Aloha Tower Drive, Honolulu, HI 96813, United States
Hours: Monday to Saturday 9 am. to 9 pm. and Sunday 9 am. to
6 pm.
Website: AlohaTower.com
Aloha Tower Marketplace is located down by the harbor area of
Downtown Honolulu. The focal point of this area is the Aloha
Tower, and you can go up here for free to enjoy some nice
panoramic views of the city. This is a lovely area to walk around,
especially where there is a nice sea breeze, and there are plenty
of options for shopping as well as dining. There is live music
here throughout the week at different times throughout the day
(see their calendar for details). There are shops selling every type
of item imaginable including: clothing, accessories, home décor
items, candles, sarongs, local art, jewelry, Hawaiian print bags,
children's toys, and macadamia nuts. There is also an abundance
of places to eat and drink.

Kapolei Shopping Center

91-590 Farrington Highway, Kapolei, HI 96707
Hours: Individual shops set their own hours. Some open 24 hours
Website: InKapolei.com

There are about thirty stores at Kapolei Shopping Center including options such as: Safeway, Radio Shack, Longs Drugs, AT&T Wireless, Jeans Warehouse, GameStop, and Kapolei Jewelry. It is a convenient place to shop, but there can be a problem finding a parking space when it is busy – it is best to come here early in the morning or late in the evening if you have a car. Dining options at Kapolei Shopping Center include: Taco Bell, Tasty Korean Barbeque, Subway, Sushi Bay, Baskin Robbins, KFC, McDonalds, and Chili's Grill & Bar.

Best Markets on Oahu

One of the real joys of shopping in Oahu is visiting the farmers markets and swap meets. Some of the best options for this would include:

International Market Place

2330 Kalakaua Avenue, Honolulu, HI 96815, United States
Hours: Monday to Sunday 10 am. to 9 pm.
Website: InternationalMarketplaceWaikiki.com
The International Market Place arguably offers the most interesting shopping experience in the whole of Hawaii. The best day to go here is usually Thursday when the place is in full swing. There does tend to be many stalls selling similar things, but this level of competition also makes it easier to pick up a bargain. This is the place to go if you are looking for cheap souvenirs, clothing, knick-knacks, traditional crafts, jewelry, beach wear, and new age products. It is highly recommended that you haggle hard here – if you accept the original price you will be paying more than you need to. There are also many stalls where you can pick up some tasty snacks or food to take home.

Aloha Stadium Swap Meet

99-500 Salt Lake Boulevard, Honolulu, Oahu, HI 96818

Hours: Wednesdays and Saturdays 8 am. to 3 pm. and Sunday 6:30 am. to 3 pm. (some Saturdays closed for the UH Football Season).
Website: AlohaStadiumSwapMeet.net
It costs one dollar to gain admission to Aloha Swap Meet and for that price you have the opportunity to pick up some of the best bargains on the island. Souvenirs can be significantly cheaper here than you will pay in the resort areas, but you have to be willing to haggle. This is the largest open-air market in Hawaii with usually around three hundred sellers. Vendors set up their stalls in a ring shape around the stadium, and it can take a few hours to do this market justice.

KCC Farmers' Market

Kapiolani Community College, 4303 Diamond Head Road, Honolulu, HI 96816
Hours: Tuesday 4 pm. to 7 pm. and Saturday 7:30 am. to 11 am.
Website: HFBF.org/markets/markets/kcc/

KCC Farmers' Market is a superb option if you are looking for fresh fruit and vegetables. It is best to get here early if you want to have a good selection of products. There are also plenty of cooked food options and snacks if you want to eat something on the go. You can also pick up flowers and plants here including orchids. It does get crowded here, but it has a nice atmosphere.

Haleiwa Farmers' Market

Beautiful Waimea Valley, 59-864 Kamehameha Highway, Haleiwa, HI 96712
Hours: Thursday 3 pm. to 6 pm.
Website: HaleiwaFarmersMarket.com/haleiwa.html
Here you will find a good selection of locally grown products. They also usually have some live music, so it can be a pleasant place to visit for a couple of hours on a Thursday afternoon. On busy days a lot of the fruit and vegetables will be long gone before six, so it is a good idea to get here as early as you can.

Kai Farmers' Market

Kaiser High School, parking lot, 511 Lunalilo Home Road,
Hawaii Kai, HI96825
Open Hours: Saturday 9 am. to 1 pm.
Website: HaleiwaFarmersMarket.com/hawaii-kai.html
One of the nice things about Kai Farmer's Market is that it
doesn't get too packed, and it less touristy than some of the other
options. There is a good selection of products on sale including
fresh fruit and vegetables, fresh baked goods, pastries, and even a
fire oven pizza wagon. The market is made up of stalls as well as
product tents.

Best Places to Buy Books on Oahu

You will have no problem finding reading material during your
stay on Oahu. The most popular bookshops include:

Barnes & Noble has a number of stores on the island including
branches at Waialae Avenue (Honolulu), Kahala Mall, Ala
Moana Mall, and Keawe Street (Honolulu).

Bookends can be found at Kailua Town Center Mall

Jelly's Honolulu (98-023 Hekaha Street #9, Aiea, HI 96701)
sells new and used books.

Revolution Books (2626 South King Street, Honolulu, HI
96826) offers an eclectic mix of titles.

**Best Places to Buy Computers, Appliances, and Electrical
Goods on Oahu**

There is an Apple store in Ala Moana Shopping Center, Royal
Hawaiian Shopping Center, and Kahala Mall Shopping Center.
Radio Shack has branches all over the island – including in most
of the malls. Best Buy has a branch on Alakawa Street in
Honolulu. It is also possible to pick up some reasonably priced

computers and electrical goods at Costco. Wal-Mart has branches at Keeaumoku Street (Honolulu), Kuala Street (Pearl City), and Lanikuhana Avenue (Mililani).

Where to Buy Souvenirs on Oahu?

All of the main resorts areas will have an ample selection of shops selling souvenirs, but they can be more expensive to buy here. The International Market Place offers the most choice, and you can pick up some great deals here as well. Another option for souvenirs would be the Aloha Stadium Swap Meet – if you know how to haggle, you will be able to get the best deals here. If you are looking to take back food items, the best option will be the farmers' markets.

One of the most popular souvenirs that people will take back home with them from a trip to Oahu is a ukulele. These are on sale everywhere, but they are not always good quality. If you want to be sure of getting something decent, you might try somewhere like Easy Music Store (1314 South King Street, Honolulu) – they have about fifty different quality models. It is also possible to buy directly from the factories on the island, if you want to get the best possible deal.

Where to Buy Food on Oahu?

If you are looking for cheap groceries you might try Costco – there are branches at Alakawa Street (Honolulu), Ka Uka Boulevard (Waipahu), and Kapolei Parkway (Kapolei). Safeway has branches at Kapahulu Avenue (Honolulu), East Manoa Road (Honolulu), and Farrington Highway (Kapolei). Anyone staying in Waikiki will be able to pick up reasonably priced groceries at the Food Pantry on Kuhio Avenue. If you are looking for fresh goods, the farmers' markets will be the place to go. The Whole Foods Store has branches on Waialae Avenue (Honolulu), and Kailua Road (Kailua).

Where to go shopping with Kids on Oahu?

Kahala Mall Shopping Center has 'toddler time' every Wednesday (10:30 am. – 11:30 am.), and this involves things like crafts, toddler yoga, and fairy stories. Children tend to enjoy the International Market as there are plenty of street performers and interesting stalls, but it might be worth giving this place a miss at peak times. The Rhelm Adventure Theater at Aloha Tower Marketplace is like a cross between a theme park and a children's museum. Haleiwa Farmers' Market puts on activities to keep kids entertained such as arts and crafts.

Shopping on Big Island

The Big Island can be a great place to go shopping so long as you have reasonable expectations. If you are looking for souvenirs, traditional crafts, and local food items you are going to be impressed. There are also a few large malls on the island where you can find the usual chain stores that you find elsewhere in the US. The one shopping experience you won't want to miss on the Big Island will be the farmer's markets – this is the place to go for exotic fruit and vegetables as well as plenty of other fun stuff.

What to Buy on Big Island?

One of the nice things about going shopping when you are on holiday is you get the opportunity to purchase things you would not normally find at home. There are plenty of unique products to look for on Big Island. The local coffee is famous all over the world, so this can be a nice thing to stick in your suitcase. You will also find plenty of exotic fruits and vegetables in the local markets (see below). If you are interested in art, you will find paintings, sculptures, and figurines by local artists – it you are looking to save money it is best to avoid buying these items in the resort areas. You can also find something unique like a paperweight made from the lava of one of the Big Island volcanoes.

Best Shopping Areas on Big Island:

Hilo

Hilo is the largest settlement on Big Island, and you will find a reasonable selection of shops in the downtown area. This is a pleasant area to walk around, and there are some interesting art galleries, restaurants, and cafes. If you are looking for cheap groceries, you will probably want to check out Hilo Farmer's Market on the corner of Mamo Street. If you are looking for books, you might try out Basically Books (see below).

Banyan Drive Area/ Prince Kuhio Plaza Area

The Banyan Drive pedestrianized shopping area is about a mile outside of Hilo. The Prince Kuhio Plaza (see below) is located here, but there are also other shops along this road. If you are looking to buy fabrics, you will certainly want to have a look inside the Discount Fabric Warehouse where they have the largest selection on the island. Visitors with a sweet tooth can check out Big Island Candies where they serve tasty treats like hand-dipped chocolate cookies.

Kailua-Kona

If you have the itch to purchase luxury items, one of the best places to do this will be Kailua-Kona on the west coast. This is where most of the top resorts on Big Island are to be found and so most of the shops are designed specifically to target tourist dollars. There is a mall here called Kona Inn Shopping Village (see below), and this can be a convenient place to go shopping.

Waikoloa

Waikoloa is a resort area in South Kohala. There is where the Hilton and lots of other fancy resorts are located. There is a trendy mall here called Kings' Shops. This is another good place to go for luxury goods and you will find options like Coach and Tiffany.

Honokaa

Honokaa used to be a very prosperous town, but it has witnessed a decline since the loss of the local macadamia nut industry in the nineties. The High Street is a charming place to go for a wander in the early mornings or afternoons. There is a good selection of shops and eateries. The Honokaa Trading Company is well worth a visit if you are looking for souvenirs or collectables.

Best Malls on Big Island

The malls are a convenient place to shop because they are easy to walk around, and they offer a good selection of stores. The best malls on Big Island would include:

Prince Kuhio Plaza

111 Puainako Street, Hilo, HI 96720

Prince Kuhio Plaza is the most popular indoor mall on the island, and it offers the best selection of shops. It opens from 10 am. to 8 pm. Monday to Thursday, 10 am. to 9 pm. on Friday and Saturday, and 10 am. to 6 pm. on Sundays. This is a pleasant mall to wander around even if you are only window shopping because you can escape the heat of the day. The stores here include: Macy's Department Store, Longs Drugs Store, Hallmark, Jeans Warehouse, Radio Shack, Sears, and Toys R Us. You will also find plenty of eateries including: IHOP, Hot Dog on a Stick, KFC, Chen's Chinese Kitchen, Maui Tacos, and Starbucks. Prince Kuhio Plaza also has a large multiplex cinema.

Kawaihae Harbor Shopping Center

Highway 270, Kawaihae, HI 96743

This small mall is close to the seafront in Kawaihae. It is in easy reach of many of the island's top resorts such as the Hilton Waikoloa, Marriott Waikoloa, and Mauna Kea Resort. If you fancy something to eat, you can choose from Avenue (locally made ice-cream), Kawaihae Kitchen (seafood dishes), Cafe Presto, or Kohala Burger and Taco. You can find more food at the Kawaihae Market & Deli. There is also a gallery featuring locally made items, a jewelry shop, and scuba diving shop.

Kings' Shops

Waikoloa Beach Resort, 250 Waikoloa Beach Drive, Waikoloa, HI 96738

King's Shops Mall is inside of Waikoloa Beach Resort, but it is open to the public. There is a shuttle service that runs from many of the nearby hotels, and it operates from 10 am. to 10 pm. Some of the higher-end stores on the island are to be found here including Tiffany & Co, Coach, Baron and Leeds Swiss Watches, and Louis Vuitton. There are also plenty of other stores such as Macy's, The Walking Company, Sunglass Hut, and the Big Island Motorcycle Company. King's Shops Mall is also a good place to go to eat and you can choose from options like The Three Fat Pigs, Island Fish & Chips, Merriman's Market Café, and Kona Brothers Coffee. There is free Wi-Fi throughout this mall, so it can be a good place to go and check up on your email.

Kona Inn Shopping Village

75-5744 Ali'i Drive, Kailua-Kona, HI 96740

The Kona Inn Shopping Village is right on the beach in Kailua-Kona. There are a great variety of shops here – small stores selling local items alongside bigger names like ABC. If you are a bit of an adventure traveler you will find shops here that sell things like surfboards and hiking gear. As you might expect, many of the stores here sell souvenirs and Hawaiian shirts. You will also find plenty of options for refreshments such as Kona Coffee.

Best Markets on Big Island

The most enjoyable shopping experiences on the Big Island are to be found by visiting the local markets. There is a great selection of these to choose from including:

Kona International Market

74-5533 Luhia Street, Kailua-Kona, HI 96740

Kona International Market opens every day of the week from 9 am. to 5 pm. One of the most impressive things about this venue is the huge food court where you can pick up a tasty Hawaiian food plate. The stalls here sell an eclectic mix of items, and you are likely to pick up knick-knacks that you won't find anywhere else on the island. This is nowhere near as big as the International Market in Honolulu, but it is worth a visit – especially for the food court.

Keaau Farmer's Market

16-550 Old Volcano Road Keaau, HI 96749

Keaau Farmer's Market is open on Tuesdays to Saturdays between 7 am. and 5 pm. They have a good selection of locally grown fruits and vegetables. There are also baked good available and some vendors where you can sit down and enjoy a meal. One of the nice things about Keaau Farmer's Market is that it a great place to mingle with the local people.

Ali'i Gardens Marketplace

Ali'i Drive, Kailua-Kona, HI 96740

Ali'i Gardens Marketplace is open Wednesday to Sunday between 9 am. and 5 pm. It is like a mix between a market and a swap meet. There are usually about fifty stalls here selling a wide variety of items such as food, clothing, local crafts, natural soaps, jewelry, flowers, and local coffee. This market is located in a nice setting with plenty of shade. On some days it can be very quiet here, and this means that many of the stalls won't bother setting up.

Hilo Farmer's Market

400 Kamehameha Ave, Hilo, HI 96721

Hilo Farmer's Market is the busiest market on the island, and it was voted as the top US farmer's market by the Huffington Post. It opens Wednesday and Saturday from 6 am. until 4 pm. (these are the best days to come because this is when they have the most stalls open) – the rest of the week it opens from 7 am. to 4 pm. There are about two hundred vendors selling their goods here. If you love food, you are going to love this place. You will also be able to pick up things like local crafts, souvenirs, and fresh flowers.

Best Places to Buy Books on Big Island

Big Island has a good selection of bookstores to choose from such as:

Kona Stories (78-6831 Ali'i Drive, Kailua-Kona, HI 96740) is an independent bookstore offering over 10,000 new and classic titles. They open Monday to Friday from 10 am. to 6 pm., Saturday 10 am. to 5 pm., and Sunday 11 am. to 5 pm.

Basically Books (160 Kamehameha Avenue, Hilo, HI 96720) is a family owned store that specializes in Hawaiian books, but also has a good selection of travel, fiction, science fiction, and children's books. They open Monday to Saturday from 9 am. to 5 pm.

Kona Bay Books (74-5487 Kaiwi Street, Kona, HI 96740) offers the largest selection of used books in the whole of Hawaii – they also sell used DVDs and CDs. This store opens Monday to Sunday from 10 am. to 6 pm.

Mandarin Books (340 Kilauea Avenue, Hilo, HI 96720) sells rare and collectable books as well as printed art.

Best Places to Buy Computers, Appliances, and Electrical Goods on Big Island

You will be able to find most appliances and electrical goods on Big Island, but there is much less choice than you would find in Honolulu. If you are looking for Apple products, Mac Made Easy (73-5618 Maiau Street, Unit B105, Kailua-Kona, HI 96740) is the place to go – this is also the place to go if you need repairs on your Apple devices. There are a few computer shops and electrical goods stores in Prince Kuhio Plaza including a Radio Shack. There is also Bay Side Computer Shop in Hilo (108 Kalakaua Street, Hilo, HI 96720) – they have a great selection of computer accessories, and the members of staff are very knowledgeable and helpful.

Where to Buy Souvenirs on Big Island?

There are plenty of shops selling souvenirs in all of the main tourist areas such as Kailua-Kona and Waikoloa, but you will usually end paying more in these touristy areas. The better option would be to try to pick up a bargain at Hilo Farmer's Market, Kona International Market, or Ali'i Gardens Marketplace (see above). There are also small shops in Downtown Hilo where you can pick up some interesting souvenirs at a reasonable price.

Where to Buy Food on Big Island?

If you are looking to purchase fresh fruit and vegetables, the best place to go will be a Farmer's Market – the one in Hilo (see above) offers the best selection. If you wish to pick up some cheap groceries, you can go to Safeway (75-1027 Henry Street, Kailua-Kona, HI 96740). There is also a Costco (73-5600 Maiau Street, Kailua-Kona, HI 96740), which is often cheaper than Safeway on popular items.

Where to go Shopping with Kids on Big Island?

Kawaihae Harbor Shopping Center is a good option with kids because there is not only the large multiplex cinema, but they also have a kids arcade located close to the food court. Kona International Market will sometimes have performances on their stage that kids will like – they also provide free Beginner ukulele lessons here every Friday between 11 am. and noon (you need to bring your own ukulele).

Shopping on Maui

Maui offers a great range of shopping options including swap meets, farmer's markets, boutique stores, and modern department stores. Visitors to the island will have the opportunity of trying out some of the local goods, and even just window-shopping can be a fun experience in this part of the world.

What to Buy on Maui?

One of the nice things about shopping on Maui is you will find plenty of items that are hard to come by outside of Hawaii. As well as traditional style clothing and souvenirs, you will also find things like Maui coffee, local fruits, Kula onions, dark chocolate with macadamia nuts and specialty cookies. If you intend to spend a lot of time on the beach, it is a good idea to purchase a straw mat like the locals use – this is much better for dealing with sand than a towel. It is also well worth checking out the handcrafted jewelry and handbags, as you will likely pick up something really special for a nice price.

Where to Buy Souvenirs on Maui?

The most popular souvenirs that visitors will pick up during a trip to Maui will include things like Aloha t-shirts and hats. If you are looking for something a bit more unique, you could choose to buy some local coffee, island specialty soaps, local perfumes, or a Maui calendar. You can also pick up some traditional crafts such as a koa wood bowl or jewelry box. One of the best places to pick up Maui souvenirs would be Maui Swap Meet (see markets below) or Maui Hands (an art gallery shop with branches all over the island).

Best Shopping Areas on Maui

There are a number of locations on Maui where shopaholics can really go wild including:

Wailea

Some of the most expensive shops on the island are to be found around Wailea Resort. There are about seventy boutique stores here along with some fancy restaurants. If you enjoy art there are six galleries to choose from where you will be able to pick up work created by some of the local artists. Some of the big name stores with branches at Wailea include: Banana Republic, Coach,

Gucci, Malibu Shirts, Gap (also Baby Gap), Louis Vuitton, L'Occitane En Provence, St John's Boutique, and Tiffany & Co.

Lahaina Main Street (Front Street)

The main street in Lahaina is a mile long, and it offers a good selection of shops and restaurants. The buildings here mostly date back to the early nineteenth century when Lahaina functioned as the capital of Hawaii. It was predominately a whaling town in those days, and it is easy to imagine what it must have been like. This has to be one of the most laid-back shopping streets in the world, and there are plenty of spots where you can just sit down and enjoy the sun.

Ka'anapali

Some of the best shopping in Ka'anapali is to be found at Whaler's Village Mall (see below). There are also plenty of small shops in the area as well, and it is often cheaper to buy from them than go to the mall.

Wailuku

Wailuku was the most popular tourist town on the island a hundred years ago, and it is currently undergoing a bit of a revival. There are some nice boutique shops and mom-and-pop diners to be found on the main street and the alleys. This is a particularly good option if you are on the lookout for antiques. These days Wailuku feels more like a regular town, and this is what can make it such a nice place to visit if you want to get away from the tourist-circus.

Kahului

Kahului is right beside the airport so almost all visitors will at least pass through here. The best shopping options are to be found on Dairy Road (Highway 380), and this is where you will find stores like Wal-Mart, K-Mart, Office Max, Costco, and Eagle Hardware. This tends to be where the local people go for their weekly shopping trip, but it often gets missed by tourists who usually just stick to the resort areas.

Best Malls on Maui

Maui has an impressive selection of modern department stores to choose from. This is the place to go if you are looking for the big-name brands or you just want to escape the heat of the day by shopping in an air-conditioned environment. The most popular malls on the island would include:

Queen Kaahumanu Center

275 West Kaahumanu Avenue, Kahului, HI 96732

The Queen Kaahumanu Center is the biggest mall on Maui. It opens daily from 9:30 am. until 9 pm. – except for Sundays when the opening time is 10 am. to 5 pm. There are well over a dozen shops to choose from including Macy's, Toys R Us, The Walking Company, T-Mobile, Sears, Game Stop, Forever 21 and the Fun Factory. There are also plenty of places to eat such as McDonalds, Panda Express, Fernando's Mexican Grill, Starbucks, and Ben & Jerry's.

Maui Mall

70 East Kaahumanu Avenue, Kahului, HI 96732

Maui Mall is the best department store when it comes to entertainment options. They have a large 12-screen Megaplex Cinema (all digital), and a great choice of restaurants including: Dragon Chinese Restaurant, Tasaka Guri-Guri, Thailand Cuisine, Wendy's, IHOP, Subway Sandwiches, and Pizza Hut. Shopping options include the Whole Foods Market, Longs Drug Store, The Pet Shop, and the YNVU Clothing Company. This is a nice place to go with the family and every week they have 'Family Sunday' when there are extra activities for kids to enjoy.

Whaler's Village

2435 Ka'anapali Parkway, Lahaina, HI 96761

Whaler's Village is probably the most attractive mall on Maui, and it is right beside the Ka'anapali beach. This is an open-air mall so it can get a bit hot if you are walking between shops during the day. The most pleasant times to come here is in the evenings – they open every day from 9:30 am. until 10 pm. There is a small museum on the premises, and this can be a good place to take the kids – they have an impressive whale skeleton on display. There is also a stage in the mall where they have daily activities such as Lei making, hula-hoop lessons, and coconut husking. They have a cultural performance on Monday's Wednesdays, Saturday, and Sunday at 7 pm. There are many high-end stores in Whaler's Village such as Louis Vuitton, Coach, and Tori Richard.

Lahaina Cannery Mall

Lahaina Cannery Mall is completely indoors, so this means that it is a great option on a hot day because of the air-conditioning. This building was once a functioning cannery, but it was converted to a mall almost a quarter of a century ago. They have a Safeway grocery store that stays open twenty-four hours. They also have many clothes shops and a couple of jewelers. Bikers will want to check out the West Maui Harley-Davidson store. There is also a Starbucks. Lahaina Cannery Mall also has a number of dining establishments including: Chopsticks Express, Edo Japan, Casa Maya Mexican Restaurant, Dairy Queen, and Lulu's Lahaina Surf Club & Grill.

Best Markets on Maui

The best deals in Maui are usually to be found at the markets. Even if you don't plan on buying anything, it can still be nice to go to these places to just to enjoy the sights, sounds, and smells. Some of the best markets on Maui would include:

Maui Swap Meet

Grounds of the University of Hawaii Maui College, Kaahumanu Avenue, Kahului, HI 96733

The Maui Swap Meet takes place every Saturday between 7 am. and 1 pm. There are over two-hundred vendors here, and they sell every type of product including: baked goods, fresh fruit and vegetables, fresh flowers, souvenirs, knick-knacks, traditional arts and crafts, carvings, cosmetics, clothing, organic food, and hats. There are also plenty of food concessions here as well.

Farmer's Market

3636 Lower Honoapiilani Road, Lahaina, HI 96761

The Farmer's Market is open every day from 7 am. to 7 pm. This is the place to go if you are looking for healthy organic food or vegan products. This is a family run business, and the staff will usually go out of their way to help customers. The prices here are also very reasonable, and most of the food here is locally grown. There is also a nice salad bar with a good selection of options.

Kula Country Farms

375 Koheo Road, Kula, HI 96790

Kula farms can be found right of Kula Highway. It is another family run business, and they also allow other local farmers to sell here as well. They do not officially certify their fruit and vegetables as organic, but they do use integrated pest control which they claim means they can avoid using toxic chemical sprays. They open between 11 am. and 5 pm. on Tuesday to Thursday and 11 am. to 4 pm. on the weekends.

Maui's Fresh Produce Farmers Market

Queen Kaahumanu Center, 275 West Kaahumanu Avenue, Kahului, HI 96732

This farmer's market is open on Tuesdays, Wednesdays, and Fridays between 8 am. and 4 pm. All of the fruit here is locally grown and very good value. There is also usually a good selection of backed goods and other edibles on sale here as well.

Kihei Farmers Market

61 South Kihei Road, Kihei, HI 96753

Kihei Farmers Market opens on weekdays between 8 am. and 4 pm. The vendors take great pride in providing some of the freshest produce on the island and most of it is organic. You can also pick up things like salsa spreads, banana bread, and granola. It is a very laid-back kind of place, and it never really gets busy.

Best Places to Buy Books on Maui

There are few things better in life than spending the day on the beach with a good book. The popularity of the eBook has meant that most of the small bookstores on the island have closed. The best selection of books is to be found at **Barnes & Noble** (325 Keawe Street, Lahaina, HI 96761), and they open every day from 9 am. until 9 pm. Another good option for reading material would be to go to **Kahului Public Library** (90 School St, Kahului, HI 96732), which is close to Maui Mall. There is also a group called **Maui Friends of the Library**, which sells second-hand books at their small shop (Puunene School, Wailuku HI 96793), and occasionally at the local markets.

Best Places to Buy Computers, Appliances, and Electrical Goods on Maui

If you are looking for digital or electrical goods on Maui, you will have a few good options. Fans of the Apple brand can visit **MacNet** (444 Hana Highway, Kahului, HI 96732) – they are an authorized Apple service provider. There is a **Home Depot** on Pakaula Street in Kahului, and this store offers a good selection of home audio equipment and other electrical products. There are also shops Lahaina and Wailuku where you will be able to pick up digital products like cameras and video recorders.

Where to Buy Food on Maui?

If you are looking to do some cheap grocery shopping the best option would probably be Wal-Mart or Costco. For fresh fruit and vegetables, the best option will be one of the Farmer's Markets (see above) – this is also the place to go for organic food. Foodland (1881 S. Kihei Road, Kihei, HI 96753) also offers a good selection of products. Another good place to pick up some food would be Maui Swap Meet – this is only open on Saturdays (see above).

Where to go Shopping with Kids on Maui?

All of the large department stores are kid-friendly on Maui. The Queen Kaahumanu Center offers a large indoor play structure. Maui Mall regularly puts on special activities to attract families – especially on Sundays. Whaler's Village is a good option with kids because they have activities like learning to hula-hoop – there is also a similar show at Lahaina Cannery Mall. If you want to go shopping at Foodland in Kihei, you can stop off at Kalama

Park playground and there is a play structure here that younger children tend to love.

Shopping on Kauai

They call Kauai the 'Garden Isle', but there is a lot more to do here than just stare at the vegetation. If you enjoy shopping, you are going to find plenty of options for expressing your passion on the island including farmer's markets, shopping malls, and boutique stores.

What to Buy on Kauai

Interesting things to buy on the island of Kauai include:

- Poke (a type of local raw tuna salad)
- Local jewelry
- Local artwork
- Ni'ihua shell necklaces
- Kauai coffee
- Kauai honey
- Lilikoi butter
- Kauai cookies
- Chocolate with macadamia nuts
- Island soaps

Best Shopping Areas on Kauai

Kapaa

Kapaa is a small town, but it is a popular tourist destination so there are plenty of shops aimed at enticing visitors to spend their dollars. There are a number of shopping malls in the area including Wailua Shopping Plaza, Kinipopo Shopping Village, and Coconut Marketplace. Kapaa is also home to many small boutique stores, tour operators, and nice places to eat.

Lihue

Lihue is the second largest town on the island, and this is where you are going to find decent shopping options such as the Kukui Grove Center, Wal-Mart, and Harbor Mall. There is also a good selection of restaurants in the local area.

Hanalei

Hanalei is probably the most beautiful town on Kauai. The shopping options here include ABC Stores, The Hanalei Center, and Kong Lung Trading.

Best Malls on Kauai

Harbor Mall

3501 Rice Street #50, Lihue, HI 96766

Harbor Mall can be found within walking distance of Kalapaki Beach on Rice Street. If you are staying close to Nawiliwili Harbor (or you are arriving by cruise ship), you can use the fun and free trolley shuttle service to travel to this venue - there are also special tours of the island using this shuttle trolley on certain days (check at Trolley Stop Tours & Gifts for details).

Harbor Mall gives a unique shopping experience because it offers options not available anywhere else on the islands such as: Beachrail Hobby & Collectibles, Elite Hunters Hunting Shop, Kauai Island Treasures, Twisted Turtles Yarn Shop, and Blue Hawaiian Helicopters (they can arrange helicopter tours of the island).

This mall is also a good option if you are looking for something to eat. There are a number of options to choose from including: Put it in a Pita, The Feral Pig, Mariachi's Mexican Restaurant, Rocco's Pizza, Splash Cafe, and Kalapaki Joes.

The Harbor Mall offers free Wi-Fi to visitors. If you want to use this service, you need to obtain the daily password from inside Trolley Stop Tours & Gifts.

Kinipopo Shopping Village (aka Kauai shopping mall)

4-356 Kuhio Highway, Kapaa, HI 96746

Kinipopo Shopping Village is a tiny mall, but it is fairly popular because it offers a good mix of tourist-orientated boutique shops and interesting places to eat. This is an outdoor shopping experience with a charming garden courtyard.

Shops and services at Kinipopo Shopping Village include: The Main Attraction (hair studio), Goldsmiths Kauai, Old Republic, Some Like it Hot, and Sacred Waters Healing Arts.

Eateries at Kinipopo Shopping Village include: Korean BBQ, Monico's Taqueria (Mexican Food), Passion Bakery Cafe, Tutu's Soup Hale, and Cake's by Kristin.

Kukui Grove Center

3-2600 Kaumualii Highway, Lihue, HI 96766

Kukui Grove Center is the largest mall on Kauai - if you are in the mood to do some serious shopping, this is the place to go. Kukui is open-air, and it can be particularly nice to wander around here in the mornings and late afternoons. This mall opens most days between 9:30 am. to 7:30 pm. - except on Fridays when it remains open until 9:30 pm. and Sundays when it is open between 10 am. and 6 pm.

The Kukui Grove Center has some of the big-name stores including: Kmart, Longs Drugs, Times Supermarket, GameStop, Radio Shack, and Macy's. There are also smaller shops like: Jeans Warehouse, Sunglass Hut, Kay's Jewelers, Vitamin World, Zales, Verizon Wireless, and The UPS Store.

Restaurants at Kukui Grove include: La Bamba Mexican Restaurant, Ho's Chinese Kitchen, McDonald's, Quiznos Subs, Starbucks, and Sone's Deli and Catering.

Hanalei Center

5-5161 Kuhio Highway Hanalei, HI 96714

The Hanalei Center once served as a schoolhouse, but it has been renovated into a charming mini-mall. Most of the outlets here sell souvenirs and memorabilia from the first half of the twentieth century, but there are also a few places to eat and drink. You can buy food inside and eat at the picnic tables in the park around the center. They have yoga classes here on the second floor, and they also have a well-stocked health food store.

Coconut Marketplace

484 Kuhio Highway, Kapaa, HI 96746

Coconut Marketplace offers a unique shopping experience and the kiosks here offer a good selection of products. This is one of the best places to pick up souvenirs or gifts – although some items can be a bit overpriced. Coconut Marketplace has its own farmer's market on Tuesdays and Thursdays (9 am. to noon), but there are vendors selling fruit and vegetables throughout the day.

Some of the most notable outlets at Coconut Marketplace include: Crazy Shirts, By the Sea (clothing and jewelry), Del Sol Hawaii (beach clothing), Mystical Dreams (gift items), and Paradise Music (CDs and DVDs).

If you are feeling hungry there are a number of eateries to choose from including: TC's Island Grill, the Fish Hut, Harley's Tropical Barbecue, and Zack's Famous Frozen Yogurt and Café.

Poipu Shopping Village

2360 Kiahuna Plantation Drive, Koloa, HI 96756

Poipu is a tourist-focused mall that is open-air and nicely designed. There are 22 shops to choose from including: Honolulu Surf Co., By the Sea, Whalers General Store (souvenirs and gifts), Sunglass Hut, Sand People (beachwear), Overboard Clothing, Crazy Shirts, Elephant Walk (art and jewelry), and Xan Designer Jewelry.

The dining or drinking options at Poipu Shopping Village include: Puka Dog (the tastiest hot dogs on the island), Papalani Gelato, Starbucks, Poipu Tropical Burgers, Keoki's Paradise, and Roy's Poipu Bar & Grill.

Best Markets on Kauai

Koloa Fish Market

5482 Koloa Road, Koloa, III 96756

If you are a lover of seafood, you are probably going to want to check out Koloa Fish Market – this is also where you are going to find the best poke on the island. This is primarily a fish market, but they also sell a good selection of cooked dishes, so it can be a good option if you are feeling hungry. There is nowhere really to sit at Koloa Fish Market, so your best bet is to pick something up and have a picnic elsewhere.

Kalaheo Sunshine Market

Paplina Road, Kalaheo, HI 96741

This small farmer's market is open on Tuesdays between 3 pm. and 4 pm. The vendors in stalls here sell locally grown fruit, vegetables, and flowers. There is also a farmer's market at Coconut Marketplace (see above).

Best Places to Buy Books on Kauai

You can find reading material at a number of locations on the island including:

Talking Book Store (3785 Hanapepe Road, HI 96716) has the honor of being the most westerly located bookstore in the US – it also offers a good selection of new and used books.
Blue House Booksellers (4504 Kukui Street, Kapaa, HI 96746) is open every day between 10 am. and 8 pm. This store is located inside of the dragon building, and they have a wide selection of titles to choose from.

Best Places to Buy Computers and Other Electronics

If you are looking for electronics or IT equipment, the obvious choice would be **Kukui Grove Center**. There are also some small outlets and repair shops in Lihue and Kapaa. If you are looking for Apple products, you might try **Mac Made Easy** (4480 Ahukini Road, Lihue, HI 96766).

Where to Buy Souvenirs on Kauai?

Besides the malls, souvenir shops are plentiful on Kauai. If you are looking for a wide selection of options, you might want to try Coconut Marketplace – just keep in mind that you can probably find the same items cheaper elsewhere. It may also be worth checking out the small boutique gift shops in Hanalei, Lihue and Kapaa if you want something a bit different.

Where to Buy Food on Kauai?

If you are looking fresh fruit and vegetables your best bet will be one of the farmer's markets (see above). **Koloa Fish Market** is the place to go for fresh seafood. Cheap groceries can be purchased at **Whalers General Store**, **Safeway** (Kapaa), or **Foodland** (5-4280 Kuhio Highway, Princeville, HI, 96722).

Where to Go Shopping with Kids on Kauai?

Shopping with kids can be a bit of an ordeal if they become bored. There are some good options to keep them entertained while you shop including:

• A **Fun Factory** at Kukui Grove Center.
• **Coconut Marketplace** offers cultural shows.
• Live entertainment at **Poipu Shopping Village** every Monday and Wednesday at 5 pm.

There is a kid's reading hour every Wednesday between 10 am. and 11 am. at **Blue House Booksellers** in Kapaa.

Shopping on Molokai and Lanai

At first glance, the Hawaiian Islands of Molokai and Lanai might not seem to have much to offer shopaholics. There are no large malls or department stores, and you are not going to feel overwhelmed with merchants selling souvenirs. What you will mostly find is small shops where you can browse at your leisure. Here you may find unique items not available anywhere else in Hawaii.

What to Buy on Molokai and Lanai

- Locally grown macadamia nuts (see Purdy's Nut Farm below)
- Local coffee
- Traditional arts and crafts
- Poke (raw tuna salad)
- Kites (see the Big Kite Factory below)

Best Shopping Areas on Molokai and Lanai

Lanai City

Lanai City is the main commercial center on the island of Lanai, but it is more like a village than a city – the population is just over 3,000 (source: 2010 U.S. Census). The town is focused around Dole Park. There are some charming old-fashioned general stores, as well as some boutiques and small outlets selling gift items. If you are interested in vintage clothing, you will definitely want to check out Cory Labang Studio on 7th Street.

Kaunakakai

Kaunakakai is the main shopping area on Molokai. You don't have to worry about getting lost because almost all the shops are to be found on Ala Malama Street. There are two large general stores to choose from, as well as a few smaller shops mostly selling gift items. The Molokai Pizza Café is a popular hangout, and if you are feeling thirsty, you might try Paddlers' Inn. Most of the shops close by 4 pm. and there and they don't open on Sunday.

Best Markets on Molokai and Lanai

Purdy's Natural Macadamia Nut Farm

Lihi Pali Ave, Hoolehua, Molokai, HI 96729

Purdy's Nut Farm is the perfect destination if you enjoy eating macadamia nuts. When you arrive here, you can expect to be given a tour of the farm – you will learn about how this produce is grown and harvested. The most fun part of the tour is when you get to crack open your own macadamia nuts. There is a small gift shop where you a few bags of this delicious treat. They also sell honey which goes well with the nuts.

Friendly Market Center

90 Ala Malama Avenue, Kaunakakai, HI 96748

The Friendly Market Center is more like a general store, but they offer a good selection of locally grown fruit and vegetables. The prices of items tend to be cheaper here than other stores in Kaunakakai.

Lanai Ohana Poke Market

834-A Gay St, Lanai City, Lanai, HI 96763

The best poke on Lanai is to be found in Lanai City at the Poke Market. There are many different types of poke to choose from (ten at last count), but you need to get here early in the day because the popular dishes tend to sell out fast. The Poke Market is hidden away on a residential street, but any of the locals can point you in the right direction.

Richard's Market

434 8th Street, Lanai City, HI 96763

This is another general store that has a good selection of local products – and a good option if you are looking for organic food on Lanai. They tend to close the shop early on the weekends.

Farmer's Market Lanai City

Lanai Culture & Heritage Center, Dole Park, Lanai City, HI 96763

The Farmer's Market in Lanai City takes place every Saturday between 8 am. and noon. It is very easy to find because it is right in the center of town at Dole Park. This is a very small market, but you can purchase fresh fruit and vegetables as well as some cooked food here.

Best Places to Buy Books on Molokai and Lanai

Kalele Bookstore & Divine Expressions (64 Ala Malama, Kaunakakai, Molokai, Hawaii 96748) has a good selection of new age books and the recent bestsellers. They also sell crafts and gift items and operate a cafe.

Where to Buy Food on Molokai and Lanai?

Most of the resorts have small shops selling at least a limited selection of food items. If you are looking to buy a lot of groceries, the best option is going to be to go to general stores in either Kaunakakai or Lanai City.

Where to Go Shopping with Kids on Molokai and Lanai?

Most kids are going to get a kick out of Purdy's Nut Farm (see above). Big Wind Kite Factory (120 Maunaloa Highway,

Maunaloa, Molokai, HI 96770) not only sells kites but also provides free kite-flying lessons.

One of the nice things about shopping on Molokai and Lanai is the pace is so laid-back and shop owners usually make a fuss over kids – this should mean your child is less likely to be bored while you shop.

25 – SOCIAL PROBLEMS

Attitudes

This one is a catch-22. If your own attitude is poor, you'll meet some of the nastiest people you ever didn't want to know in Hawaii. That's just the way it is everywhere, right? However, if you've got a cool attitude and are open to learning how things work before and during your time here – and you are friendly, outgoing, and a decent person all around, you'll be happy to meet the coolest bunch of people you ever knew.

Give first, and you'll get more in return. Such has been my experience meeting new people in Hawaii. The Hawaiian spirit of Aloha is really a wonderful philosophy of life and I hope you get to experience it in heaps during your stay. If you're not the type of person that deals well with cultural diversity or have a lack of common sense, you may not do well in Hawaii and it can be a very cold place for the ignorant, clueless, and heartless.

Racism

I haven't experienced it much. When I do experience it, it's usually a frustration by locals in regards to something I'm doing. Maybe I don't know a road as well as they do and I do something stupid as I drive. I might hear – 'Stupid haole! Go back to the mainland!' I've heard that one before, at night, by a drunk Hawaiian girl late on a Saturday night.

I've had locals hold knives up so I could see them on a couple of occasions. I've never been attacked, and I don't know anyone that has personally because they were visitors to the island.

There is a tension that can exist between locals and some visitors that take Hawaii for granted, and that don't treat others with respect. Locals will put you in your place in some cases… and it isn't a reason you shouldn't move to the islands. It's just something to be aware of. Like I said before, four guys held knives up to me and the girl I was with – but I didn't really feel threatened like they were going to jump out of the car and attack us. It was more like an empty threat designed to scare us into staying out of their neighborhood. We were off on the wrong road, and we sure knew it then!

If we hadn't turned around, would be have been attacked? No, I don't think so. But, I have this philosophy that people who want to be left alone in Hawaii in their own little world, should be allowed to be left alone.

Crime

Assault, rape, and murder are less of an issue in Hawaii than on the Mainland. It does happen, but the most common types of crime in Hawaii include car and home break-ins, stolen cars and purse snatchings.

Theft

On a couple different occasions as I was far out on the waves bodyboarding, I've watched guys looking through my bag on the beach. I yelled, but who's going to chase down a young kid on drugs for you? Not many. Not me!

Auto smash and grabs, purse snatches, wallet snatchers, bike thieves… they're all here in Hawaii. It has to be expected, as there is a huge gulf between the haves and have-nots. The have-nots get theirs too, but before it's theirs, it was *yours*!

You will have some of your things taken. Be smart and try to limit your losses. What I usually do when I park by the beach is I roll down all my windows and take whatever is valuable with me in a backpack.

I've never had my car stolen, nor had a window broken. Friends I know have had windows broken numerous times because they insisted on locking their car doors.

Traffic Congestion

Traffic is worst on Oahu, during rush hours. Hawaii residents that need to commute somewhere, or that travel during rush hours or lunch hour often complain about traffic being bad. Highways H1, H2 on Oahu and the Honoapiilani Highway on Maui are frequently jammed up during this time. Sitting in traffic is no fun.

Why is traffic so bad?

On Oahu, there are a few reasons for the traffic problem:

1. The overwhelming majority of jobs are in town. Not everyone can, or wants to, live in town, so they commute from wherever they are. Most people are coming from the west side, Pearl City and further west. This results in huge crowds on the road during rush hours.

2. There are over one million vehicles registered in the state. I heard a figure a while back; I'll repeat it, not knowing the truth of it... "There are two vehicles for every person on Oahu." I know it can definitely seem that way.

3. The roads are under built. Meaning, there are not enough roads for the area of Hawaii, so everyone must use the same roads. This is largely a function of topography, with mountainous regions covering the islands and leaving little space for flat roads or roads up through the mountains. Hawaii legislators are cautious about building roads up through areas that retain their natural beauty. This is a good thing in most people's opinions.

4. The roads are not wide enough in many places. Tight roads mean longer lines, and Hawaiian roads were not really built with

the idea that they'd need to expand their width for some reason. There is little room to expand the width of most roads in town because building structures are already too close to the street. There is just no space.

The state has various programs in place to help the flow of traffic including contraflow lanes, high occupancy vehicle lanes (two or more people in the vehicle), coordinated stoplights, and improving public transportation like TheBus.

For more than twenty years there has been talk about creating a sky train system, but the cost up to this point has been prohibitive. Such a train would definitely take some of the traffic off the roadways because some people I know would do anything to have an alternative to driving into town in the bad traffic daily.

Driving and Getting Around

I used my mountain bike quite a bit while living in Waikiki.

Was it dangerous? Sure it was, most tourists are looking around at the amazing scenery and not paying attention to bicycles on the street. Still, I preferred it to driving my Honda around a lot of days.

Rush hours and weekends where there is an event of some kind going on can be a real nightmare. You will not want to live far from where you work unless you live in downtown and work in Kapolei, or somewhere else there is no traffic. Traffic goes toward the downtown and Waikiki areas in the morning and away during evening rush hour.

If you're working far from where you live on Oahu, then traffic is going to be an issue. This is a big issue for some. It never bothered me that much because how upset can I really get sitting in an air-conditioned car listening to my favorite music, drinking amazing Kona coffee and looking at all the people around me?

Not that bothered. Hawaii traffic can really get some people worked up into a tizzy though. It's atrocious during rush hours on Oahu. On Maui, it isn't that big a deal, there are some small spots of traffic during rush hour in Kahului. On Kauai, traffic is non-existent; ditto that for Molokai and Lanai. On Big Island, it isn't really a problem often at all.

Directions (Mauka, Makai, Diamond Head, Ewa)

Directions are often given using words other than north, south, east and west. Hawaii locals have followed their tradition by talking about direction in terms of places on the islands.

Mauka means toward the mountain.

Makai means toward the ocean.

Ewa means toward Ewa beach – past Pearl Harbor.

Diamond Head means toward the volcano in Waikiki.

Police Everywhere?

Add to the poor driving situation the fact that the Honolulu police seem to be everywhere. There is a higher police presence in Waikiki than I have experienced anywhere else in the nation.

If you are late putting your seatbelt on, there they are, standing in the middle of the street looking for people who put on the seatbelt late! If you coast through a stop sign, even slightly, they're on you. If you speed – they got ya! If you ride in the wrong lane on the highway – you're toast. It seems that you cannot win driving a vehicle in the islands. This in particular was no fun for me at all. As I said, I used the bike or walked a lot while living in the islands.

Parking

I mentioned parking above, but it deserves its own section. Parking on Oahu, Hawaii is a serious inconvenience. On the other islands it is not so bad, but still, it's no joy!

For instance, if you drive down to Waikiki to swim at "The Wall." There is a parking lot close to it. It is jam-packed every weekend, and weekdays too unless you get there before about 9 am. There are parking meters. You'll get just ten minutes for one quarter (or less now). There is a maximum of two to three hours you can stay before the meter runs out. If you happen not to remember the meter is running out as you're bodyboarding, bodysurfing, surfing, sunning, or whatever you're doing – you'll get a $35 parking ticket the very instant the meter expires because there are meter-maids camped-out at that parking lot trying to earn their daily pay.

The parking situation in town is quite bad, and you should expect to pay every time you park. You won't have to, but, if you expect it and then do not have to pay sometimes, you'll be in a better mood. Oh, one more thing. If you park on private property, your vehicles will be towed very quickly, and it costs $100+ to retrieve it. The towing service will charge you for keeping your vehicle for every night you leave it at the impound facility.

I can't count the number of times I parked on private property at night as I was going to clubs in downtown. Sometimes I didn't see the sign, other times I thought, *who is going to care if I park here*?

The owners care. Boy, do they care!

Homelessness

Like all over the U.S., there are homeless people living in Hawaii. Some are happy to be homeless, and some are not, but they are here and increasing in numbers.

Homeless folks live at the beach, on the west side of Oahu near Kaena Point, in the parks, on the streets, under highways, and even underneath Hawaiian Schools portable facilities.

Some have cars, and you might see a whole family loving in one. Small tent cities pop up from one place to another, and various plans for a large tent city have been introduced over the years, but are usually shot down by neighboring communities afraid crime will increase in their neighborhood.

Across the state there are about 15,000 people who are homeless at some point during the year. On any given day, there are about 6,000 homeless folks, including many children.

The number of homeless people in Hawaii has increased by more than sixty percent since 2000. U.S Census data shows that Hawaii's increase in poverty is among the highest in the USA.

At least 11.5% of Hawaii's population is living in poverty. Even though Hawaii has a warm climate year-round and there could be worse places to be homeless - robbery, assault, rape, and other crimes exist and are a threat to homeless people.

Why are their so many homeless people living in Hawaii?

1. The Welfare Reform Act, 1994. This act limits the number of years families on federal welfare can collect benefits to just five years. In many cases, it is impossible for the family to do anything else to come up with money in Hawaii's limited economy.

2. High cost of living. Housing costs are the highest in the U.S. here in Hawaii, and there are precious few low-income homes for those that can't afford the $500K+ three bedroom, two bath home.

3. Drug addiction and underfunded mental health programs.

Illegal Drug Epidemic

Drug abuse and addiction is a large factor contributing to crime in the islands. Crimes involving illegal drugs comprised over half of the total convictions in the state in 2001.

The national average for the USA is 41.2%.

Methamphetamine (crystal meth, ice) is the most commonly used illegal drug in Hawaii, besides marijuana. Of all the criminal convictions that were related to drug abuse, ice made up over half of all cases.

Social workers expect the range of problems caused by crystal meth to eventually reach everyone in the islands. Not that everyone will be addicted, but, the effects of those using it, break ins, traffic accidents, friends or family using it, will touch each of us on the islands at some point.

There is no doubt it's use is rampant. I remember in 2002 I was met at the airport by a woman I had befriended online. She was taking me to my hotel when she pulled out some white rocks and proceeded to light them up in a pipe she had.

I was aghast to say the least. I'd never been around anyone that smoked the stuff, nor did I want to start! That was the end of that brief friendship!

Apparently, it is used so commonly that many locals think it's just like smoking pot and they are just as open about it.

Though there are no hard numbers to point to regarding crystal meth use or addiction in Hawaii, something can be said about the extent of the problem by looking at the number of addicts that attended addiction treatment for its use. 2,730 people entered treatment facilities for the drug in 2002. That is higher than for all those that attended alcohol and marijuana treatment programs the same year. Estimates range from 8,000 - 120,000 users in a population of 1.36 million in the state.

Noise

Before moving to Thailand, I had thought that Hawaii, Waikiki in particular, was loud and noisy. Now I have a new perspective on things. Thailand's noise levels make Waikiki seem like a three-person church eulogy service.

You may not have the same perspective, and you might think that the part of Hawaii you stay in is loud. There is a lot of construction going on in Hawaii, and sometimes it is right next-door. If they're building a 50-story condominium, you're likely to be hearing noise for a couple of years before it stops… only to be replaced by someone building something else within hearing range.

Living in town is not going to fill your ears with Mynah birds and soft rain showers… Instead, the sounds of the city prevail – construction, traffic, horns, and car alarms. If you're not prepared for the noise, it can all be a big and unwelcome surprise. Come prepared if you plan on living in or next to a city on the islands.

It's almost funny how clearly you can hear the garbage trucks around the islands come at 4 am. to 6 am. They are very loud, and there is no other sound going on to drown out their roar. Then, to top it off, they have the beep-beep-beep going on every time they reverse, as a safety precaution. Get used to it! It will probably affect you wherever you are in Hawaii. I can't remember not being affected by it, even staying 22-floors up in a condo on the Ala Wai Canal.

Garbage

Another problem, that has been a problem for twenty-five years since I started coming to Hawaii, so probably forever, is where to put Hawaii's garbage. Hawaii landfills are nearly full, as they have been every time I hear about this issue. Well, they've been almost full for twenty-five years now, and they still keep putting garbage in them. I don't know that anyone has a good solution for what to do with all the trash. Other U.S. states sure don't want Hawaii's trash, and we can't ship it to the moon. Yet.

One of the main problems is that garbage dumps need to be in an area where they won't contaminate the ground water. It is difficult to find such a place in Hawaii.

26 – MARIJUANA

No, pot is not legal in Hawaii. We do have a medical marijuana law, but anybody without cancer, HIV, or other qualifying conditions, is not supposed to be touching the stuff.

For the record, I'm not a fan of the substance, but I still *get* that I'm probably in the minority of people living in Hawaii! Marijuana, pot, herb, pakalolo, budz, Kona Gold, Maui Wowie, all refer to same thing. When touring around one of the Hawaiian Islands and you see a local guy standing in the middle of the road on a particularly deserted stretch, he isn't there to rob you or ask you to jumpstart his vehicle. He will likely be holding up a massive bunch of freshly culled pot and asking you whether you want to buy some *buudzz*.

I can't tell you how many times this happened to me on Maui. I loved to cruise over around the west side of the island; it's virtually barren and so beautiful. A great Sunday morning drive. A great place to buy pot too, if that's what you're into.

My stand on legalizing pot, is – *sure, why not?* Why not give people an alternative to alcohol? They are similar, both give a fun high, but alcohol can cause a state of mind that can totally incapacitate people regardless what they're doing. Driving for instance. I've never seen pot do that, or anything remotely close.

Hawaii will likely make pot legal in the next couple of years. They just ratified law legalizing medical marijuana treatment. Full legalization is on the way for sure.

27 – BUGS and OTHER CRITTERS

One problem many people contemplating a move to Hawaii consider is how many and what types of bugs they are going to encounter in their new home. Though I can catch a cobra, krait, or coral snake with my hands, I'm no fan of bugs that bite. I avoid them like the plague. Hawaii doesn't have any venomous snakes, but they do have some biting and stinging bugs, some of which you are likely to encounter (fire ants, centipedes) and some you likely won't see, like scorpions.

Centipedes

Ok, lets start with the worst thing I can possibly imagine getting bitten by in Hawaii – the lowly centipede. Centipedes come from the family, *Scolopendra*, and there are three types in Hawaii. *Scolopendra subspinipes* is the only centipede to fear. The other two are harmless – *Lethobius sp.* and *Mecistocephalus maxillaris* (*Gervais*). A large and a small *Scolopendra* have bitten me. Both hurt a lot, and I can't say which hurt worse. I do know the orange *S. subspinipes* centipedes can get to nearly a foot long. I'm not joking; I've seen numerous ten to eleven inch centipedes on the sidewalk in Maui at dusk, near my home. I thought they were snakes they were so big. They range in size from one to twelve inches. Centipedes scare me more than spiders, much more.

I have had centipede families living under my carpet in Hawaii – twice. Both times it was near the restroom, where the floor is frequently wet. I must have killed twenty of the *buggahs*, they were hard to see at only about an inch and a half in length. One got me in the morning as I had my coffee; it ran across my sandal-covered foot and got my ankle. Not a great way to start the day.

Probability of Encountering - High. They are very common in Hawaii and they seem to not mind a bit moving in with you to your home. They also enjoy cruising through the grass at night concerts – I have seen a couple people bitten while sitting on towels and blankets and watching musical events outside on the grass.

Bites – A bite that lasts a second or more, and they all do because centipedes don't let go until you beat them senseless, starts with a slow burning in a very small spot at the bite-site. The pain location then grows to a couple inches in diameter. It can be excruciating, depending where it bit you – if it got you where you have a lot of nerve endings like the fingers or toes, it will hurt more.

Prognosis – Good. I'd say more than 90% of centipede bites heal up without any sort of complication. It's like a strong bee sting. If you are allergic to the venom, or if the beast got you good, you could possibly end up in the hospital with an infection. I have seen feet swelled up very large from a bite in the case of allergies or sensitivity. My bites healed in three to four days.

Precautions – Keep your residence clean. I mean, clean it at least weekly. If there are any damp spots in your home, make sure you caulk whatever you need to, or dry it up some other way to keep centipedes from camping out there. They love warm, and dark environment. Block the area under your doors so they can't slip in from outside. Don't sleep on the floor.

Cockroaches!

There are nineteen different species of cockroach in Hawaii, and only three of them are often near humans. The three types are the American (*Periplaneta americana*), the German (*Blattella germanica*), and the Surinam (*Pycnoscelus surinamensis*).

I don't know why people are so afraid of cockroaches, they don't bite very often. This is one thing I'm not very scared of, I've seen so many I am accustomed to them I guess. One time I was coming out of a dream in my bed at my dorm room at Hickam Air Force Base, and I was kissing a girl in my dream. It was heavenly. Her lips were soft like pineapple, or something. As I came to and opened my eyes, I realized I wasn't dreaming. But why were my lips still tickling? I had a giant cockroach on my lips, probably trying to get at the pieces of food stuck between my teeth. I smacked my own face and jumped off the bed cussing a storm. My roommate woke up horrified he was going to die because he didn't know what had transpired. True story. I hope you know I'm giving you my worst stories ever for these bugs; you are not likely to have the same experience. ;)

So, cockroaches are all over the place. They fly. They crawl. They eat whatever food is around, even if it's stuck in your teeth. They don't have venom, but apparently, they can inflict some sort of bite. I have not been bitten by one, and I'm knocking on wood right now.

Probability of Encountering – High. Guaranteed. Most residential buildings have a routine spraying schedule. You can be sure that nice accommodations are spending good money to keep the place bug free. Still, you'll see some.

Bites – They bite, but rarely. I think only when you're sleeping and roll over on them or something. OK, a bit of research turned this up from Orkin – the pest control specialists – "Cockroaches are omnivores that eat plants and meat. They have been recorded to eat human flesh of both the living and the dead, although they are more likely to take a bite of fingernails, eyelashes, feet and hands. The bites may cause irritation, lesions and swelling. Some have suffered from minor wound infections." So there, nothing major. Apparently, roaches don't bite people unless there is a shortage of other food to eat.

Prognosis – Minor wound infections as a worst-case scenario.

Precautions – Like centipedes, you have to block up every hole in the walls or under doors, around light fixtures, and windows. Do not sleep with the windows open without a screen, or you WILL be visited by flying bugs at night. Cockroaches are known to spread disease and they are generally very dirty bugs. If you have an infestation, don't ignore them, get them cleaned out right away.

Scorpions

There is one scorpion in Hawaii, it is the 'lesser brown scorpion', *Isometrus maculates*. A sting causes pain and swelling and is similar to a bee sting. If you are allergic to the venom, you will require immediate hospital care – so watch for any symptoms out of the ordinary swelling and pain.

Probability of Encounter – Low. I've only seen one while camping at the beach. One in six years.

Bites – Cause swelling and accompanied by bee-sting like pain.

Prognosis – As long as you're not allergic to the venom, you'll be fine.

Precautions – Don't leave shoes outside. Check shoes for resident scorpions, dirty laundry, anything that touches the ground. If you camp, zip the tent.

Note – there is a bug called the *Pseudoscorpionida*, or 'pseudo scorpion.' It lacks a tail and venom stinger, but otherwise looks very much like a scorpion. If in doubt, don't pick it up!

Caterpillars

In particular, the Stinging Nettle Caterpillar (*Darna pallivitta*) is a real pest in Hawaii.

Caterpillars are cute and fuzzy, but there are some species, the D. pallivitta is one that will make you scream in pain if you are stung by it. The spiny hairs release an irritant to the skin that causes intense burning and itching later as the burning wears off. A caterpillar in Florida that was intensely painful has stung me.

Caterpillars can cause more pain than any bee I've ever been stung by. Beginning in 2001, these caterpillars have made their way across the Hawaiian Islands and are now on Oahu, Maui, Big Island, and recently, Kauai. If you are allergic to the irritant, you can have trouble breathing and require emergency care. Problem is, you won't know whether you're allergic to the chemicals the caterpillar produces until you are stung.

Probability of Encounter – Low. Even if you are hiking a lot on the trails, you probably won't encounter this caterpillar. I hiked often, over fifty times per year, and was never stung by this stinging caterpillar.

Stings – There is no stinger like a bee, rather, the irritants are located on the spiny hairs of the caterpillar. All it needs to do is touch your skin lightly to cause intense pain.

Prognosis – Most people will be fine after the pain and itchiness goes away. Some will have allergic reactions and require medical treatment. If stung, pay attention to odd symptoms like breathing problems, sweating, and cloudiness of mind. These things may indicate you are allergic to the venom and should get help immediately.

Precautions – Cover up your legs and arms when hiking, and be extra cautious as you are gardening. These have been found on palms, weeds, grasses and other foliage, so they could be just about anywhere.

Bees

While hiking on a couple of occasions I've heard the low hum of what seemed like six million bees in a hive close by. I started seeing bees flying around me every minute or so too. I quickly reversed on the trail. Though you don't have to be aware of snakes – there are bees on your hikes!

Snakes

There are no snakes native to Hawaii but every now and again one is found, no doubt either coming to the islands as a stowaway on a boat or plane, or brought in illegally as a pet or for sale.

Mosquitoes

Yes, and they are plentiful. Keep standing water around your home to a minimum, or eliminate it entirely. There are things you can add to your decorative waterfalls or ponds that kill the mosquito larvae - like fish.

Geckos

There are small house geckos that hang around the lights to catch insects that are drawn to the light. They are not harmful except they do leave droppings you'll notice. They squawk and chirp like little birds. I got used to it after a couple of weeks – you should too – they're basically harmless and they eat some of the mosquitoes and other bugs around your home.

Coqui Frogs

There are what some people call "infestations" of these little frogs with a big mouth. They can be heard croaking in a chorus of noise that will either not bother you at all as you get used to it – or, drive you stark raving mad and bent on their destruction. When buying a home, you will want to ask your realtor about these frogs in the area!

Termites

Yes, and in big numbers. Termites are a major cause of damage to homes in Hawaii. You'll want to have your new property checked for them.

Other Bugs – Bees, Wasps, Spiders, Bed Bugs, Fire Ants

Hawaii has a lot of other bugs obviously. Many of them bite, but I think most people are aware of bees and spiders and there is no need to go into any depth about them. Like most parts of the world, Hawaii does have the black widow and brown widow spiders – so caution should be taken when in cellars, or outdoor sheds and other dark places. Their bite is necrotic and can cause complications, possibly even death. Fire ants can cause a wicked sting for a short while, then overwhelming itchiness for a night or two.

The major harmful terrestrial pests, you'll find above – cockroaches, centipedes, and scorpions. Just be aware and take some precautions and you'll be fine, like the other 1.36 million residents on the Hawaiian Islands! Don't let your fear of bugs turn you off the idea of visiting or moving to the Hawaiian Islands. There are ways to deal with them and lessen their impact.

28 – MARINE CRITTERS

Long-Spined Venomous Sea Urchins

(*Diadema paucispinum, Echinothrix diadema, and Echinothrix calamaris*)

In Hawaiian language, "*Wana.*" Pronounced "vah-na." Though eaten by locals and considered a delicacy. They taste like *opihi*. If you've never had opihi, then you're really missing something. I remember having them freshly picked with soy sauce (shoyu), ginger, garlic, and maybe something else mixed in to make it a secret recipe – I can't recall everything exactly. I do remember the taste was absolutely lovely.

Stepping on an urchin is a very bad experience. Three species are dangerous in Hawaii, those named above in the subheading. These are wicked circular or oval spined beasts up to ten-inches across, that attach to coral, rocks, and other submerged structures directly under some of the prime surfing spots in Hawaii. This long spiny urchin is the scourge of surfers all over Hawaii. If you have lived in the islands for any amount of time, you already know someone that is living with wana barbs inside their foot, which, with time, dissolve.

The problem is, before they dissolve, you are going to go through tremendous pain from the pointy spines, the venom they carry, and possibly infection, as a result of punctured skin. I'll talk more about the risk for infection when you cut yourself in Hawaii's waters later.

Wana venom is released through the shorter hollow spines as something contacts the sharp tip. Though you may have trouble seeing them if you are snorkeling or diving because they collect organic debris, and sometimes small pebbles, you know immediately if you've stepped on one. It is nothing like a coral cut – which often isn't even felt.

The spines can break off and lodge inside the tissues of your body, and need to be removed as much as possible. The area around the punctured skin will be stained purple or black, the same color as the offending organism. This fades with time. Hospital or clinic treatment is highly advised because all medical personnel that deal with this problem have been well trained on how best to treat the site of injury. There are even substances that can be applied that help soften the barbs so they are absorbed into the skin faster than through the normal process.

Probability of Encountering – Unfortunately, if you spend a lot of time in the water, you are likely to put your foot down on a piece of coral or rock and step right onto a long-spined venomous sea urchin. *Wana* are very common. It happens. It happened to me only a couple of times, and I never suffered with them broken off in my foot like a lot of people do. It doesn't take long to learn not to put your foot on the coral in any circumstances.

Stings – It hurts a lot to step on urchins, and it will hurt for a while. Soaking the wound in warm water, as warm as you can stand, breaks down the toxins. Soaking in vinegar can also help to break down the calcium-carbonate spines so they are absorbed into your body if you can't, or the medical personnel cannot remove them all with tweezers. Eventually the spines dissolve and you're good to go. Some people may suffer infection as a complication, so keeping an eye on the wound is essential so you can have it treated by experts, not at home in your restroom.

Prognosis – Good in most cases. It is painful, and even debilitating for a while, but eventually without secondary infection, it works itself out.

Precautions – Avoid at all costs, stepping on coral with your feet – whether you have reef shoes on, tennis shoes, or fins, whatever. I have had thin water shoes on my feet and stepped on an urchin that went right through those thin rubber shoes. Don't put yourself in a situation where you are snorkeling or riding a board where you may have to put your feet down onto the reef because it is so shallow.

Coral Cuts and Abrasions

Coral is alive, but it feels like a very sharp rock when you touch it. The danger is in stepping on it or brushing against it because it is so rough, that it can scrape the skin and even cause lacerations, very easily.

Probability of Encountering – Very high if surfing, bodyboarding, or bodysurfing. There is coral all over the Hawaiian Islands where swimmers and other water enthusiasts are having fun.

Lacerations, Scrapes – Treat immediately, don't continue playing in the water until you're ready to go get it treated. If you're bleeding, you're ready to go home. If you don't know what you're doing, go to a clinic and have them clean it out. I know it sounds funny, to have a clinic clean out your scrape or cut, but you don't want it to get infected. Infection is very common after a coral cut, I'd say it's the rule and it happens every time. Did for me!

Prognosis – Probably fine, infection of some sort is normal, but most people recover fully. However, because there is usually some form of infection present, whether from the coral itself or bacteria in the water, coral cuts can take up to months to heal. Be aware that some people are allergic to the substances in coral that can enter the body through a break in the skin. Signs of infection and anaphylactic shock symptoms should be dealt with immediately.

Precautions – Of course, you don't want to ever step on coral or brush against it for any reason. Some surfing spots have coral reef under the breaking wave, that's why it's breaking! Do be careful not to be caught out on a coral reef when the tide has gone out and left you in a place you can't do anything else but crawl across or try to paddle your surfboard or bodyboard over top of the coral reef. Not a good position to be in! Been there myself in Waikiki and at Magic Island, Ala Moana Beach Park. I don't ever want to be in that position again, I probably don't need to tell you.

Conus – Deadly Sea Snails (*Conidae*)

In Hawaiian language, "*Poniuniu*." As strange as it sounds, walking along a beach or diving in Hawaii and picking up a Conus shell with a snail still inside, can lead to excruciating pain, and possibly even death. Yes, snails in Hawaii can be potentially deadly, though there have been no fatalities here yet. There are thirty to forty species of Conus snail in the waters of Hawaii.

The largest, the leopard Conus (*Conus leopardus*) can reach 9 inches in length. The three that are especially dangerous are the textile, striated and marbled cones. These dangerous snails are carnivorous and hunt marine life nocturnally. The snails have a harpoon-like 'tooth' that contains potent neurotoxic venom that renders prey helpless. The venom is also cytotoxic, destroying cells of the organism. There is no antivenin available.

Probability of Encountering - Very low, unless you are actively looking for shells on the beach or in the ocean. Only shells with live snails in them can harm you. I have heard stories of people putting shells in their pocket, and the snail stings them in the thigh, through the cloth of the pocket.

Stings - Small Conus snails can give a painful sting. Larger snails can induce respiratory failure and death. Typically stings include intense pain, some swelling, numbness, tingling, and vomiting. Symptoms can be delayed by days. Severe cases involve muscular paralysis, vision difficulty, and respiratory problems. If you are stung, watch for signs of going into anaphylactic shock and seek treatment immediately. As stated, there is no antivenin, and treatment involves providing life support until the venom is metabolized by the victim.

Prognosis - For small snails, the prognosis is usually good. For large snails, better to get to the hospital quickly. There have been no fatalities in Hawaii to date.

Precautions - Don't pick up snail shells if you are not an expert on snail species. There are only a few snails that can hurt you, but you'd better know which ones.

Portuguese Man-O-War (*Physalia physalis*)

Hawaiians call them many names, "*Ili Mane`o*", "*Pa`imalau*", "*Palalia*" or "*Pololia*." On the windward sides of all islands, there is an abundance of these purple-blue Portuguese Man-O-War, or "Blue Bottles." They are floating siphonophore (not jellyfish) that have a bubble inside their body that keeps them afloat. Unfortunately it also acts as a sail and catches the wind, so when the wind is blowing onshore, there are many of these floating pests all over the water and washed up on the beach. Their tentacles are usually between 33 and 160 feet in length, and they inject venom into your skin when you brush up against them, causing intense pain.

These are quite common on the windward side of the island. I body boarded frequently at Waimanalo, and Bellows Air Force Station. It seemed these pests were there every time I went.

Probability of Encountering – High if you spend much time in the ocean in Hawaii. If you live in Hawaii you will likely have an encounter at some point.

Stings - There are varying degrees of stings, and reactions to them. I spent many hundreds of hours in he ocean in Hawaii. I was stung repeatedly by tentacles of these jellyfish-like monsters. I remember getting stung and just staying in the water because it wasn't that bad. I think I just wasn't that allergic to the venom after a while and so many stings. I remember having red welts across my back, legs, arms, cheek, and other places, and they stung a bit, but nothing like what many people describe as the worst pain of their lives. Do be exceptionally careful though, because you might be a person that reacts very badly to the venom. Most people urinate in a cup and pour it on their stings. It appears to help.

Prognosis - Red welts and some pain, some itchiness is apparent for up to two to three days for most people. If you're going to have an allergic reaction, it usually happens within the first few hours of exposure to the toxins.

Precautions - These pests are present in greater numbers when the wind is coming onshore and blowing them into the beach. You can usually find some on the beach first, and that will notify you that they are also in the water. If you see one man-of-war floating on the water, get out immediately, there are likely hundreds more around. I don't remember being stung through a shirt or shorts, so covering up with a long-sleeve surfing shirt can help mitigate the extent of a sting.

Winged Box Jellyfish (*Carybdea alata*) – and Other Jellyfish.

The winged box jellyfish is one to three-inches long with tentacles around two feet in length and appear approximately seven to ten days after the full moon. They are present for a couple of days, and then aren't usually to be found. There is the occasional oddball that can be found anywhere, so caution is always indicated. They show up a week after the full moon on the leeward shores of the Hawaiian Islands.

Lifeguards display signs warning if jellyfish are present. This is another reason to swim at beaches that have lifeguards. Not all Hawaii beaches do.

Probability of Encountering – High if you spend a lot of time in the water, especially during windy periods with onshore wind.

Stings - Stay calm and remove the tentacles if you can see them, using something other than your finger. Use something like a piece of cardboard, tweezers, sock, or something else. Do not touch the object again once used to brush away the jellyfish flesh. Flood stings with vinegar or isopropyl alcohol for at least thirty seconds, for minutes if possible.

Once you have done that, apply the "Safe Sea Jellyfish After Sting" gel. You can get it from BuySafeSea.com.

Don't rinse with freshwater, as the nematocysts of the jellyfish will continue to release toxins into your skin. Do not use ice or hot water either.

Transport victim to hospital if any serious breathing or consciousness problem occurs.

Prognosis - The pain from the winged box jellyfish is much more intense than that of the Portuguese man-of-war or other jellyfish for most people. The other way you can tell is that the pain from the box jellyfish lasts for around eight hours, and not just fifteen minutes to an hour as with the man-of-war. Scarring can last for years for the box jellyfish, and only days for the man-of-war. Keep in mind that nobody has died from a box jellyfish sting in Hawaiian waters. You will likely be fine. Treat stings with vinegar and see a doctor or emergency room for any severe symptom related to anaphylactic shock.

Precautions - Lifeguards keep a vigilant look for box jellyfish and sometimes close entire beaches if there is a threat. If you are swimming on a beach without lifeguards, you must be aware that jellyfish, man-of-war, sharks, and other dangers might be present (undertows, large surf, etc.). It is better, if you don't know the ocean well, to attend only beaches with lifeguards present.

Beaches that are prone to having winged box jellyfish: Ala Moana Beach, Waikiki Beach, Hanauma Bay, Makaha Surfing Beach and Pōka'i Bay.

My Hawaii Box Jellyfish Story

I had been snorkeling at a deserted beach on Maui for a few hours. As I came in to the shallow water I sat down and pulled off my fins. I felt an excruciating pain on the inside of my left thigh. I instinctively jumped up and ran in to the beach, slapping my thigh to get whatever was burning my leg, off of me as fast as possible. When I got to the beach my leg was on fire with pain.

Up to that point the only pain I had ever felt that was comparable was being stung by the barbs of a stingray that ripped open my foot after I stepped on one while wade fishing in Florida. The pain in my thigh was almost making me lose my mind, it was so strong. I felt my breathing become labored and I wondered if I was going to die right there in front of my friend. I can't even describe the pain, but it was like someone had poured battery acid from a car on my leg and it was eating through to my bones. It was that intense. Peeing on it didn't help. Fresh water didn't help.

We went to the doctor, who watched me closely for signs of going into shock. I was treated and released in a few hours. I had a five-inch diameter road map of thick lined welts on my leg for about six years. It slowly faded away and today I can only see a slight mark where that box jellyfish got me. I have been stung by many things in the past. The box jellyfish and stingray are two that you could not pay me enough to ever endure again. The pain was excruciating. Do be careful in Hawaii's waters!

Dangerous Bacteria – *Staphlococcus, Streptococcus*

I have had my share of cuts made by coral while surfing and bodyboarding at various spots on the islands. When I first arrived on Oahu I was fearless and stupid, emphasis on the latter. I'd go wherever the waves were without much consideration for the sharp coral reefs underneath. I had a coral cut or scrape a couple of times per month on average. After two years of this foolishness I noticed I was getting a boil every now and then, somewhere on my body. The location was different all the time, but usually on my upper torso, not my legs so much. If you've had boils, you know they are no fun. They're an annoyance. However, I began having them on average once per month, every single month, without fail. This went on for about two years, even after I moved up to New York City. Multiple rounds of very strong antibiotics eventually put a stop to the recurring infection.

It was then I learned from some of the best dermatologists in the world, that the Pacific Ocean around the islands of Hawaii – especially Waikiki, is filled with opportunistic bacteria like *Staphlococcus and Streptococcus*! If you get a coral cut, you have a good chance of getting an infection from some nasty bacteria in the water. It is essential to have your wounds cleaned out professionally, and still, you have a chance of coming down with boils or something else.

Probability of Encountering - Very high if you are swimming in the waters of Waikiki and cut or scrape yourself.

Infection - Infection usually occurs with lacerations that occur in the water in Hawaii. That has been my and others' experience. Do take care to clean any wound very thoroughly, and it definitely wouldn't hurt to have it done at a hospital or clinic where they know what they're doing. The risk of infection is great.

Prognosis – As I mentioned above, I've had many coral cuts while surfing and bodyboarding, and all my friends have too. The worst thing I've ever seen happen was my own recurring staph infection that took many courses of antibiotics to fix. Usually infections are mild to moderate and hospitalization is not necessary.

Precautions - Be cautious of the coral reef and urchins (*wana*) while in the water. If you have open sores or other wounds, don't get in the water as bacteria can infect easily when there is a break in the skin's surface.

Sharks!

We gave an entire chapter (below) to sharks in Hawaii because it is such a major, and mostly irrational fear, that most of us have.

Summary

As you can see there are a few dangerous marine animals and bacteria to keep up to speed about if you are planning on spending time in the oceans around the islands of Hawaii. Most things can be avoided by being smart – including sharks. There are times of day and night they can be found, and preferences they have for feeding which you can be aware of that will help you avoid them. Probably the biggest risk of injury you face in the water is a sting from the abundant Portuguese man-of-war that floats on the surface and come into shore during onshore wind periods.

29 – SHARKS!

Sharks attacks happen at the usual rate of three to four per year in the Hawaiian Islands. When sharks attack, they don't usually eat the entire body of a person, they usually bite and let go. Sometimes they take an arm or part of a leg, or something else, but they usually don't hang around and pick a person apart. It's actually remarkable, considering the extent of some of the injuries suffered by shark-bite victims, that more people don't die as a result of shark attacks considering the damage that can be done.

There are some very dangerous sharks in Hawaii; the worst is the Tiger Shark (*Galeocerdo cuvier*). But, unless you are spending day after day surfing or spearfishing, you are very unlikely to ever be attacked by a shark at all, or even see one. Read more about these incredible creatures below.

Sharks scare people to the core. Galeophobia is the fear of sharks and most of us have it to some degree. JAWS, the movie, sure didn't help people get over that fear, and this article will likely only exacerbate whatever fear you have in your own head about sharks in Hawaii, though I can assure you, my intention is to help you get a more realistic picture of the shark situation around the Hawaiian Islands.

Shark Basics

Sharks are top-level vertebrate predators that fear nothing and eat whatever they can catch. The average shark life expectancy is of between twenty and thirty years, depending on the species. A few species like the Great White and Tiger sharks in Hawaii can grow to over twenty feet long, are heavy, and have a large turning radius so they would have trouble catching their usual prey if they didn't have some great sensory organs to help them find it. Sharks have no problem finding things to eat, even in total darkness or muddy water. If it's dark, the shark has cat-like eyes, which clarify the image. It's actually a row of small reflective plates that redirect the light through the retina a second time that allows sharks to see their prey even in the extreme light-deficient depths of the ocean.

A shark's sense of smell is fine-tuned for blood. Sharks can sense one particle of blood in a million. It can track the blood through the water to the source in a short time, in part because the shark can distinguish the strength of the smell in each nostril and turn toward where the scent is strongest. This is one reason nobody with an open wound or females during menstruation should enter the ocean where sharks could be lurking.

So many things give the shark the extra edge in hunting prey: lateral line, smell, sight, hearing, and *ampullae* of Lorenzini.

Special Sense Organs of Sharks

Ampullae of Lorenzini – This specialized organ gives the shark a sixth sense, giving it the ability to detect electromagnetic fields as well as temperature gradients. Sharks could possibly be more sensitive to electric fields than any other animal. With a centimeter-long ampulla, they can sense five one billionths of a volt of electricity. That is approximately five million times stronger than what humans can sense.

Lateral Line – these receptors in this organ help the shark sense movement of water, and vibrations in the water. Using the lateral line, a shark can feel movement in the water surrounding it up to 330 feet away.

Sharks are fast enough to catch a lot of different prey. Great White sharks can reach a swim speed of 50 kilometers per hour (30 miles per hour), when preparing an attack, though most sharks max out around 12 mph.

Shark Species in Hawaii

There are forty-one distinct species of shark in Hawaii's warm Pacific Ocean. As far as we know, these are the most dangerous: Tiger Sharks (*Galeocerdo cuvier*); Great White Sharks (*Carcharodon carcharias*); Galapagos Sharks (*Carcharhinus galapagensis*); Bull Sharks (*Carcharhinus leucas*); Mako Sharks (*Isurus oxyrinchus; Isurus paucus*); and Hammerhead Sharks (*Sphyrna zygaena; Sphyrna lewini*). Of the other thirty-five species, most are smaller reef sharks, and some have bitten people, but those mentioned above are ones to be concerned with in Hawaii. Identification of a shark as one of the less harmful species does not mean you should fail to take it seriously when in the water. Do be careful with every shark, they all have large mouths, many teeth, and can cause significant wound damage with a bite.

The most frequently encountered Hawaiian reef sharks are the White Tipped Reef Shark, Scalloped Hammerhead Shark, Tiger Shark, Galapagos Shark, Gray Reef Shark, and the Sandbar Shark. The Tiger Shark and the Galapagos Shark are the most aggressive of the Hawaiian reef sharks. The other known Hawaii sharks don't typically attack for any reason, but when provoked or when blood is in the water from spearfishing, anything goes.

What Do Sharks Eat?

The typical shark diet includes fish, turtles, squid, sea snakes, rays, Hawaiian monk seals, and dolphins. Occasionally they'll eat birds, dogs, trash, and pieces of boat, human beings, and even each other.

Sharks are more active for hunting during the time right before sunset and sunrise, and night. They prefer murky unclear water because they can use their *ampullae* of Lorenzini organs to sense the electrical fields in their prey and attack them easily, though they cannot see it. In turn, sharks can be invisible to their prey, a good thing when they are a couple of meters long and hundreds of pounds. Their size makes them easy to see and avoid for prey in the clear water.

Sharks typically hunt for fish, turtles, dolphins and seals during the low light times of dusk and dawn. Sharks can detect the faint electrical fields given off by all living organisms, and even by the magnetic field of the earth! As they recon the water, receptors on the sharks' snouts allow them to locate their prey without seeing it.

Sharks in Old Hawaii

Hawaiians called the god of the sharks, *Kauhuhu*. They have many stories about sharks they have passed down through generations. The Hawaiian word for shark is, *mano*.

Why Do Sharks Attack People?

The experts say sharks attack people as a case of mistaken identity. I take issue with this. After thousands of shark attacks worldwide, some in which the sharks consume some or most of bodies of the victim, I have to disagree with that statement. Sometimes sharks know what you are, and know they can eat you, and do. There are enough people in the water that sharks know what we are. We are a food source. We may not be a preferred food source, but, over countless millennia, anything soft enough that enters the ocean is eaten by sharks. They don't care all that much what it is. They are opportunistic feeders. They eat what is present. If you are present, they will eat you if they are hungry. It isn't personal. Seems to me ridiculous to say that all cases of shark attack are *misidentification*.

Sharks have sensory organs that enable them to sense the electrical fields of animals. They have eyes. They have lateral lines. They know what turtles move like in and on top of the water. They know how seals move. They know what fish look like. They know what humans look like.

Sharks attack people for many reasons. Primarily, they have either decided a human in the water is a valid food source, or, is a potential food source, and give a little nip before deciding. Often, sharks decide they don't want to eat a person, and they don't finish the job. Other times, sharks eat the entire person. It isn't mistaken identity at that point. They know it isn't a seal or turtle. They eat it anyway.

If you look up "shark attacks usa wiki" – you'll quickly get the idea that sharks eat humans often. Keep in mind, that is just attacks in the USA. There are another hundred or so nations with borders on an ocean with sharks. There are thousands of documented attacks worldwide, and some are scarier than any movie depiction.

Shark Attacks in Hawaii

There are usually three to four shark attacks in Hawaii per year and usually no fatalities result. However, just a couple of days ago a man kayak fishing off Maui was bitten on the foot and died on the boat back to shore. Just before this, a German tourist lost her arm to a shark off Maui. She died in the intensive care at Maui Memorial Medical Center after being treated for a week. She was bitten while snorkeling off Maui at Hamoa Beach. Most shark attacks involve arms or legs and there is no further bite after the first one. The last fatal attack in Hawaii before these two was in 2004.

I created a Google Docs spreadsheet called, Hawaii Shark Attacks, covering the years 2001 to present-day, to see if it would help me get a better idea of the reality of shark attacks in Hawaii. What I found was surprising.

Maui had twenty-six attacks since 2001. Oahu? Just sixteen. That's strange itself. Right? There are so many more people in the water around Oahu, and yet Maui had ten more attacks over this nearly thirteen-year period. Kauai had ten attacks, and Big Island Hawaii only eight.

I was also interested in what time of day sharks attack most often, so I could ascertain if there was a time of day worth avoiding. (See hours of day below)

Sharks appear to be consistently on the hunt from 6 am. to 6 pm. The numbers of attacks are fairly constant. There is a lull around 8 am. to 10 am. This might be because few people are in the water during that time. The 6 am. to 8 am. time period has a lot of regulars on "Dawn Patrol" – surfers that meet every morning before work when the crowds are non-existent. Here's a look at the number of attacks during each two-hour period:

6 - 8 am.: 12 attacks

8 - 10 am.: 6

10 - 12 pm.: 12

12 - 2 pm.: 13

2 - 4 pm.: 10

4 - 6 pm.: 10

Does the clarity of the water have any bearing on the attacks in Hawaii? It seems to. Out of sixty-three attacks over the past almost thirteen years, there were attacks during clear water – twenty-six times. Seems like sharks bite whenever they are hungry, regardless of water clarity. They might prefer sandy, turbid, muddy water by a two-to-one margin, but they bite plenty of times when the water is clear.

In the last almost two-hundred years, there have been eight deaths attributed to sharks around the Hawaiian Islands. But there have also been numerous events where people have been lost at sea while swimming or surfing, boating, where a shark attack was non-conclusive. Some of these are likely shark attacks and involved fatalities. There have been over one-hundred and sixteen attacks during this time period. So, roughly one out of twenty attacks has resulted in human death.

Thirty-four of the shark attacks in the islands were either identified as tiger sharks by witnesses or victims, or the conclusion of the shark's identity as a tiger was drawn after examining evidence post-attack.

Researching further, I found the Wikipedia entry for shark attacks in the United States. If you are an avid surfer, snorkeler, diver, spear-fisher, or anybody that gets in the ocean around Hawaii for any reason, I have to caution you before you read the descriptions of attacks at this link. I just spent twenty minutes reading it and soaking it all in, and I don't know whether I'll ever ride a surfboard again. Some of the attacks are just mind numbing. Here's the link. I'm not joking when I caution you not to read this page if you want to continue spending time in the water, because some of you might change your mind after reading this:

Wiki Shark Attacks in USA (click if connected to the internet)

Precautions - It isn't all bad though. There are many things you can do to avoid shark encounters, or at least lessen the probability of being attacked by one. Here are some of the most highly recommended tips by experts.

1. Avoid murky water. When it rains, the run off of freshwater over the land and into the ocean creates a very murky marine environment, which sharks love. They love it because their prey cannot see them before they attack, so they can eat as much as they want. They sense their prey using the electric impulses all living creatures emit. If you look at my spreadsheet you'll see that about two thirds of attacks occurred in turbid water (crashing waves usually), the water is not clear because of bubbles and sand being stirred up.

2. Do not enter the water when bleeding, however slight. Sharks sense blood in very low concentrations and can follow the scent.

3. Avoid spearfishing, which puts significant amounts of blood in the water. If spearfishing, don't attach your fish to a stringer and then attach it to your body, and change your location often.

4. Avoid swimming near someone netting, or using chum for fishing.

5. Use low contrast colors and patterns. It's like fishing, you don't fish with camouflage lures, you fish with high-contrast colors and patterns so the fish can see it and attack it. Well, with sharks you want to be as invisible as possible. Choose low contrast clothes, scuba equipment, and surfboards. Remember, it's the bottom of the board the shark can see, not the top. Dark blue surf or diving gear is probably best.

6. Don't enter the water alone.

7. Don't swim or surf too far from shore.

8. Don't enter the water at night.

9. Be alert for signs from other animals that may signal sharks nearby. Dolphins in close to shore, baitfish jumping out of the water, etc.

10. Avoid swimming close to the mouths of rivers or streams where they empty into the ocean.

11. Avoid swimming or surfing near jetties, piers or other structures in the water. Sharks often feed at such places.

12. Avoid loud splashing, hard physical splashing, and jumping straight into an area that might have sharks. All these activities attract sharks. Don't swim with dogs, horses, or other animals, their movements may attract a predator.

Anti-Shark Systems

There have been various inventions that are said to reduce shark attacks by repelling them with electronic pulses, scents, and sounds. Over the years I've seen very, very few people ever surfing with one of these contraptions. I don't know why surfers are so against them. Personally, I'd use it every time I went out, if I knew it would work.

Here's a wearable shark repellent system for around $600 at Amazon.com. When you see it, you'll think like I did that it looks a little clumsy to wear while surfing, but still – the benefit probably outweighs that!

Seachange Shark Shield

The devices work by causing discomfort to the sharks through their *ampullae* of Lorenzini – as I mentioned earlier, this is the electrical sensing organ sharks use to size up prey. This seems like the best way to go about it. I saw a photo of a guy on a boat putting the palm of his hand on the nose of a large shark, which is said to short out the shark's brain a bit because there is too much stimulation coming through the *ampullae* of Lorenzini. If sharks can detect these very faint electrical impulses, then blasting them with some strong signals that overwhelms them seems like a great strategy. Some devices can be placed in the leash for your board, or on the board itself.

On another note, if you are able to hit the shark in the nose, you have a better chance of persuading the shark to leave the area. A number of victims have done this, and lived to tell about it.

Vern's Comments

The owner of one of the companies I worked for on Oahu told me about a weekend trip to Waimea Bay on the North Shore of Oahu one time. He and his family were all sitting there on blankets on the sand eating food at a picnic, when all the sudden, about forty yards off the beach, a giant tiger shark jumped out of the water, high in the air. The shark had a dolphin (like flipper, not mahi-mahi), in its mouth. It then tore the dolphin apart in front of a hundred or so onlookers – having a picnic of its own.

Welcome to the real world kids. Pull up a chair, grab yourself a chicken leg and watch the show, right?

I've seen it stated a couple of times that the odds of being attacked by a shark in the United States are about one in six million. If you live in Hawaii and spend time in the water every day, I'm going to say that the odds increase considerably, and not in your favor. Most people never see a shark while surfing, or swimming. I saw shark fins while surfing twice in Hawaii. They were very small, and I wasn't really afraid at all at the time. Usually a shark attack isn't preceded by a fin you can see coming at you like it is in the movies.

I've swam and surfed at many of the spots listed on my spreadsheet where people have been attacked by sharks. Kihei, Ka'anapali, Sunset Beach, Makena, Baldwin Beach, Ewa Beach, Nimitz, Bellows AFS, Velzyland, Honokowai, Sandy's, Kapalua, and these are just beaches where attacks have taken place over the past twelve years. Kihei and Ka'anapali, Honokowai areas seem to be a couple of hotspots that I'll likely avoid in the future. However, Makapu'u on Oahu still looks good!

Ok, that wraps it up. Have a look at my Hawaii Shark Attacks Spreadsheet here when you get a chance: A History of Shark Attacks in Hawaii.

30 – OTHER CAUTIONS

Approximately seven million people per year visit the Hawaiian Islands. I wish all of them could read this list of cautions because it would save them some trouble, sometimes without much effort.

Hawaii is different from where you grew up, wherever that was. The ocean and other weather events can be dangerous at times. An atmosphere of free-for-all fun might exist during your first couple trips to Hawaii – or first few months living here and you might not be aware of dangers.

Here is a list of what I think is important for everyone to know when visiting or living in Hawaii.

Water Cautions

I mentioned Flash floods and big waves already and won't cover them again here. Those are probably the two biggest concerns you should have when around water in Hawaii.

Tsunamis

One natural weather phenomenon that has the potential for absolutely devastating effects is a tsunami. Recently Thailand and much of Southeast Asia experienced a devastating tsunami caused by an underwater earthquake in Indonesia. Hundreds of thousands of people died in that event, and it gave us all something to think about. I had left Patong Beach, Thailand, one of the hardest hit areas, just two days before the tsunami struck. Having lived in Hawaii for years I knew what receding waters meant. Who knows, maybe I could have warned a lot of people to get to higher ground if I was still there.

If you live in Hawaii you will see tsunami cautions mentioned frequently in the newspapers, and on television. When the water recedes far past what it typically does, and you see fish, octopus, or other sea life stuck in the sand wondering what happened, you'll know that a tsunami is about to take place. Get to as high a place as you possibly can. If there is nothing near you, climb a strong coconut tree! Sure, it's difficult, but not more difficult than it would be trying to stay alive in the turbulent waters as a tsunami rushes in.

A tsunami could wreak havoc on Honolulu – which remains, largely – at a meter or so above sea level.

On average a tsunami hits the Hawaiian Islands about once each year. There is not necessarily damage wrought with each tsunami, it could amount to little more than a ripple. Damaging tsunamis hit about once every seven years.

Tsunamis almost always occur after an earthquake near the ocean – or actually under the ocean.

The worst tsunami in recent times occurred in 1946, April Fool's Day, when a large tsunami hit Hawaii and killed nearly 160 people. There was no warning system in place, and many died exploring the sea life flopping around on the beach after the water pulled away from the beach.

How high was the tsunami surge? On the Big Island, it hit 55 feet high. Some of the waves (surges) made it over a half-mile inland from where it usually hit.

Tsunamis travel across the open ocean at 400-500 miles per hour, though they slow down a lot by the time they reach the shallows bordering the beaches.

The biggest wave of a tsunami?

It's never the same numbered wave, but it's somewhere in the middle of the set of waves. So, knowing that, if you see the first wave come in – and it hits the parking area where your car is –

get out fast because the next one, or the next one after the next one – could be 55 feet high.

Get to higher ground immediately.

Many people surviving the Boxing Day Tsunami in Southeast Asia survived by climbing up higher than the second story of sturdy (concrete) hotels on the beach. They were able to watch the devastation with front row seats. There is no telling how big the waves will get – so, over two stories of climbing may not be enough. If you can, go higher.

Don't forget – once the waves come in, they have to go back out… when they do – a whole lot more destruction takes place as the wave carries wood, trees, boats, cars, people, and everything lighter than the rushing water itself. Even though the water may seem shallow – one to two feet high once the waves come in, DO NOT get in it, because the rip currents will be incredibly strong and might sweep you off your feet and to your death.

Yes, it's that serious.

Blowholes

Blowholes are some of the coolest natural phenomena to experience, and yet they can be deadly. A blowhole is a hole in the cliff face near the ocean that sprays water when waves come in and go under the lava cliffs and up and out the hole in front of onlookers. They are great fun, but also can be quite dangerous. The force of the water coming through the hole can pick you up and drop you head first down the hole – where you drown. This has happened numerous times in the past. Some blowholes are closed for this reason.

Remote Beaches

Though picturesque, swimming at secluded beaches where you are the only one in the water is not a good idea for a couple of reasons.

The best reason for swimming where there are lifeguards is the rip current that is sometimes present. Many people have died in Hawaii after being sucked out away from the beach in a rip current that exhausted them as they tried to swim against it or tread water until help arrived.

Rip Currents

What to do if you're caught in a rip current that is pulling you away from the beach and you're helpless to swim back to the beach where you want to be?

Don't fight it directly – it's a losing battle. The strongest swimmers in the world cannot fight the strength of a powerful rip current.

You can start by swimming parallel to the beach. This may take you out of the current, and then you can swim back to the beach.

Or, if that isn't working, you can try just going with the current until it weakens and releases you so you can swim back to the beach.

Anyone can get caught in a rip current. I was caught in a very bad one at Sand Island one time as I bodyboarded with a friend. Good thing I had bodyboarding fins on and a board to float on. I had to use all my strength for twenty-five to fight the rip current and swim at an angle to the beach. I was completely exhausted and had to sit on the beach for an hour to regain enough strength to stand up!

Shore Breaking Waves

A special mention goes to *Sandy Beach* because the place is treacherous for those playing in the surf. There are more broken, strained, and sprained necks, knees, elbows, and ankles at this beach than at any of the other beaches.

Why?

The culprit is the wicked shore-break. This is where the waves break right at the beach – and into the hard-packed sand. Every time there are waves at Sandy's you'll find people in the dangerous surf. Stay all day and you'll probably see someone hurt by it.

I've been thrown into the sand very hard at Sandy's and I just don't even enjoy the place anymore. Couple that with the strong localism of the teenage crowd – and it's just not a fun place for too many people but the teens themselves!

Territorial Surfers

Not just locals, but primarily the locals, can be unwelcoming to put it mildly. If you don't understand the common courtesy that takes place as you vie for position to catch a wave – you are best to learn it before putting your board or "okole" in the water.

Local surfers will let you know when you're not playing by the accepted rules. Sometimes there are no rules and the locals will gripe no matter what you do – just because you're there at their spot – and in the way.

Up to you how you handle that, I've fought for a spot on a couple of occasions, because I'm equally as passionate about catching waves as they are! Other times, I'm way outnumbered and take my board and go to a less crowded spot.

Once I had a teenage duck his surfboard down in front of me – and it popped up and hit me as I rode my bodyboard down a wave. The next time he caught a wave I grabbed his board and threw him off it. It shouldn't get to this point – but it sometimes does. In a perfect world, these situations don't exist... Hawaii is NOT a perfect place; so take off your rose-colored glasses before you arrive!

Hurricanes

In recent memory, and since Hawaii became one of the United States, there were a couple of hurricanes that tore through Hawaii. There was a lot of devastation and some people even died as a result. The first hurricane was Hurricane Iwa on November 23, 1982 that hit Oahu, Kauai, and Ni'ihau. This was not a major hurricane, it ranked only as a Category 1.

The next hurricane, Iniki, was a more powerful Category 4 storm, and hit Kauai on September 11, 1992. Hurricane Iniki caused six deaths and nearly $2 billion dollars in damage to the island.

In addition to the strong winds – the storm surge caused significant flooding.

Other Cautions

Hiking Ridge Trails

There are some amazing hikes on the islands that result in being at the peak of a very high ridge. On Oahu the Ku'ulao mountain ridge is the summit of many hiking trails – and well worth the hike to reach it.

The ridges of Hawaii mountains are steep, treacherous, with loose lava, dirt, and plants that hide holes and steep drops. This is the norm.

Do not go off the trail, you might regret it!

Falling Rocks

Rocks falling off high mountains can happen at any time. I remember hearing about some that fell and ripped right through a home in that was not far from where I was staying!

There was once a wonderful hike on Oahu, Sacred Falls, that was very popular with locals and tourists alike. Over 50,000 people visited the attraction each year. It was a beautiful walk down a forest trail under overhanging limbs and vines... and the reward was a cool (and I mean cool as in frigid!) dip in the pool of water at the base of the waterfall. It was one of my favorite places to visit and I had been there almost a dozen times over the years. In 1999, on Mother's Day, there was a rockslide and eight people at the falls lost their lives. Another group of fifty was injured, some severely.

Volcanoes

We won't cover volcano dangers here, except to say that you need to follow the cautions laid out by your guide, signs, and other officials that explain what proper and safe behavior is as you walk around active parts of a volcano.

Earthquakes

Hawaii does have earthquakes, but most are not noticeable. There are thousands per year on the Big Island of Hawaii.

The most destructive earthquake in Hawaii occurred in 1868 with a magnitude of 7.9 on the Richter scale. It killed eighty-one people.

Skin Cancer

A big risk because the sun is closer to you than in other parts of the world, and because it is so warm and so few clothes are worn.

Use a 30+ rated sun block if you'll be in the sun for more than an hour. For children – it's more important to lather them up with sun block or keep them out of the sun for extended periods.

31 – PLAN B

Nearly everyone who moves to Hawaii thinks they're going to make it over the hump, and pull out a win, staying in the islands forever.

If that doesn't happen, you *will* need a fallback plan.

You might try to look at it from another perspective, so it doesn't become all that big a deal if you do have to return to your previous home or go somewhere else in search of the ultimate place to live.

Look at living in Hawaii as a temporary move and tell yourself you'll try living on one of the islands for a year. See if you can make it that long. By then you'll have a good idea what the island you're living on is like… you'll also have some idea what the other islands are like. Hopefully you've visited them too.

You might choose to move to another island or you might continue on living where you are. Or, you might move back to the mainland US after a year. No harm done, right? You just spent a year in Hawaii while many people dream of that experience. You'll have many people ask how you did it because they too are starting to get that question in the back of their mind…

"Is Living in Hawaii Possible for Me?"

32 – MAKING THE DECISION TO GO

You go around once in this game of life as far as we know. It would be a shame, if your personality and expectations were a good match for Hawaii and yet you didn't go and try living in this most amazing place.

There are positives and negatives to everything. You probably have noticed that when you focus on the positive side of things you take action more, and you experience new things that you otherwise wouldn't have.

Life is full of big and small experiences that can bliss you out or bring you down, and you'll never know until you try a new experience, which it will be.

Look at it this way…

Knowing what you now know about moving to and living in Hawaii… *what is the worst experience you could possibly have?*

You could have some bad days. But, I think it would be near impossible to have a bad week, month or year in Hawaii.

If you can make it work with your money situation, which is the major issue for nearly everyone considering the move, you should give it a try.

Your Hawaii experience will be different from every other person that decides to move to the islands this year. Out of all the people who have read past versions of this book, there are hundreds now living in Hawaii and loving it. Others have moved back home where they started. Some move on to try another place.

You'll never know until you make the move!

Best of luck and life to you!

Aloha Nui Loa!

Vern L.

APPENDIX

Some Interesting Facts About Hawaii

Hawaii is the most isolated population center on the face of the earth. Hawaii is 2,390 miles from California; 3,850 miles from Japan; 4,900 miles from China; and 5,280 miles from the Philippines.

More than one-third of the world's supply of pineapples comes from Hawaii.

There are only twelve letters in the Hawaiian alphabet:

Vowels: A, E, I, O, U; Consonants: H, K, L, M, N, P, W

Hawaii is the widest U.S. State measuring from east to west.

Honolulu is the largest city in the world, having the longest borders. The reason is the state constitution declares all unnamed Hawaiian Islands as being part of Honolulu. This makes it 1,500 miles long or more distance than halfway across the forty-eight contiguous United States.

Honolulu's zenith star, (the star that rises directly above it) is Arcturus. The Hawaiians called it Hokule'a.

All of Hawaii is the result of underwater volcanoes that erupted thousands of years ago.

Hawaii was the 50th state admitted to the union on August 20th, 1959.

Highest recorded temperature in Hawaii – ever – was only 96° F.

The lowest temperature ever? 56° F. (under 3,000 feet altitude)

More than 100 world-renowned beaches surround Honolulu.

Iolani Palace on Oahu is the only royal palace in the United States.

The world's largest wind generator is on the island of Oahu. The windmill has two blades 400 feet long on the top of a tower twenty stories high.

The island of Oahu draws more visitors than any of the other islands.

One-third of the state's best surfing beaches are on Oahu.

On Maui, Haleakala Crater is the world's largest dormant volcano.

Molokai Island has the world's highest sea cliffs, Hawaii's longest waterfall, and the largest white sand beach in the state.

On Lanai, Hulope Bay is a marine preserve and considered one of the best diving spots in the world.

Kahoolawe was used for target practice by U.S. Navy and Air Force fighter planes and bombers. No one is allowed to go ashore without permission. The island consists of an uninhabited area of forty-five square miles. The author of this book had a chance to go while stationed in the Air Force, on a cleanup detail, but instead assigned someone else to go in his place!

At 800,000 years the Big Island is the youngest of the island chain. However, it was the first island discovered by voyaging Polynesians.

Kilauea volcano on Big Island is the world's most active volcano.

On Big Island, Ka Lae is the southernmost point in the United States. It is located at 18:54:49 N, 155:41 W. There is a constant 27 knot per hour wind blowing east to west, 24 hours per day and 365 days per year.

Most of the world's macadamia nuts are grown on Big Island Hawaii.

Big Island is home to the world's largest telescope and more scientific astral observatories in one place than anywhere else in the world, and recently there is another one being built that is the cause of a lot of problems with locals who insist enough is enough.

Highest Mountains?

Mauna Kea rises 13,796 feet and Mauna Loa 13,679 feet above sea level. The mean elevation of all the islands is 3,030 feet above sea level. Hawaii's tallest mountain, Mauna Kea, stands at 13,796 feet but is taller than Mount Everest if followed to the base of the mountain, which, lying at the floor of the Pacific Ocean, rises about 33,500 feet.

Size in Comparison to Other States?

Hawaii is bigger in landmass than seven other states.

Land - Hawaii's total land area is 6,423.4 square miles.

Coast - Hawaii's total coastline stretches 750 miles.

Highest Waterfall?

The highest waterfall is Kahiwa, a 1,750 foot (533 m) cascade on the island of Molokai.

Hawaii's Main Islands Biggest to Smallest in Land Area?

- Big Island of Hawaii: 4,028.0 miles²

- Maui: 727.2 miles²

- Oahu: 596.7 miles²

- Kauai: 552.3 miles²

- Molokai: 260 miles²

- Lanai: 140.5 miles²

- Niihau: 69.5 miles²

- Kahoolawe: 44.6 miles²

Elevation of the Highest Mountains on Each Island

Big Island of Hawaii:

- Mauna Kea - 13,796 feet

- Mauna Loa - 13,679 feet

Maui:

- Haleakala (Red Hill) - 10,023 feet

Oahu:

- Kaala - 4,003 feet

Kauai:

- Kawaikini - 5,243 feet

Molokai:

- Kamakou - 4,961 feet

Lanai:

- Lanaihale - 3,366 feet

Niihau:

- Paniau - 1,250 feet

Kahoolawe:

- Puu Moaulanui - 1,483 feet

HAWAII FAQ

This section covers material not already mentioned in the previous section.

When is the best time to visit Hawaii?

Between January and May, and between September and November. Avoid June, July, August and December because those months the rates for everything get higher. There are more tourists to compete with for things to see and do during this time.

What is the "coconut wireless"?

Word of mouth. Some say the gossip flies around Hawaii very fast. Judge for yourself!

What clothes should I bring?

It is always warm, occasionally a night or morning is cool enough – because of the wind usually – to require a long sleeved shirt or pants to stay comfortable. Plan on dressing for warm (80's) weather daily.

What islands should I visit before deciding to move to Hawaii?

If you know you need a big city, good shopping, nightlife, or it will be tough for you to get a job – visit only Oahu before you plan your move to Hawaii.

If you are not tied to Oahu for a job, for nightlife, shopping and the rest of it, you should probably have a look at Maui and Big Island too.

If you are prepared for seclusion and a very low-key lifestyle go see Kauai as well.

Visit Molokai and Lanai if you think you could live in the ultimate in seclusion and quiet.

Which islands have active volcanoes and flowing lava?

Just Big Island Hawaii. Visit the "Volcanoes National Park" and hopefully you will see the lava flow during the time you are there. Tip – it is not constant.

What is the approximate rate for accommodation?

The whole range is present. There are hostels in Waikiki for $30 per day. Budget hotel rooms for about $75 per day. Some hotel rooms go for $1,000 per day, and there are three to four-bedroom condominiums on the beach that run into the tens of thousands of dollars per day.

How long is the flight to Hawaii?

From east coast USA, about non-stop is ten hours from New Jersey, or with stops about twelve or thirteen hours. From west coast USA, five or six hours. From Japan, six hours. From Thailand, seven hours.

How likely am I to be attacked by a shark in Hawaii?

How much do you surf, dive, or spear fish?

Those activities have a higher probability of a shark bite. Most people who just swim in Hawaii's waters have an astronomically low chance of ever seeing or being bitten by a shark. I do know a guy that was bitten on the forearm by a barracuda in the murky water of Maui surf as he was putting on his fins to snorkel in about three feet of water.

The island of Maui is currently (2013) experiencing a higher than average number of shark attacks and resulting deaths. Just the other day another man died from a bite to the foot.

How can I minimize the risk of shark attack?

Read the shark chapter above, all this is covered.

How many people drown in Hawaii each year?

About sixty.

What languages are spoken in Hawaii?

Since Hawaii is a U.S. state, English is the official language. However, Hawaiian is spoken by many locals as well. Hawaiian is taught in schools and universities. Pidgin is a dialect that is spoken frequently among locals, and it is a colorful and fun language to learn. If you live on the islands for any amount of time, you'll hear certain words spoken often.

Should I learn to speak Pidgin'?

Up to you. If you want to understand what the locals are saying sometimes you might pay attention and try to figure it out. There are some websites online that have Hawaiian pidgin dictionaries and sound clips.

The language is based on English, but it's a slangified English that you probably won't understand unless you really try for a while. There is a lot of variety to it. If a local is using it with you, he or she either thinks you are local or have lived in Hawaii a long time, or is being rude to you so you can't understand. Usually it's the first one.

Here is a dictionary of pidgin sayings:

E-hawaii.com/pidgin

Here are some audio clips of Hawaiians speaking pidgin from National Public Radio:

Audio Clips (click)

Can I visit the island of Niihau?

Not without an invitation from one of the locals living there or, the Robinson family. Some snorkel tours leave Kauai and take snorkelers to waters around Niihau, but nobody is allowed to step foot on its shore.

What is "Da Kine"?

This is a phrase in pidgin that is used often. Some people it seems like, can use it in every sentence! It can mean anything, but it is used when someone cannot think of the proper name for something – or when they are being lazy to think of the proper word, or when they are being funny.

Someone can say – "Lucy, where's da kine for my shirt?" Meaning "iron." Or just about any situation... it can be a person, place, situation, and experience, really, just about anything. It's up to the person being spoken to, to figure it out!

What is considered proper tipping in Hawaii?

Restaurant staff: 15-20%. Taxi drivers: 10-15%. Hotel maids: $5/day, or $10-20 if your room is over $300 per night.

Is aloha attire required for all social events?

No. For some events they may request aloha attire. Many people wear it daily for work or play. It's a laid-back style that doesn't require much thought. The shirts are light and keep you cool in Hawaii's sometimes stifling hot weather, and, of course there are many styles to choose from.

Usually you just cannot go wrong by wearing the aloha style – no matter what the event.

That's all for the FAQ section. If you have a specific question email me at address found at the end of this book.

EMAIL AND ANSWERS

Here are some of the emails I've had from people who were considering moving to Hawaii, and my response to them. I've changed the names to preserve anonymity.

The following is an email – slightly edited – that I received a short while back from someone wanting to move to Hawaii. I didn't think she had a realistic chance for success. Sometimes the truth is hard to face. Hawaii can be an unforgiving place. While living in the islands, money goes fast and dreams die faster in some cases.

Email #1

Hello Vern,

I am a 42 years female, single mum of a beautiful 8-year-old boy and currently living in the UK.

I am a part-time self employed Holistic Therapist, and Reiki Healing Master Teacher. Since I have been studying it, practicing and opening many doors of the Universe, I have been having this urge, call and desire of living in Hawaii.

Therefore, for many days and months I have been doing my research for me and for my boy about living in Hawaii. That's when I saw your page, which I love. I thought your website was well-done and straight to the point. I have been doing the research again today, I started at 9 pm. and it's now 2:30 am. here.

I am contacting you and asking your advice on the matter of moving to Hawaii, for me professionally and as a single mother, for my boy and his education. Do you know how it is to start up a holistic practice? What is the situation of living in Hawaii now?

There are many things that concern me about the crime, drugs, etc.

My son wants to be a computer Lego (games) designer. *What opportunities does he have?*

We both love the laid-back life (that's what I am hoping for), the love feeling, the friendly way, the beaches, the clean air and nature. We both love Japanese food.

I am a Buddhist and I believe in the Law of Attraction. Therefore I feel that Hawaii is the place for me forever but of course as a parent (you are one, you know) I need to know, research and see all the options to decide if this is a good move overall. How much is going to cost me? With my life in the UK, I am struggling.

I believe nothing is worse than here in the UK right now except maybe Africa.

What I am asking you is if you give me an overall and extensive (if you can) picture of the Living in Hawaii, please.

I would appreciate it and very grateful.

Thank you very much! I look forward to hearing from you soon.

Aloha,

Kim

* * * * * *

My response to her…

Hi Kim,

Thanks for writing…

I have a book at Amazon, it's at Amazon in the UK too, called, "Moving to Hawaii – The Good, Bad, and Ugly" that you should get as soon as possible. It is less than $10, and I highly recommend it. It will answer questions you didn't know you had. This book will give you the greatest insight as to what it's actually like to move to Hawaii and live there.

Beyond that, Hawaii is not a great place to start a business in any area that I can think of. It is a VERY tough atmosphere to understand… the market is different than any other I know. It's not welcoming. It takes a while to feel like you fit in. Though you are in a space (holistic living) where people are generally friendly, easy going, unselfish and inviting, there are not really that many people like this in Hawaii. Hawaii is not like palm trees and shacks and people living off the land. That was decades ago, nearly 100 years ago. People can't afford that way of life any longer. Now, there are places on Big Island and Kauai where you can work on the farm and they'll give you a place to stay for a couple weeks or months, if that's something you're thinking about. Not sure where your son will attend school though. In Hawaii everything is so expensive. Please don't discount that fact before you decide to come over.

We are living in Thailand, rather than Hawaii for two reasons:

1. Expenses. Though I could make a lot more money in Hawaii, it is still a big price to pay (working full time) to move back to the Hawaiian Islands. Here in Thailand I can work online and we are OK with that income without my having to get a full-time job.

2. Education for our daughter. She's only four years old, but I am unsure about Hawaii education unless I can put her in Punahou or some other $1K+ per month tuition private school as she gets older.

Would I suggest you go to Hawaii to start a business?

No.

Really, I just wouldn't suggest you even try it. It's a tough environment for a single parent with a child. To add starting a business to that situation, would be far too much stress and I think failure would probably result.

Please reassess moving when you have all the info you need about moving to and living in Hawaii.

Sorry I can't be more optimistic. Maybe the time isn't right, but you can make it right with some effort. I'd suggest accumulating as many skills as you can to enable you to work in the tourist industry, or some other essential job area.

Aloha,

Vern

* * * * * *

Email #2

Sometimes I like to answer email within the body of the original email. When formatted, it's easy for the person submitting the email to me to read. Here on the eBook, it isn't so easy. I'll preface lines with who said them.

* * * * * *

Hi Vern,

Thanks for all your amazing info on Hawaii!

Vern - You're welcome, I love to write about Hawaii!

Mike - I live in England (U.K.) and am into alternative medicine...have been for thirty-five years.

The idea of living in Hawaii has been calling to me... mostly the weather, I guess.

I was born and brought up in Kenya until I was nineteen. I still love the idea of good weather. However, Kenya is a dodgy place to live. Life is very cheap and daily life is dangerous. I lived here for thirty-five years, and I'm at the age where I'm thinking I want to enjoy myself, and the weather here is somewhat lacking in luster you could say!

Vern - Yes, i couldn't imagine. I know quite a few expats living in Thailand from U.K. and they all tell the same weather story.

Mike - Your info gave me a much better idea than it just being a fantasy. But, in truth, it is a fantasy because I haven't even been there!

Vern - Living in Hawaii is a very different way of life. It is impossible to give you the real feeling. You'll either love it - or be on a plane moving somewhere else in a year. Most people can make it a year. It's truly paradise for some of us.

Mike - My work is my passion. I love helping people become more authentic, more themselves, having worked hard on myself for all these years. What became clear from your writing is the perspective that I'm not that much of an outdoor type. Or maybe it's just because of the mainly cold weather we have here.

I remember waking up at 4 am. (because I had to travel later) in Australia, and just being blown away that I could do my Tai Chi outside without being frozen!

I guess I could easily enjoy walking if the climate is kind.

Vern - Yeah, nice weather can make a so-so life pretty nice. Hawaii weather is to die for.

Mike - However my focus is on my work. My mission is helping people, the bigger the groups the better.

I teach Biodanza, which you've probably not heard of. I love it - it combines three of my passions, self-development, dancing and music. I was thinking though, if people are that laid-back in Hawaii maybe this kind of thing is not for them!

Vern - Well sort of. There is a group of people who are all laid-back. A group that's working their butts off to survive. And a group that's even stressed out in Hawaii.

People are usually working hard because it's so expensive. Their free time is theirs and they want to spend it doing free activities, not paying for them. I'm saying, for the majority. There are also obscenely wealthy people who can spend it on whatever they wish.

Mike - Also I love teaching Tai Chi. I've been a practitioner of Acupuncture and Shiatsu for twenty-two years, but it would probably be too complicated to do there. I'd have to sit all sorts of exams. I'm more into group work than 1:1's, it pays more and gives me a better buzz. I'm now fifty-four and realizing there's more to life than killing yourself for work. I love the laid-back lifestyle.

Vern - Don't we all, my friend!

Mike - Are properties expensive to buy? All depends on what you want I guess. You mention places are small and expensive. (to rent)

Vern - To buy on Oahu, you won't find anything livable for under $250K USD. That's a studio to 1-bedroom in a high-rise. A house is more. Much more. To rent, you can find something $800 - 1K per month – a no-frills studio apartment in Waikiki.

Mike - From your perspective of how far it is from the US, made me re-think.

I would like to teach Biodanza in the US as well. There are a few teachers, but numbers are still very small. I would love to teach it in the US because Americans are so much more enthusiastic than the Brits. My focus is on helping society shift to a more holistic lifestyle, removing masks.

Given what I've mentioned what would you say re: idea of moving?

Vern - Hawaii wouldn't work for the business. That's just my guess. You could prove me wrong. I don't see anyone making money that way, or with meditation classes, or anything similar. If it happens, it happens at the high end, those with a lot of free spending money. It is hard to find those folks though. Better chance of that working in California.

Even better chance of doing video training, or classes on the internet where you could create it all and then focus on marketing it and selling it.

Now, as a supplement to whatever else you're doing, like doing work supporting the tourism industry, yes, it can be good for that if you work at it.

Mike - I would be grateful for your feedback about whether it is feasible for me to be thinking about moving to Hawaii from the UK.

All the best!

Vern - I think it's very hard for an American living in the mainland to go to Hawaii and create a business that works. It is very difficult for a person that has lived in Hawaii over their lifetime, to create a business that works there. For foreigners coming? I think quite difficult. That isn't to say you couldn't pull it off, but you'd need a lot of savings in the bank and you'd need to work really hard for a couple years to get your business going.

Visit first, yes! See what you think. Search twitter.com to see if anyone's talking about Hawaii and Biodanza in the same conversation.

Good luck to you!

Aloha,

Vern

* * * * * *

Email #3

Which Island Might Be Best?

I received a letter from "Sam" in Connecticut. Sam and his fiancé are considering moving to Hawaii within five years, and wanted to know what I thought about the right island to look at, with some considerations about lifestyle given. Here is Sam's email to me, and my response.

* * * * * *

Vern (if you do not mind my being presumptuous and calling you by your first name), my name is Sam. I have been fiddling around with the idea of maybe retiring in Hawaii. As having never lived there before and only visited the main island once for business purposes, I have no clue where to look for housing. If you do not mind offering an opinion on the subject, I would like to give you an idea of what I am looking for and a little of our personalities.

Looking for a newer home that will last without much work until I pass on or longer priced in the $300K range or less. If that is not feasible then, a condo may be the next best bet, as I do not like making tons of repairs and like my bills to be very predictable.

My fiancé and I are both in the fifty-year-old range and will not be doing this for about five more years but might be willing to start looking now and if we find something, grab it earlier than the move.

We have a bit of a slower lifestyle and love reading books and spending time on the computer. She loves the beach or sun bathing and I like a good sports bar with satellite TV for watching our favorite teams play.

We both like to shop and walk around in nice areas.

We are not too much into the nightlife but would love to have places nearby for live music, a good glass of wine and some great restaurants.

Of course, safety and security is a must.

Do you have any opinion on which Island and what area of that island would be the best place to start our search?

Kindest regards,

Sam

* * * * * *

Hi Sam,

Thanks for writing – sounds like a lovely plan to live life in Hawaii!

It sounds to me like Maui is what you're looking for – but you might have difficulty, no, you will have difficulty to find a place for that amount.

Maui would be my first choice if I were in your situation – and I'd be looking hard to find a place to live that is in that price range, and in a safe neighborhood...

Big Island would also be quite nice.

On Big Island, $300K homes are widely available, and you'll have to figure out where on the island you would like to live. Sounds like one of the bigger cities would suit you and your fiancé. The main problem I would have with Big Island Hawaii is the vog… volcanic fog. It is not constant, but it is something you would deal with on some level depending where you chose to live.

BigIsland-BigIsland.com covers vog pretty well – they say this:

Health effects: Health effects from vog exposure vary greatly among individuals. People with pre-existing respiratory conditions such as asthma, emphysema and bronchitis are more prone to the adverse effects of the vog. Common symptoms related to Big Island Vog Index include the following:

- headaches

- breathing difficulties

- increased susceptibility to respiratory ailments

- watery eyes

- sore throat

Another problem is the great distance between places. At least in relation to Hawaii – there are big distances between things on Big Isle. Everything is spread out – the island is quite big compared to the others.

Best advice? Go visit and see whether Big Island is for you – or not. You might like it just as well as you would Maui. If there is something about Big Isle that rubs you the wrong way, try Maui. Oahu has $300K places in Kapolei and other areas outside downtown, so those might be other options.

Best of luck to you and your fiancé…

Aloha,

Vern

* * * * * *

Keep in mind that living in Hawaii is different for everyone who plans to make it a reality. There is no one island that will suit every type of person. Hawaii is so variable – weather, people, traffic, costs… that you really have to be there to see the different areas and whether it will work for you. Living in Hawaii is so different from living wherever you are on the mainland USA. Go to Hawaii and experience as much as you can on each island.

Figure out your top choices and start looking for a place to live. It might take a year or more to find the right place to live that fits your lifestyle and budget.

But, when it's all done – it will have been worth it!

ABOUT THE AUTHOR

I grew up in Southwestern Pennsylvania and really disliked the weather. The winters were depressing for me every year, and yet it was all I knew. That is, until we took a trip as a family to Ocean City, New Jersey. The beach there was dirty and the ocean was dark green and murky. I didn't know clean water from dirty, but I loved playing in the waves and pretending like I could bodysurf them. I was captivated by the beach and the people there who could enjoy them anytime they wished. I knew then at fifteen-years-old, I would spend the rest of my life in close proximity to a beach.

After I graduated high school in 1984, I joined the U.S. Air Force and was stationed at Hickam Air Force Base on the amazing island of Oahu. After my tour of duty ended and I left the Air Force to pursue undergraduate and later graduate studies, I dreamt often about Hawaii. It felt like my true home. I think a lot of people say that after living there, or even visiting for a short time.

Since then I've been back to the islands to visit and to live for a couple more years. Currently my wife and I are planning to move back to the Hawaiian Islands within two years.

Thank you for purchasing this Moving to Hawaii guide. If you have any comments – good or bad - *would you please let me know?*

I love receiving comments from readers because it helps me understand what was helpful and what wasn't, and what I missed that you really wanted to see. I want this to be the best moving to Hawaii guide published. Help me make it so!

If you really enjoyed this book, could I trouble you for a couple minutes to help me out by leaving a review for it at Amazon? Authors live and die by their reviews, and since I revised my book with some new information, the 60+ reviews I had, disappeared! Now I'm starting over, and it would be so great if you could write a sentence or two about whether you enjoyed the book!

My email is: AimforAwesome@gmail.com. Don't forget to check out a great website about Hawaii - Aim for Awesome - AimforAwesome.com.

I wish you the best of luck if you move to Hawaii! I'd love to hear from you in that regard. Let me know how you're doing and if it was a struggle, or everything went smoothly.

Aloha Nui Loa!

Vern Lovic

Who knows? Next year at this time you might be walking on the beach in Hawaii… Make it happen!